HOW HITLER WAS MADE

HOW HITLER WAS MADE
GERMANY AND THE RISE OF THE PERFECT NAZI

CORY TAYLOR

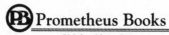 Prometheus Books

59 John Glenn Drive
Amherst, New York 14228

Published 2018 by Prometheus Books

Cover design by Jacqueline Nasso Cooke
Cover design © Prometheus Books
Map illustration by Andrew McCormick
All interior photographs are from the
Fotoarchiv Heinrich Hoffmann, Bayerische Staatsbibliothek.

Inquiries should be addressed to
Prometheus Books
59 John Glenn Drive
Amherst, New York 14228
VOICE: 716–691–0133 • FAX: 716–691–0137
WWW.PROMETHEUSBOOKS.COM

22 21 20 19 18   5 4 3 2 1

Library of Congress Cataloging-in-Publication Data Pending

Printed in the United States of America

To Julie and Liam

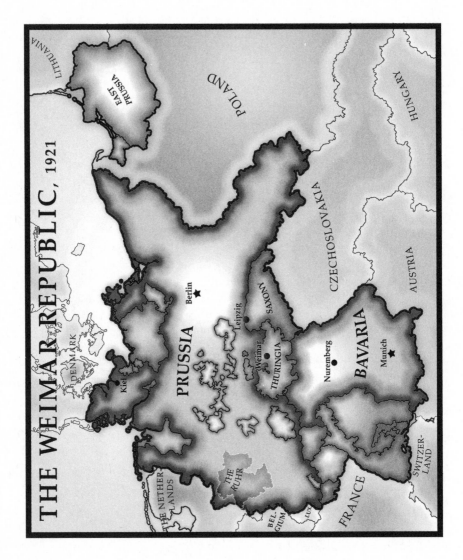

THE WEIMAR REPUBLIC, 1921

LITHUANIA

EAST PRUSSIA

POLAND

HUNGARY

DENMARK

CZECHOSLOVAKIA

AUSTRIA

Berlin

Kiel

PRUSSIA

Leipzig

SAXONY

Weimar

THURINGIA

Nuremberg

BAVARIA

Munich

THE NETHER-LANDS

THE RUHR

BEL-GIUM

LUX.

FRANCE

SWITZER-LAND

CONTENTS

INTRODUCTION

One of Germany's most popular tourist destinations is Munich's Hofbräu-haus. Founded in 1589, the massive beer hall attracts tens of thousands of thirsty customers nearly every day. Upstairs in a large banquet hall called the Festsaal, groups are seated at long wooden tables under a vaulted ceiling with enormous chandeliers. As an oompah band plays traditional music, servers dressed in Bavarian costume bring customers beer, sausages, and other local dishes. Sounds of cheerful conversation, toasting, and clinking steins reverberate through the chamber. The festive atmosphere reflects the warm, fun-loving, and down-to-earth spirit of the Bavarian people. But most visitors are unaware that the Festsaal also has a sinister legacy.[1] There are no signs posted to inform them otherwise.

On February 24, 1920, thirteen years before he became German chancellor, Adolf Hitler led the inaugural meeting of the Nazi Party in the Festsaal before two thousand guests. Outlining the party's anti-Semitic agenda in twenty-five points, the future Nazi dictator informed his audience that only people of "German blood" would be considered citizens if the Nazis ever came to power.[2] No one in the hall outwardly opposed Hitler's idea of institutionalized anti-Semitism, and history's most reviled political movement was underway.

In the ensuing years, the Nazis would rent the Festsaal for mass meetings, until it was no longer large enough to accommodate Hitler's followers. "During that period the hall of the Hofbräuhaus in Munich acquired for us, National Socialists, a sort of mystic significance," Hitler wrote in *Mein Kampf.* "Every week there was a meeting . . . and each time the hall was better filled than on the former occasion."[3] Why did so many people gather to hear Hitler speak?

Germany was severely traumatized by the First World War. Not only had millions of young men died in the trenches of Europe, but defeat had wrought great injury to national pride. Founded in 1871, the German Reich (Empire) came to prominence considerably later than the great powers of Europe. Longing for respect and acceptance in the international arena, Germany was suspicious of its European neighbors, including France, Russia, and Great Britain. Though they had defeated the French in the Franco-Prussian war of 1870, the Germans still felt denied the "high esteem, which is due to them."[4] Anticipating conflict in Europe, the German war historian Friedrich von Bernhardi predicted in 1911, "Our next war will be fought for the highest interests of our country. . . . World power or downfall! will be our rallying cry."[5]

Three years later in the summer of 1914, Germany resolved to make a stand. That June, when Serbian nationalists assassinated the Austro-Hungarian heir Franz Ferdinand in Sarajevo, Germany's leadership took a bold step. Pledging unconditional support to Austro-Hungary, the Germans encouraged a war with Serbia, which was backed by Russia. Consequently, when the Russians mobilized their forces and refused an ultimatum to stop, Germany declared war. That same day, August 1, France began mobilizing its forces against Germany. To gain a strategic advantage, Germany invaded Luxemburg and Belgium while declaring war on France. This brought Great Britain into the war on the side of the French and the Russians. Desperate to avert bloodshed, US President Woodrow Wilson sent an urgent plea for peace, but nobody was listening.[6] Europe was prepared to see the conflict through. Looking back with our modern sensibilities and rapid-cycling news media, we sometimes forget that this war was arguably the most complicated and multipartied that Europe had ever experienced. Add to that the common person's limited access to objective news, and it wasn't difficult for Germans to be misled and to believe that their enemies had started it all.

The First World War, which lasted from 1914 to 1918, was in many ways the most brutal conflict in human history. New and terrifying weapons of the industrial age eviscerated and maimed millions of young men on the battlefield. When it ended, the victorious French, British, and American armies returned home to peace and security. But in defeated Germany, soldiers came home to a postwar revolution.

In 1914, the German people had been led to believe that the war would be over by Christmas. Promised peace through victory by military leaders, including First Quartermaster General Erich Ludendorff, they endured four and a half years of famine, suffering, and heartache before strikes and protests erupted in towns and cities across the country. Then, antiwar sentiment coalesced into Communist and Socialist revolutionary movements that threatened to turn Germany into a Soviet state.

The inaugural meeting of the National Socialist German Workers' Party (NSDAP) in the Hofbräuhaus Festsaal in February 1920 was as much a reaction to defeat and revolution as it was Hitler's first opportunity to introduce his party's platform. Like other far-right nationalists who opposed leftist revolution, Hitler wanted to restore Germany's national pride. Unlike Munich's stuffy politicians, who bored their audiences by reading their speeches and spoke condescendingly with status-conscious attitudes, the Austrian immigrant sounded as if he were speaking extemporaneously in a way that "responds to the vibration of the human heart with the delicacy of a seismograph . . . enabling him . . . to act as a loudspeaker proclaiming the most secret desires, the least admissible instincts, the sufferings and personal revolts of a whole nation."[7]

In the Festsaal, the thirty-year-old Austrian immigrant appealed to people's sense of pride by demanding equal status for the German people among all other nations and a repeal of the humiliating Treaty of Versailles. Playing on their emotions, he invoked long-entrenched anti-Semitic attitudes and suggested a restructuring of society without the Jews. Hitler would eventually blame Jews and Bolsheviks for all of Germany's problems, including defeat in war, the postwar revolution, the armistice, and the devastating terms of the Treaty of Versailles. Though it hinged on the absurd premise that the Jews created Bolshevism to subvert the German race, the assertion captured the mood of the times. In fact, the simplicity and repetition of his message began to resonate with a growing number of Germans eager for a scapegoat. But in February 1920, Hitler and his anti-Semitic ideology were in no way fully formed. It would take several more years and a confluence of fateful events, including a *putsch*, a trial, and imprisonment, for the Nazi leader to discover the full power of his megalomania, and his path to dictatorship. Yet, according to Hitler, the inaugural meeting in the Festsaal, was an important turning point: "When I finally closed the meeting, we were not alone in feeling that a wolf had been born which was destined to break into the herd of swindlers and misleaders of the people."[8]

Unlike the many books that focus on the Nazi leader after he took power in 1933, this one examines the early years of 1918–1924 to reveal how Hitler the future Führer was made, and how his devastating movement coalesced. Contrary to Nazi propaganda, which characterized Hitler as a savior, this work tracks the fateful convergence of those intimate associates that surrounded him in the early years and prepared him for leadership. Further, it reveals how they began to doubt him when the hour was already too late and they could no longer control him. The book also depicts the idealistic postwar revolution, its leadership of Jewish descent, and the role of propaganda and fake news in shaping the political attitudes that propelled Hitler into the mainstream.

The horrors of Nazi genocide and the Second World War would prompt several generations in the international community to suspect that the Germans had a special proclivity for evil. But the story of Hitler's early rise tells us that the problem of evil is universal and can occur anywhere and at any time, given the confluence of the right conditions. When tested by adversity, people and nations are often compelled to choose between self-interest and the greater good. In the case of Hitler and the Nazis, the stakes couldn't have been higher.

CHAPTER ONE

THE HORROR OF WAR

In October 1918, Adolf Hitler, while serving as a private in the German army, was temporarily blinded by a mustard gas attack. "We were subjected for several hours to a heavy bombardment with gas bombs," Hitler later wrote in *Mein Kampf*, "and about seven o'clock my eyes were scorching as I staggered back and delivered the last dispatch I was destined to carry in this war. A few hours later my eyes were like glowing coals and all was darkness around me."[1] Transported to a military hospital northeast of Berlin, Private Hitler was treated for "war hysteria,"[2] not blindness. He had served for more than forty months near the front lines, far longer than most, and was now suffering from battle fatigue and psychological stress.[3] At the hospital, when he learned of Germany's surrender, his blindness reportedly returned with a vengeance: "Has all this been done in order to enable a gang of despicable criminals to lay hands on the Fatherland?" he asked in *Mein Kampf*.[4]

Hitler claimed he decided right then and there to enter politics.[5] But this was an embellishment: *Mein Kampf* was written six years later, and the story was enhanced to create emotional resonance between the author and the German people. Who were the "despicable criminals" that Hitler spoke of? What happened in the six years between Germany's surrender and the writing of *Mein Kampf* to radicalize this lowly private and allow him to become the most popular up-and-coming figure on the nationalist scene? Why were so many Germans susceptible to his point of view? To answer these questions, one must take stock of the terrible impact of the First World War. And consider the trenches of a battlefield Hitler never stepped foot in.

"THE BROTHER OF THEM ALL"

In the winter of 1916, the western front of the First World War extended four hundred miles from the North Sea in Belgium to the Swiss border of France. Facing one another in a series of trenches extending along the line, French, British, and German forces had reached a deadlock. To break the stalemate, the Chief of the German High Command, Erich von Falkenhayn, a handsome and distinguished Prussian senior officer, set his sights on Verdun, where he hoped to deliver a decisive blow. Situated in the French countryside, two hundred and fifty kilometers east of Paris, Verdun had come to symbolize the spirit of French resistance since the Franco-Prussian War of 1870. Falkenhayn had no intention of seizing the medieval city and its fortifications. Instead, he planned to lure the enemy into combat and kill them in massive numbers until they lost the will to fight. To make them "bleed to death" were the general's infamous words.[6]

Among the Germans fighting on the front lines at Verdun was a pale young poet with deep-set eyes named Ernst Toller. At the time, no one could have known that the shy twenty-year-old would go on to play a key role in Bavaria's postwar revolution, become a world-renowned expressionist playwright, and a vociferous opponent of Adolf Hitler. Toller, who had been studying law at the University of Grenoble when the war was announced, departed France for Germany on one of the last trains before the French sealed the border in August of 1914.[7] On his homeward journey, he read a newspaper arguing that Germany's declaration of war had been prompted by a surprise French attack. "French airmen," Toller later wrote, "had dropped bombs on Bavarian soil, and Germany had been invaded. I swallowed it all."[8] The report was false. Convinced

Ernst Toller.

that the French had initiated the hostilities, Toller opted to volunteer for military service in Munich rather than return home to Prussia. In August, he was accepted into the First Bavarian Artillery Regiment.[9]

Toller had grown up in Samotschin, a town three hundred and forty-six kilometers east of Berlin, in present-day Poland, where he had the unpleasant childhood experience of being maligned as a "dirty Jew."[10] Born to Jewish parents, Toller had always considered himself German, and bristled at the hurtful anti-Semitic insults thrown his way. Volunteering for service in the German army offered him the chance to gain the acceptance he'd never received growing up. Toller wrote of his enlistment, "I thought of . . . my terrible joy when I realized that nobody would recognize me for a Jew . . . and my passionate longing to prove that I was a real German by offering my life to my country."[11]

Apart from the institutional prejudices, which curtailed his rise in rank, Toller found acceptance in the German army and seldom encountered anti-Semitism while in uniform.[12] Then in 1915 he won the respect of his peers when he volunteered for frontline service. It wasn't every day that a man freely undertook an assignment that meant almost certain death. At the front, soldiers were being torn apart by the terrifying new weapons of the industrial era. Those who served there, and lived to tell about it, joined an elite brotherhood of survivors. Toller's decision resulted not from heroism but from boredom. "At last to be allowed to take one's part!" he recorded in his diary, "To prove one's thoughts, one's feelings with one's life."[13]

But Toller, relegated to a muddy, rat-infested frontline trench, where the men of his unit were dying so quickly there was no place to dispose of the bodies, became soul-shocked. "We did not bury our dead," Toller wrote. "We pushed them into the little niches in the wall of the trench cut as resting places for ourselves. When I went slipping and slithering down the trench, with my head bent low, I did not know whether the men I passed were dead or alive; in that place the dead and the living had the same yellow-grey faces."[14] Some soldiers had been blown to bits; others were caught in the barbed wire between trenches, their bodies rotting in the elements. Pieces of torn flesh littered the ground, and when the rats weren't stealing the soldiers' food they were eating the dead. Then came Verdun.

Falkenhayn's strategy was simple: He intended to pound the French lines at Verdun with massive artillery fire, decimate the enemy, and then send in the infantry. Everything had been prepared in advance. The Germans had brought forward a fearsome number of artillery pieces: 1,220 field guns.[15] They outnumbered French artillery at a ratio of four to one. To maintain the element of surprise, the Germans dug a bunker complex beneath the front lines, called *Stollen*, to conceal their infantry. At the anointed hour, they would emerge from the depths and charge the enemy in terrifying numbers. High above in the clouds, German planes kept French reconnaissance aircraft from reporting on German preparations by blowing them out of the sky.

Falkenhayn had originally intended to attack on February 12. But driving snow and bitter cold had delayed the assault. Finally, at 8:12 a.m. on February 21, the Germans began their offensive by shelling French positions for eight straight hours. Then at 4:00 p.m. the order was given to attack, and a restless German infantry poured out of their Stollen and advanced on the French. Crossing a landscape destroyed by artillery, the Germans brought forward a new and terrible weapon: the flamethrower. French soldiers reportedly fled in panic when their comrades were set ablaze.[16] But somehow the French did not allow themselves to be completely overrun.

The following day, the Germans repeated their fearsome artillery bombardment. French forces were literally vaporized: The smell of their shredded, gastric entrails filled the air, causing waves of nausea among the survivors. And the shelling continued. Soldiers were in constant danger of being buried alive. But when the Germans sent in the infantry, again the French refused to yield, and they inflicted severe casualties. Falkenhayn's offensive wasn't going according to plan. However, two days later, on February 24, German fortunes changed when the constant pounding of artillery allowed the infantry to break through at several positions. The French were losing heart, particularly at the sight of hundreds of wounded men left unattended in the confusion. Things were about to get worse.[17]

French generals were deeply concerned that battle fatigue and low morale was crippling the front lines. Fearing that a French retreat might lead to capitulation, an entire army of French reserves was sent to Verdun as reinforcements. It seemed the German commander's foresight was coming true. Now Falkenhayn could make them "bleed to death."[18] But what he didn't anticipate was the appointment of a military genius to command his enemy's forces: Philippe Petain. The French commander, who later achieved infamy by collaborating with the Nazis as prime minister of Vichy France, arrived at Verdun and quickly deduced how the Germans could be stopped. In a well-coordinated counteroffensive with French guns, Petain decimated German positions and inflicted severe casualties.

To keep their gains, the Germans tried to move their artillery forward. But a spring thaw had turned the pockmarked battlefield into a slippery bog, and they were ill-equipped to cross the muddy landscape. In the lapse between Petain's bombardment and retaliation, German gains were compromised and stalemate set in. For ten excruciating months, the two adversaries exchanged deadly volleys of artillery fire along a thirty-kilometer front, turning the verdant French countryside into a barren wasteland. Estimates suggest two shells were fired every second for the duration of the conflict, and one man died every minute.[19]

In the trenches, rain and soil mixed with the bloody entrails of the dead, making a putrid stew. Pinned down by enemy fire, soldiers cowered in the mud among the grisly, dismembered corpses of their countrymen. The wounded shrieked, wailed, and moaned, sometimes for hours at a time. Those left maimed in no-man's-land—areas too dangerous for a rescue mission—called out for days on end, until death finally claimed them. Soldiers did anything they could to blot out the screams. Many went mad. These were the horrors that began to erode Ernst Toller's sense of purpose.

At Verdun, Toller was ordered to pinpoint the location of French artillery. His work took place at night. Like a person in a thunderstorm trying to calculate the proximity of lightning, Toller would join the infantry in a frontline trench and count off the seconds between the flash of enemy artillery and its thunderous detonation. From this, he could determine the exact bearings of French batteries. It was extremely dangerous work. Night after night, as shells rained down upon him, Toller would brave enemy fire as he scrambled back and forth between the front lines and the communication trench, where his coordinates could be relayed to German artillery.

On March 3, 1916, Toller became a noncommissioned officer. Two weeks later, he was promoted again. Considering his intense desire for acceptance as a Jew in the German Army, the promotions must have been gratifying. But in his autobiography, all Toller wrote of the subject was, "I was promoted to corporal."[20] At Verdun, other thoughts preoccupied his mind. Toller was losing his appetite for war. The relentless killing was forcing him to reevaluate nationalism, and to consider things from a different perspective.

Among the changes in Toller's thinking was his growing respect for the enemy. The shared horrors of the front line caused him to identify more with the Frenchmen on the other side of the line than the German officers in the rear, who were calling the shots at a safe distance. Reading German publications on the front, the poet expressed disgust for the incessant propaganda articles deprecating the French, the English, and the Russians.

Toller's intolerance of the barbarity of war came to a head in late March 1916. One day, while digging a trench, his pick got stuck in the mud. When he pulled it out of the ground, he discovered that human entrails had wound their way around his pick. The poet had stumbled onto the anonymous burial site of a fallen soldier. Given his constant exposure to death, there was nothing particularly unusual about the discovery. But on this day, Toller found himself frozen.

"A dead man," he later recalled of the experience. "I tried to thrust the words out of my mind. What was there about them that they should so overwhelm me?" Toller could not move. "And suddenly," he continued,

> like light in darkness, the real truth broke in upon me. The simple fact of Man, which I had forgotten, which had lain deep and buried out of sight; the idea of community, of unity. A dead man. Not a dead Frenchman. Not a dead German. A dead man. All these corpses had been men; all these corpses had breathed as I breathed; had had a father, a mother, a woman whom they loved, a piece of land which was theirs, faces which expressed their joys and their sufferings, eyes which had known the light of day and the color of the sky. At that moment of realization I knew that I had been blind because I had wished not to see; it was only then that I realized, at last, that all these dead men, Frenchmen and Germans, were brothers, and I was the brother of them all.[21]

Toller had reached his breaking point. In an army whose business was killing the enemy, his revelation was tantamount to madness, and he could no longer continue. After some 361 days at the front, he was removed from the battlefield on April 3, 1916. Just four weeks later, he arrived at a hospital near Strasbourg, where he was treated for "war neurosis,"[22] known today as post-traumatic stress disorder. The poet would never see the front line again.

When the battle of Verdun ended in the fall of 1916, the French and the Germans had lost nearly half a million men each. Yet no ground had been gained: It seemingly had all been for nothing. Seizing the opportunity to advance their careers, General Erich Ludendorff and other German officers lobbied against Falkenhayn, who was then demoted.[23] From that point forward, Ludendorff and his superior, Field Marshal Paul von Hindenburg, commanded the German war effort. Ludendorff, it was said, was now the most powerful man in Germany.[24] In a written postwar analysis of his own decision-making, Erich von Falkenhayn showed no remorse.[25] The commander appeared aloof to the human suffering that marked Ernst Toller's frontline experience.

Following the stalemate at Verdun, some angry Germans, looking for a scapegoat, vented their frustrations by accusing German Jews of malfeasance. Prevalent among the charges was the claim that Jews had avoided military service, particularly at the front. Two months after General Falkenhayn's dismissal in 1916, a study was authorized to determine the extent of Jewish participation in the war.[26] The census provoked outrage among outspoken German Jews, and the government eventually decided to withhold its findings. In retrospect, it's unfortunate the census wasn't published. According to the statistics, Jews were well represented in the German army and the front lines. Among these patriotic German Jews was Ernst Toller.

"THE TERRIBLE PERVERSITY OF THE LAW"

Toller's journey into the postwar period is a striking counterpoint to the path of Adolf Hitler. While the two men were exposed to similar perils, they arrived at vastly different conclusions and followed divergent paths. Indeed, taking stock of the poet's trajectory puts Hitler's rise in a new and uncommon perspective.

In January 1917, Toller was released from the army and returned to his studies, not in Grenoble but at Ludwig-Maximilians-Universität (LMU) in Munich. In his new surroundings, Toller kept his distance from newspapers, sensing that he might be retraumatized by reports from the front. In the streets of the Bavarian capital, disabled veterans and widowed women served as constant reminders of the war. At LMU, Toller remained silent about his military service, took trips to nearby lakes, and went to concerts, later reporting that the pulsing music of Bach, Beethoven, and Schubert allowed him to blot out the screams of the wounded in his head.[27]

Toller's return to Munich that spring coincided with significant developments on the home front. In April, a handful of antiwar politicians split from Germany's largest political party, the Social Democrats, and formed the Independent Social Democratic Party (USPD). Though tiny by comparison, the fledgling USPD aimed to champion the antiwar cause and press for democratization. After close to three years of war, many Germans were growing weary of the conflict. Strikes had erupted in various cities and an estimated two hundred thousand workers walked off the job in Berlin. Widespread famine was a daily reminder that Germany's military leadership had miscalculated when they boasted that the conflict would be won in just a few months. The lack of food was so acute that some German pet owners were forced to eat their own cats and dogs.[28] To appease dissent, Kaiser Wilhelm II delivered an Easter message, in which he promised a softening of autocratic rule when the war ended.[29] In truth, neither the Kaiser nor his top generals, Ludendorff and Hindenburg, had any intention of altering Germany's war footing or relinquishing the reins of power.

In Schwabing, the bohemian quarter north of Munich, Toller spent time with a group of ambitious students questioning the old values of German society and hoping to create something new through literature. They embodied the youthful, antiestablishment spirit later epitomized by rock and roll. "Each of us had a drawer full of manuscripts," Toller later wrote, "each dreamed of fame; each deemed himself specially favored and chosen."[30] Since the turn of the century, Schwabing had been a mecca for artists and performers. Even the idealistic postcard painter Adolf Hitler came here to take up residence before the war. Through the assistance of a fellow war veteran and professor of theater history, Toller gained acceptance in Schwabing's influential avant-garde circles, inhabited by notable literary figures including Thomas Mann, author of *A Death in Venice*, and Frank Wedekind, who penned *Spring Awakening*. The promising young writer received personal guidance from Mann, who took time out of his schedule to go over his poems line by line. Through these encounters and others, fate seemed to be grooming Toller to contribute important literary work of his own. However, his politics remained undefined. Then, in the summer of 1917, the poet experienced something of a transformation when he read *Aufruf zum Sozialismus* (Call to Socialism) by Gustav Landauer.

A German Jew and an anarchist, Landauer had been one of the few pacifists to oppose the war since its inception. Teaching that anguish leads to redemption, Landauer's book seemed to suggest that Toller's crisis of conscience at the front was an opportunity for rebirth: The discovery of the dead man's entrails at Verdun not only triggered Toller's war neurosis, it signaled a tectonic shift in his thinking; one in which human solidarity took precedence over German nationalism. This was a realization that would escape Adolf Hitler throughout his life. Landauer had called for the spiritual awakening of the German people.[31] Thoroughly inspired, Toller incorporated his ideas into a play he was writing about his wartime experiences entitled *Die Wandlung* (*Transformation*) and started to consider whether he might be fated to play a leadership role in the rebirth of German society.

In July, developments in Berlin set the stage for Toller's first foray into political activism. That month, ministers of the German Reichstag (parliament) issued a majority statement in which they suggested that the war be ended through "a peace of understanding and permanent reconciliation."[32] Further, they proposed that Germany abandon her territorial gains. This dovish proposal was a blatant refutation of the High Command and contradicted Erich Ludendorff's resolute commitment to victory. While parliament lacked the authority to impose its will on the Kaiser, Ludendorff, and the military, the nonbinding statement outraged Germany's Far Right and provoked the establishment of an extremist party dubbed the Vaterlandspartei (Fatherland Party).[33] In a society at war, where the acceptance of state authority had, since the time of Chancellor Otto von Bismarck, formed the bedrock of social contract, it is no wonder that the Vaterlandspartei became exceptionally popular. Its staunch opposition to the Reichstag's majority statement was headline news. Soon, the party commanded over one million supporters. However, the reaction of Ernst Toller and a growing minority of restless students was decidedly different.

For his winter term, Toller relocated to the University of Heidelberg to pursue his doctorate. When news came from Munich that a pacifist professor at LMU had been assaulted for speaking out against the war, Toller coauthored a pamphlet defending him. The playwright was incensed that the nationalists had used physical violence to suppress the professor's freedom of speech. Signed by 135 students, the tract was published in Bavaria and distributed to various universities. Inspired to take further action, Toller led the creation of an antiwar student league, which attacked the Vaterlandspartei for opposing the Reichstag's majority statement and drafted a pamphlet entitled *Aufruf* (Appeal) that called "for a deepening of culture in the name of human morality."[34] But Toller was offending those Germans who saw his activities as undermining the troops.

When the Vaterlandspartei became aware of *Aufruf*, Toller and his fellow students were castigated as a "traitors"[35] and accused in a newspaper of lacking "patriotic sentiment."[36] Students and professors distanced themselves from the former frontline soldier. Shortly thereafter, the military intervened, threatened Toller's male colleagues with conscription, and issued a warrant for his arrest. However, when they arrived at his Heidelberg flat to take him away, the playwright was nowhere to be found. Toller had received a tip from a fellow student and fled to Berlin by train.

In the German capital, Toller read Socialist literature and acquainted himself with recently published memoirs, which claimed that Germany had started the war and kept the public in the dark. "I read in these books that the imperial government had betrayed the nation," he later wrote. "I had been as credulous as everyone else in Germany . . . [But after reading the memoirs] I felt that the land I loved had been betrayed and sold."[37] Toller now felt he had incontrovertible proof that he'd been duped in 1914, when he put his faith in a newspaper report that blamed the French for starting the war.

While in Berlin, friends brought Toller to a meeting with a man who was to play the most decisive role in his life. Visiting the Prussian capital was Kurt Eisner, a charismatic Socialist journalist and prominent leader of the antiwar USPD in Bavaria. An advocate for revolution, the Jewish-born Eisner had opposed the war since anyone could remember, and he hoped to spark a democratic movement that would overturn Germany's authoritarian state. In Eisner, Toller found an ethical activist, sincere in his commitment to people-centered politics, who took the time to listen to the ideas of young people. The meeting had a profound impact on the young playwright. Within weeks, he followed Kurt Eisner back to the Bavarian capital, where he resumed his studies at LMU.

In late January 1918, with the war still raging, Eisner and the USPD held a series of meetings in Bavaria to organize a massive antigovernment labor strike. Workers in Munich were angry about the government's stubborn refusal to negotiate for peace. Feeling that they could no longer endure Germany's ongoing famine, they were increasingly prepared to join Kurt Eisner, Ernst Toller, and the USPD and air their grievances against the government. On January 31, 1918, an estimated eight thousand workers from local munitions plants and other Bavarian factories walked off the job. Police authorities arrested Eisner that evening.

Vowing with the workers to prolong the strike, Toller launched a strategy to win Eisner's freedom and penned a leaflet entitled *Kameraden* (Comrades) to appraise Munich of the strikers' true motives and intentions. The following day, thousands met at the Theresienwiese (the traditional location of Munich's Oktoberfest) to continue the strike. The crowd was so massive that the police stood down. But their restraint was short lived. In the coming weeks, strikers were targeted for military conscription and sent to the western front. Shortly thereafter, Toller was arrested and brought to a police station in handcuffs, where he was instructed to put on a military uniform. "[But] I've been invalided out," the playwright protested to his abductors. "Well, you've been called up again," they replied. "Put that on!"[38]

After lengthy interrogations, Toller was exposed as the author of *Kameraden*. Led away by soldiers with fixed bayonets, he was deposited in a military prison on Munich's Leonrodstraße. Incarcerated in a filthy, lice-infested cell behind the prison's brick walls, the poet was denied access to Eisner and the other strike leaders, and subjected to daily abuse. Of his confinement at the military jail, Toller would later write, "For the first time I saw clearly the true structure of society today, the conditions that make war inevitable, the terrible perversity of the law that allows the masses to go hungry while a few grow rich."[39] Little could his jailers have known that they were priming him for the day he would leave prison and take leadership of a Bavarian revolution.

Germany would transform in the months following Toller's arrest. By the time Kurt Eisner was released from prison nine months later, the nation's First Quartermaster General, Erich Ludendorff, would be suing for peace. The changes would be so earth shattering that a lowly, unknown private named Adolf Hitler would start looking for scapegoats and blaming the antiwar strike leaders— many of them Jews—for sabotaging the army and betraying the Fatherland.

The future Nazi dictator could not, or would not, countenance the real reasons Germany would lose the war.

CHAPTER TWO

THE GREAT DECEPTION

"THE BLACK DAY OF THE GERMAN ARMY"

In a rose garden on a hill overlooking Spa, Belgium, Germany's top commander, Erich Ludendorff, drew deep breaths as he paced the grounds of his appropriated villa in September 1918. Suffering from depression, the fifty-three-year-old was in a state of extreme agitation. For the past four years, he'd shouldered a punishing work schedule of eighteen to twenty-three hours a day. In all that time, he'd taken only three days off.[1] Then in early August, he suffered a nervous collapse.[2] When a consulting psychologist diagnosed his condition as exhaustion, Ludendorff was encouraged to get more sleep, practice deep breathing, take walks in the rose garden, and even sing folk songs from his childhood. While these therapeutic practices noticeably improved his demeanor, they couldn't resolve his crushing crisis of leadership.

Ludendorff grew up in

First Quartermaster General Erich Ludendorff.

Prussia in the nineteenth century, the product of military cadet schools that emphasized discipline and self-sacrifice in the spirit of the ancient warrior culture of Sparta. His work ethic and mastery of mathematics were considered exceptional, and he received his first commission at the age of twenty. Ludendorff's ambition as a military careerist made him the sort of man to shovel food into his mouth without tasting it so that he could get back to work as soon as possible. Married with three stepsons, he denied himself idle pleasures and had few close friends. During the early years of the First World War, Ludendorff's name became legendary when he orchestrated stunning military victories in Belgium and Poland. In August 1916, when Erich von Falkenhayn was sacked for failing to achieve a breakthrough at Verdun, Kaiser Wilhelm II appointed Ludendorff to lead the general staff under Paul von Hindenburg.

With no one to answer to except the Kaiser and Hindenburg, Ludendorff took sole command of the military in his new position as First Quartermaster General. In the years since that appointment, like Falkenhayn before him, he'd been trying to deliver a knockout punch against his country's enemies. But the odds were stacked against him. Germany's forces were engaged in a two-front war, with Russia in the east and France and Great Britain in the west. Hindsight suggests that Ludendorff could have made peace and avoided war reparations. But the ambitious First Quartermaster General wanted more. "If Germany makes peace without profit," he'd told Austro-Hungary's foreign minister, "then Germany has lost the war."[3]

Believing that the French would lose heart if he could strangle the English, Ludendorff authorized unrestricted submarine warfare to cut off supply shipments to Great Britain in January 1917. But instead of demoralizing the enemy, the carnage provoked America to join the Entente (the alliance between France and Great Britain). On April 6, 1917, President Woodrow Wilson and the United States of America declared war on Germany. Recognizing that he lacked the manpower to sustain a war on two fronts once trained American forces arrived in Europe, Ludendorff sought to conclude the conflict in the east.

The war was not going well for the Russians. That spring, massive casualties, famine, and economic ruin had provoked major unrest and forced the abdication of Russia's last tsar, Nicholas II. Pushing its luck, the country's provisional government vowed to continue the war against Germany until its "glorious conclusion,"[4] and Russia's embittered populace was sent careening toward revolution. On April 9, three days after the Americans joined the war, Ludendorff arranged for the exiled Communist leader living in Switzerland, Vladimir Lenin, to board a sealed train bound for Russia through German-occupied territories.[5]

The First Quartermaster General calculated that if Lenin were to succeed in sparking a Bolshevik revolution, he would likely be required to conclude the war with Germany in order to consolidate his power. To sweeten the prospects, the Germans provided Lenin with 40 million gold marks in financial assistance.[6] When Lenin and the Bolsheviks seized power in Russia seven months later, true to Ludendorff's expectations, the Communist leader announced his intention to end the war with Germany. American forces had not yet arrived in significant numbers to alter the stalemate in France and Belgium. Secretly planning an offensive on the western front for the spring of 1918, Ludendorff hoped that peace with Russia would free up his army in the east to join his forces in the west.

In December 1917, German and Russian negotiators began peace talks at Brest-Litovsk, in Belarus. The Germans wanted to annex most of Poland, gain control of the Baltic States, and declare Ukraine a free country. The Soviets were unwilling to give up any territories. Two months into the talks, Soviet representatives staged a walkout. But when Ludendorff's army resumed its advance into Latvia, Russian negotiators returned to the table. German negotiators were now insisting that their counterparts also give up Finland, Estonia, Latvia, Lithuania, and Belarus.[7] The Soviets stood to lose a significant portion of the former Russian Empire. However unacceptable these terms may have been, Lenin pressed for resolution, and on March 3, 1918, the Soviets signed the Treaty of Brest-Litovsk. Ludendorff had engineered what no other European general, not even Napoleon, had been able to achieve in the east. But his success came at a price. While thirty-two divisions and five hundred thousand soldiers were now available to join the war in the west, an estimated one million more would have to remain in the east to occupy Germany's new territories.

In March, the Americans shipped sixty thousand servicemen to Western Europe. Understanding that time was running out, Ludendorff readied his forces to deliver a knockout punch before the United States sent any more. On March 21, 1918, wishfully thinking that his ingenuity and determination could overcome what his forces lacked in manpower and resources, Ludendorff launched an aggressive spring offensive. Supported by new artillery tactics, waves of German stormtroopers sliced through British lines on the Somme and achieved significant gains. The success buoyed Ludendorff's spirits and was welcome news back in Germany. But without sufficient operational support, and against hardened defenses, the German advances were soon halted. When the assault was called off fifteen days later, the Germans had lost 239,000 men.[8]

Erich Ludendorff suffered little torment contemplating the hundreds of thousands of men he'd just consigned to death. To him, war was a test of wills between generals, played out on maps in his military headquarters, far behind the front lines. He had no feel for the living hell Ernst Toller and other soldiers had experienced in blood-soaked trenches.[9] This indifference to suffering was not limited to his army. The First Quartermaster General also lacked empathy for the anguish caused by starvation at home. A British blockade had prevented vital food imports from reaching Germany since 1914, and hundreds of thousands of civilians were dying each year of malnutrition and associated illnesses. In prolonging the war to achieve his aims, Ludendorff hadn't really considered the consequences for the German people. However, during the first phase of his spring offensive, he experienced a personal suffering so disturbing that it forced a crack in his granite-like confidence.

On March 22, Ludendorff's beloved stepson Erich, a twenty-year-old pilot, flew behind enemy lines and never returned to base. When the wreckage and a gravesite was later identified, the general rushed to the scene and ordered his stepson exhumed. Standing over the body, he slumped his shoulders and began to weep. This was the second stepson he'd lost in the war, and marked the first of many crying episodes.[10] In the coming months, as his agitation increased, the First Quartermaster General would make repeated visits to Erich's temporary gravesite at Avesnes.

Yet Ludendorff still had a war to win. On April 9, he initiated a second offensive against the Entente close to Dunkirk, on the French side of the English Channel. Twenty days later, British resistance forced him to call it off. The death toll for each side topped 100,000 men.[11] For his third attack, Ludendorff sent his men against British positions 110 kilometers northeast of Paris, near the Marne River, on May 27. And just as it had in previous offensives, the German military stalled. Later, when Ludendorff's forces moved westward, they were stopped by a French counterattack at Compiegne. From May 27 to June 6, the Germans lost another 125,000 men.[12]

In May, the monthly shipment of American servicemen to Europe increased to nearly a quarter of a million, giving the Entente a sizeable numerical advantage. In June and July, Ludendorff mounted two more offensives, but the results were largely the same. Lacking operational support and hobbled by casualties, desertions, fatigue, and influenza, demoralized German forces were simply unable to hold on to their gains. Then, on August 8, the invigorated armies of the Entente, supported by over a million fresh American troops, began a historic counteroffensive. In just the first day of battle, thirty thousand German soldiers were killed and another thirteen thousand surrendered east of Amiens.[13] The tide of war had changed, and Erich Ludendorff knew it.

For the First Quartermaster General, August 8 became the "black day of the German Army."[14] The surrender of thirteen thousand Germans soldiers was particularly incomprehensible to him, and he concluded privately "the war must be ended."[15] This was no easy decision. Ludendorff had staked his reputation on the promise that Germany would win.[16] If he were to admit publicly that victory was no longer attainable, it would eviscerate the high respectability he felt he'd earned. For a man who had devoted his life to proving himself the ablest of generals, death must have seemed preferable to confessing defeat. Ludendorff wracked his brain to find a way out of the predicament. Even if he kept quiet and reconfigured his forces on the battlefield in a defensive posture, it was only a matter of time before they would be overrun. Finally, years of sleep deprivation and stress caught up with him, and he suffered a nervous collapse.

Witnessing their commander's erratic behavior, staff members and officers at military headquarters concluded that something had to be done to discreetly revive him. First, Colonel Wilhelm Heye was brought in to free Ludendorff from some of his less important duties.[17] Next, a retired psychologist from Berlin was dispatched to Spa to examine the First Quartermaster General. Diagnosing Ludendorff's affliction as exhaustion from overwork, he prescribed a bevy of therapeutic exercises to counteract his nervous tension.[18]

But Ludendorff refused to recuse himself from command. Six days after the Allied counteroffensive of August 8, he was scheduled to attend an imperial conference with Germany's top leadership: Kaiser Wilhelm II, Field Marshal Paul von Hindenburg, German chancellor Georg von Hertling, and Foreign Secretary Paul von Hintze. The meeting was his first real opportunity to apprise the top brass of the changes at the front. Would he tell them that the war was no longer winnable? Just a month earlier, he'd assured Hintze that his offensives would result in victory.[19] No longer feeling certain, he pulled the foreign secretary aside before the meeting and revised his position: If Germany were to achieve a satisfactory peace agreement, a defensive military strategy would now have to be employed.[20]

When the imperial conference with Kaiser Wilhelm II convened at the Hotel Britanique in Spa on August 14, Ludendorff was on edge. Just the day before, he'd impulsively offered his resignation to the Kaiser, but Wilhelm II had refused. Would the monarch have kept him on if he knew how dire the situation was at the front? For over a year, left-wing politicians back home had been clamoring for a negotiated peace with the Entente. Ludendorff had vehemently opposed them. What would the Kaiser do if his top military commander suddenly made an about-face and recommended peace negotiations?

According to official notes from the meeting, Hintze painted a dire picture of the diplomatic situation in Europe.[21] The enemy was more confident than ever, and time was no longer on Germany's side. The message was unmistakable: Ludendorff's military offensives had failed, and Germany was on the brink of defeat. A deflated Kaiser and his civilian leadership were resigned to initiating peace negotiations. But Ludendorff couldn't stomach it. Unable to concede that the war was lost, he called for a new military strategy to "paralyze the enemy's fighting spirit."[22] Backing him, Hindenburg suggested that conditions at the front were actually more favorable than anyone realized. Asserting that the army was still capable of achieving modest gains, Hindenburg and Ludendorff gave the impression that peace negotiations would likely yield better results "after the next [military] success in the west."[23] Hindenburg even went so far as to say that, eventually, the enemy would bow to their will, and that German troops on French soil were there to stay. This unrealistic report created the false impression that Germany could take its time pursuing peace negotiations. Nothing could have been further from the truth.

Six weeks later, Ludendorff's staff could no longer ignore what their commander had been unwilling to admit. Reports from the front were grim: mass desertions, influenza, and low morale were crippling an already-depleted army. The war had become a hopeless cause, and every day thousands of men continued to die. The Allied armies crept closer and closer to the German border. Yet no efforts were being made to open negotiations. Finally, when Ludendorff learned that Bulgaria—Germany's wartime ally—had decided to seek a separate peace with the Entente, he snapped. On September 28, in a meeting with fellow officers, he reportedly lost control of his emotions, suffered a seizure, and collapsed.[24] "Foam appeared on his lips and in a slow, gliding motion," he fell to the floor.[25] When he awoke, the First Quartermaster General instructed his attendants to conceal the episode and privately announced a change of heart: at last, he intended to pursue peace negotiations.

Two days later, Ludendorff confided to Hindenburg that an armistice was now necessary. Much to his surprise, Hindenburg disclosed that he had been thinking the same thing. "The Field Marshal and I parted with a strong handshake," he later wrote in his memoirs, "like men who have buried their dearest hopes and who are resolved to hold together in their hardest trials as they have held together in success."[26] But Ludendorff's comfort was probably momentary. It must have occurred to him that he was the one most likely to be blamed for Germany's defeat, not Hindenburg. When the time came to settle accounts for the failed war, there would be little to shield him from direct responsibility. Ludendorff was undoubtedly filled with dread. If only he could find someone else to blame.

"A BEAUTIFUL GERMAN HERO"

On September 29, 1918, Ludendorff met with Hindenburg, Hintze, and Colonel Heye at the Hotel Britanique. Six weeks had passed since he recommended renewed military efforts at the front, despite his realization that the war was lost. Now, facing the inevitable collapse of the army, Ludendorff recognized that it was only a matter of time before his political adversaries would seize on his failures and turn the German people against him. But his reputation was about to be saved by a twentieth century deus ex machina.

Just when it seemed that he would be blamed for Germany's defeat, Foreign Secretary Hintze introduced a deceptive scheme to reshuffle the civilian government, institute parliamentary democracy, and empower its new leadership to broker an armistice.[27] Ludendorff likely had a hard time concealing his excitement: If a new civilian leadership appeared to initiate peace talks, they would be blamed for the terms that were meted out. This would distract the public from the real question of who lost the war and Ludendorff's strategic mistakes. As Hintze laid out his plan, the First Quartermaster General realized that the strategy might save his reputation.

A seasoned foreign diplomat, Paul von Hintze was well briefed on the condition of the army and understood that Germany needed to exit the war. He reasoned that if they replaced the existing government and instigated democratic reforms, the Entente was more likely to offer favorable peace terms. Similarly, antiwar discontent inside Germany would likely subside if the government embraced reform, even superficially. The foreign secretary was, in effect, proposing a carefully orchestrated coup from the top down: Chancellor Hertling and his cabinet would be sacrificed so that the monarchy of Kaiser Wilhelm II could be saved. The Reichstag would be empowered and the center-left Social Democratic Party, which had joined the call for a negotiated peace in 1917, would be invited to share power and accountability in the new government.

Despite his later claim that he resisted the scheme, Ludendorff accepted the foreign secretary's plan wholeheartedly and was eager to see the Social Democrats and the Left held accountable for undermining the war effort.[28] Events began to unfold in rapid succession. On the afternoon of September 29, 1918, Ludendorff, Hindenburg, and Hintze met with the Kaiser to present the foreign secretary's plan, which included a diplomatic approach to the Americans. Though he feared US president Woodrow Wilson would insist on his abdication, Wilhelm II agreed. When Hertling learned of the scheme hatched behind his back, he begged for a two-week extension but was rebuffed. On September 30, he tendered his resignation. A few days later, pressures inside the government convinced Hintze to depart as well, but not before his plan was implemented.

On the first day of October, Hintze and Wilhelm II tapped Max von Baden, the Kaiser's second cousin, to become Germany's next chancellor and preside over a new government. Baden was an acceptable choice to Ludendorff because he had opposed the Reichstag politicians who had demanded a negotiated peace in July of 1917. That same day, Ludendorff gathered the section chiefs of the High Command for an announcement. According to one observer, he entered the room pale, full of worry, but with his head held high.[29] At long last, he informed the assembled officers that the war was lost. Claiming that the poison of Socialist ideas had infected the men on the front, he said he could no longer rely on the troops. With the help of the Americans, the enemy was destined to achieve victory.[30] Soon there would be revolution in Germany. Such a catastrophe, Ludendorff said, "must be avoided at all costs."[31] Therefore, he had demanded that the Kaiser and his chancellor immediately pursue peace talks with President Wilson. Ludendorff added that the war should be brought to an end "in order to avoid unnecessarily sacrificing the bravest ones, who are still loyal and able to fight."[32]

His cunning performance worked its magic. One of the assembled men, a fifty-year-old general staff officer named Albrecht von Thaer, would later record of Ludendorff, "A truly beautiful German hero. I had to think of Siegfried with the mortal wound in his back from Hagen's spear."[33] Thaer was referring to Richard Wagner's famous opera *Twilight of the Gods* and likening Ludendorff to the mythological Germanic hero Siegfried, who was lured on a hunting trip and stabbed in the back by Hagen, a cunning villain. Ludendorff's report gave the impression that he'd been betrayed by shadowy figures and that responsibility for Germany's defeat lay somewhere else. The infamous "stab in the back" theory was already taking root.

In front of his officers, Ludendorff lamented that it was "terrible" to admit defeat to the Kaiser and the chancellor.[34] He told them that Chancellor Hertling had subsequently resigned out of a sense of honor, not wanting to end his career with an armistice. Regarding the new politicians who would soon be taking over, Ludendorff said, "I have asked His Majesty to bring those people into the government who are largely responsible that things have turned out as they have. We shall therefore see these gentlemen enter the ministries, and they must now make the peace, which has to be made. They must now eat the soup, which they have served us."[35]

Ludendorff started pressuring the new chancellor to open negotiations with the US president. In a communiqué dated October 1, he instructed Baden to send an offer of peace immediately: "The troops are holding their own today, what may happen tomorrow cannot be foreseen."[36] The chancellor was understandably shocked. When he agreed to take power, no one had informed him that the situation at the front required the immediate pursuit of an armistice. In Berlin, he already had his hands full attempting to form his new government. "The army cannot wait another forty-eight hours," Ludendorff pressed in a follow-up message.[37] In hindsight, the general might have wished that he hadn't been so pushy.

On October 3, Baden dispatched a message calling for peace negotiations between Germany and the United States. In his correspondence with the US president, the new chancellor assured Woodrow Wilson that he spoke for the German people and promised that his country's parliamentary democracy was "being legally developed and safeguarded."[38] But the US president had his doubts, and replied that if America was forced to deal with the Kaiser or the High Command then he must demand "not peace negotiations, but surrender."[39] Ludendorff was outraged: Wilson had aroused the kind of anger that typifies authoritarian leaders when their pride is injured. No sooner had Baden sent a cable assuring the US president that Germany's military was subject to his authority than Ludendorff became unhinged and threatened to resign unless the Kaiser terminated the negotiations. But Germany's venerated general had miscalculated. On October 26, Wilhelm II called his bluff and accepted his resignation.

Ludendorff's dismissal coincided with Adolf Hitler's convalescence in the psychiatric ward of a military hospital on the outskirts of Berlin.[40] The twenty-nine-year-old private claimed to have been temporary blinded by a mustard gas attack on the front thirteen days earlier. But doctors at the hospital concluded that his blindness was "psychosomatic."[41] Though the Austrian immigrant would eventually recover his eyesight, he remained blind to Ludendorff's cover-up throughout his life. Like the great majority of Germans, Hitler was not privy to the First Quartermaster General's schemes and failures. He never knew that Ludendorff had initiated armistice talks while the army was still fighting at the front. Instead, he believed the German army had been stabbed in the back. Ludendorff's deceit gave rise to an essential building block in Hitler's malignant worldview.

CHAPTER THREE

A REVOLUTION LED BY GERMAN JEWS

"REVOLUTION FROM ABOVE"

In early October 1918, the German people learned that their newly appointed chancellor, Max von Baden, had initiated armistice negotiations with President Woodrow Wilson. Promised victory in war and kept ignorant of the army's decline, millions felt bitter and betrayed. Throughout the summer, Ludendorff and the High Command had insisted that the war was winnable and forbade anyone "to speak of the present position as being anything else than hopeful."[1] Now, news of peace talks were posted on every street corner. The German sacrifice to war had been massive. The conflict had left children without fathers, wives without husbands, mothers without sons, and families without brothers, uncles, and cousins. Two million Germans were dead and over four million were wounded; many of them maimed and disfigured. "This unexpected bid for peace opened the eyes of the German people at last," Ernst Toller later wrote. "They had no idea of the impending catastrophe. So it was all for nothing— the millions of dead, the millions of wounded, the starvation at home. All for nothing."[2] The catastrophe of war would trigger enthusiasm for the politics of the antiwar Left. This phenomenon is sometimes overlooked in the analysis of Hitler's rise to power. Yet it was during the initial postwar period before the rise of the Nazis that leftist politicians came to the foreground and unknowingly produced for the future German dictator several of his scapegoats.

In the wake of General Ludendorff's departure, Chancellor Baden took the bold step of amending the power structures that had governed Germany since 1871. Replacing constitutional monarchy with parliamentary democracy, he stripped the Kaiser of his power to select Germany's government and gave it to the Reichstag. Similarly, the military was subordinated to parliament, not Wilhelm II. The shift was tectonic. Since the nineteenth century, Germany's elite officer corps had enjoyed unrestricted power as a special class with special privileges. Now, they were answerable to the Reichstag's elected officials, including antiwar politicians from the Left. Baden took these steps to win over the US president and to save the monarchy. By shaking up the government, he also hoped to secure a "revolution from above"[3] in order to diminish the potential for a revolution from below. But the measures fell short of satisfying those disgruntled Germans looking to vent their frustrations.

As early as 1916, opposition members of parliament, including the far-left politician Karl Liebknecht, had tried to withhold war funds and incite the public against the conflict. However, in a system controlled by the Kaiser and the German High Command, the Reichstag had little real power, and their protestations fell largely on deaf ears. Liebknecht and others, including the Communist heroine Rosa Luxemburg, were eventually sent to prison for making antiwar speeches, and the conflict dragged on for two more years. But circumstances now were different. Confronted by the shocking news of armistice talks, many war-weary Germans were ready to join the antiwar Left. Recently granted amnesty by the chancellor and released from prison, Liebknecht and his colleagues were back in business. But it was still unclear who possessed the right stuff to effectively harness Germany's growing discontent.

Traditionally, the Social Democratic Party (SPD) had been the voice of the Left in German politics. Founded the previous century when Chancellor Otto von Bismarck banned Socialist groups, its forefathers were Marxist and ideologically radical. Later, when antisocialist restrictions were eased, and the SPD grew to become one of the country's largest political affiliations, it moved to the center-left, became moderate, and eventually dropped revolution from its platform. Instead, the SPD adopted the progressive view that Socialism would prevail as the inevitable consequence of capitalism's collapse. With over a million members, the party had built a formidable infrastructure, which included a national newspaper, a trade union, women's organizations, social clubs, a youth movement, libraries, and burial funds.[4]

At the outset of hostilities in 1914, the SPD held a majority of seats in the Reichstag and offered its full support to the war effort. Then, in 1917, the party suffered a setback when a handful of antiwar politicians broke ranks and formed the Independent Social Democratic Party (USPD). Now that Baden had reshuffled the government, making the SPD the most powerful political party in the Reichstag, Social Democrats faced an important decision: Should they support revolution, or continue in opposition to the breakaway USPD and other far-left radicals? By late October, the atmosphere in Germany was electric with the desire for change. In a country feeling betrayed by its traditional authority, those antiwar leaders who had opposed the government and gone to prison for their subversive activities suddenly possessed important credentials. Would the SPD join or undermine them? In this unstable climate, all that was required for revolution was a spark and someone with the forethought and ingenuity to ignite it.

"ALL SOLDIERS GATHER ROUND KURT EISNER!"

On October 14, 1918, the charismatic Socialist agitator Kurt Eisner, who once had inspired Ernst Toller with his antiwar speeches, was released from Stadelheim Prison in Bavaria.[5] Looking like an "old testament prophet,"[6] with wild hair and a grizzled beard, the Jewish-born Eisner returned to Munich, where USPD representatives quickly nominated him to run against the popular SPD leader, Erhard Auer, in Bavarian state elections. Eisner's eight and a half months behind bars gave him the look of a true political prisoner, and he decided to forgo a haircut.

K. EISNER † 21. FEB. 19.

Kurt Eisner.

At the time, the German empire consisted of twenty-six states under the emperor, Kaiser Wilhelm II, and his government, an array of more minor kings and royal families. Bavaria—Germany's southernmost state—had joined the empire in 1871. Ruled by the Wittelsbach dynasty for eight centuries, it retained its monarchy and much of its autonomy after unification. Known for its fertile farmlands and provincialism, Bavaria was second only to Prussia in German preeminence.

Kurt Eisner and Erhard Auer held sharply contrasting views about the future of Bavaria, and Germany as a whole. Whereas incarceration had steeled

Eisner's resolve to push for revolution, Auer was a staunch defender of constitutional monarchy. The differences between the two personified the split between the political establishment of the SPD and the breakaway antiwar USPD. Described as a "big man . . . [with a] huge frame, large hands, and wide set eyes,"[7] Auer had good reason to feel confident in his own victory. The SPD was the most organized political party in the state, with networks of support that extended deep into the countryside. In contrast, the USPD's popularity was confined to Munich and a few other cities. A standing member of Bavaria's parliament, Auer was well known and respected. In contrast, his opponent had never held political office: He was a Jew, a Socialist journalist, and a Prussian—not exactly strong selling points to voters in the Bavarian hinterland.[8] In the words of the historian David Clay Large, "it was impossible to imagine him in lederhosen."[9] But Eisner possessed one credential that Auer did not: he'd opposed the war.

On November 3, 1918, Eisner tested Munich's appetite for revolution by delivering a provocative speech at the Theresienwiese. Despite Chancellor Baden's overtures to the US president, the war had not yet been concluded. Calling for the creation of a new Bavarian government formed by the people to

Kurt Eisner's revolution at the Theresienwiese (site of the Oktoberfest), November 7, 1918.

demand peace, Eisner won the crowd. When he learned of the speech, Auer dismissed Eisner as "insane and criminal."[10] But Social Democrats feared that the opposition candidate had tapped into the public's intense dissatisfaction with the war, and that it might soon reach a boiling point. Therefore, when Eisner challenged the SPD to join the USPD in sponsoring a massive antiwar demonstration scheduled four days later, on November 7, the Social Democrats decided to accept. "Let's not continually have this talk about Eisner," Auer reassured his fellows. "Eisner is taken care of. You can be sure of that. We have our people in hand. I am going to march with the parade [on November 7] myself. Nothing is going to happen."[11] What Auer hadn't anticipated was how effectively his rival had garnered secret support in various quarters of the Bavarian capital.

In Munich on November 7, an estimated fifty thousand people gathered at the Theresienwiese for the highly anticipated antiwar rally jointly sponsored by the USPD and the SPD.[12] Two days earlier, revolutionary spirits in the Bavarian capital had been buoyed by the news that sailors in the northern German port city of Kiel had rebelled against the High Command. Refusing to participate in what they judged to be a suicide mission, the sailors had seized their vessels and formed revolutionary councils similar to those that participated in the Russian revolution. Now, on this unseasonably warm day in Munich, all along the western incline of the Oktoberfest grounds, anxious crowds encircled individual politicians, who addressed their constituents in groups.

Situated in the most conspicuous position, before the Ruhmshalle, a Greco-Roman looking temple with an imposing bronze statue, was Erhard Auer. After delivering a lukewarm address, the Social Democratic leader departed for the center of Munich among a throng of supporters, supremely confident that the rally was finished. But up the hill near the Hackerbräu tavern, Kurt Eisner was just getting started. Shortly after Auer's departure, an Eisner loyalist shot up to the platform where he stood, hoisted a red flag, and started screaming, "All soldiers gather round Kurt Eisner!"[13] When a significant number had surrounded the rostrum, Eisner declared, "The time for action has come!"[14] The decisiveness of his words traveled like lightning through the crowd. Suddenly, a group of inspired soldiers cried out in response, "To the barracks!"[15]

Flanked by rows and rows of troops, Eisner and his supporters advanced to a nearby complex of military barracks. There, something unbelievable occurred. One by one, garrisoned units declared their loyalty to Eisner. As they moved from one barracks to the next, legions of soldiers joined the mass. Stunned officers stood frozen as the crowd gained momentum. Around seven o'clock that evening, the city's war minister informed Bavaria's central leadership that he had lost control of the garrisons.[16] By 10:00 p.m. that night, Eisner and his constituents had formed impromptu soldiers' and workers' councils and taken up residence at the Mathäserbräu beer cellar, near the central train station. There, Eisner dispatched armed groups to occupy various government buildings and print outlets. Then, escorted by a military detachment and followed by a crowd, Eisner marched unobstructed to Munich's parliament building.

Inside the ornate hall, thunderous cheers greeted Eisner when he declared the formation of a Bavarian Republic and nominated himself as Bavaria's interim head of state.[17] In the span of a single day, Bavaria's leadership had been overturned in a bloodless revolution. In the predawn hours, revolutionaries hoisted red flags from the twin towers of Munich's famous Frauenkirche (Cathedral of Our Dear Lady) to announce to the public the formation of the new regime. The journalist and historian Konrad Heiden, who would later become an outspoken critic of Adolf Hitler, described the overnight revolution this way: "As though by enchantment, the king, the princes, the generals, and ministers scattered to all the winds."[18]

"EVERY HUMAN LIFE SHOULD BE HOLY"

The following day, Bavarians learned that their monarch, King Ludwig III, and the royal Wittelsbach family had fled Munich the night before. Much of Munich's population was in a state of shock. Though there had been countless voices straining for political change, hardly anyone had foreseen it happening quite like this. When Eisner's forces had arrived at the locked doors of the parliament building the night before, a porter had simply let them in.[19] Power hadn't just changed hands; it seemed as though the existing world had turned upside down. And people from every political persuasion demanded to know how Eisner would govern.

In the *Münchner Neueste Nachrichten*, the only newspaper for sale that day,[20] Eisner gave assurances that public order would be maintained and private property protected. Pointedly, the new minister-president did not intend to wage a Bolshevik campaign of terror and wanted to reassure the public that they would enjoy security. His state government was already creating a police force to prevent looting and plundering in the Bavarian capital. "In Eisner's opinion," wrote the biographer Bernhard Grau, "only a government based on the trust of the people could prevent the country from domestic and political mayhem."[21] Eisner promised to bring together a government with the moral authority to obtain peace for Germany, and he was determined to avoid violence. "In this time of wild murder," he wrote, "we abhor all bloodshed. Every human life should be holy."[22]

That afternoon, the minister-president presided over the first session of the provisional council of the new Bavarian Republic. Before an assembly of workers, soldiers, and peasant representatives, he delivered an inaugural address in which he clarified his intention to personally negotiate peace terms with the Entente. Eisner believed that President Wilson was certain to deal harshly with the government in Berlin. "But if Bavaria has a government whose leaders have ever since 1914 fought against the war policy in lonely and dangerous opposition," he suggested, "we can be confident that such a government will . . . evoke a milder response."[23] Eisner was, of course, referring to his own antiwar record.

Introducing his newly formed cabinet, which included four Social Democrats, three Independents, and one nonaffiliated representative, Eisner shocked the assembly with the appointment of Erhard Auer as minister of the interior. The minister-president had in effect given his chief political rival the second most powerful position in the cabinet and control over the police. His swift selection of a cabinet on the first day of the new republic suggested that he might be more than just a persuasive public speaker. At a time of heightened uncertainty, he demonstrated effective and expeditious leadership. On the other hand, during these seminal hours no opposition had yet appeared in war-weary Munich to counter the Eisner revolution.

"A DEMOCRATIC STATE FOR ALL BAVARIANS"

Kurt Eisner was an idealist who came of age in Berlin during the late nineteenth century. Critical of Berlin's privileged classes and Prussian militarism, he developed an interest in Socialism in the late 1880s. Fully assimilated, Eisner did not consider himself a religious Jew.[24] Inspired by the philosophy of Immanuel Kant, which encouraged moral action consistent with universal law, Eisner cultivated a political philosophy that blended Socialism with Kantian idealism.

While working as a journalist for the *Frankfurter Zeitung*, Eisner's incendiary tone had clashed with the conservatism of his readers. In 1897, he was sentenced to nine months in jail for criticizing the Kaiser in a subversive article entitled "Caesar Mania."[25] Lacking a sense of reserve that seemed to typify German culture, Eisner caught the attention of Wilhelm Liebknecht, one of the founders of the SPD, and the father of Karl Liebknecht, who gave him a job at the party's newspaper, *Vorwärts*.[26] Liebknecht hoped to use the independent Eisner on the paper's editorial board, to mediate disputes between the party's factions. However, Eisner's blunt criticisms eventually alienated him from both radicals and revisionists alike and led to his dismissal. Then, in 1907, he emigrated from Prussia with his wife and their children and settled in Bavaria. In Nuremberg, Eisner worked for a Socialist newspaper but was let go when his internationalist vision for the paper clashed with his employers.[27] Shortly thereafter, he separated from his wife and departed for Munich, where he took a young lover by the name of Else Belli.

In the Bavarian capital, Eisner became the political editor of the Social Democratic newspaper, the *Münchener Post*. In 1914, he briefly joined the ranks of Social Democrats in favor of the war. But leaked diplomatic documents subsequently convinced him that Germany's leadership was largely responsible for starting the conflict. Slowly, and with increasing outspokenness, Eisner used his columns in the *Münchener Post* to criticize German aggression. Before long, he was dismissed from that job too.[28] Then, in 1917, Eisner joined the breakaway antiwar USPD and became its leading spokesman in Bavaria. Living on meager funds he received as a drama critic, he started a discussion group at a local Schwabing tavern north of the city center. Though the authorities kept tabs on the group, they hardly considered Eisner a serious threat.

With his rabbinical look, bohemian intellectualism, and Berliner accent, Eisner wasn't likely to gain significant traction with Munich's mainstream, or so the authorities thought. But his antimonarchist, prodemocracy philosophy was attracting young followers. In January of 1918, Eisner instigated the labor strikes that landed him in Stadelheim Prison. Observing his meteoric rise to power, more than a few residents in the Bavarian capital worried that their new minister-president might turn out to be a murderous revolutionary in the Russian model.[29] Few really understood what Socialism intended[30] and were justifiably nervous about the future. What they didn't know was that Eisner's belief in nonviolence and equal rights far outweighed his revolutionary zeal. He wanted to create a democratic state for all Bavarians[31] and saw the revolution as a victory of truth over falsehood. Munich's working class loved him. The charismatic Eisner had no counterpart on the Far Right, and this would soon provoke nationalists and anti-Semites to start to look for one.

"LONG LIVE THE GERMAN REPUBLIC!"

The antiwar fervor that Kurt Eisner had so successfully harnessed in Bavaria swept across Germany with increasing momentum. In Berlin, where Chancellor Baden's coalition government still clung to power, the streets were filled with soldiers and protesters "carrying red flags."[32] Throughout late October and early November, Baden had continued negotiations with Woodrow Wilson. But there was a hold up: Despite Wilson's unambiguous signal that the Kaiser should abdicate, Wilhelm II kept refusing. To escape the surging protesters in the capital, the defiant monarch had traveled by train to Spa to be with his generals, ever unwilling to relinquish the throne.

Max von Baden couldn't bring himself to fire Wilhelm II.[33] Finally, it was too late. On November 5, President Wilson informed Baden that the French commander Marshal Ferdinand Foch was now responsible for communicating the armistice terms of the Entente and was awaiting a German delegation to cross enemy lines to meet him.[34] The news was chilling: the Germans knew the embittered French were much less likely to offer fair terms. And it was an unfortunate time to have the flu. Sick in bed with influenza, Baden was ill-equipped to deal with the mounting pressures closing in on him. Between unrest in the streets, the famine, the conditions at the front, Bavaria's revolution, and the Kaiser's refusal to step down, the chancellor likely wanted to pull the covers over his head. But fate would not allow him rest.

In Berlin on November 9, loyalist forces guarding the city joined tens of thousands of disgruntled marchers, soldiers, and workers demanding a change of government under the banners of "Peace, Bread, Freedom!"[35] To avert catastrophe in the capital, the prominent Social Democratic leader Friedrich Ebert rushed to the chancellor's side and insisted that he step down. He was not prepared for Baden's answer. "Herr Ebert," the chancellor replied, "I am entrusting you with the German empire."[36] He was deadly serious. That very day Baden handed over his authority to Ebert. As if that weren't shocking enough, the chancellor informed a journalist that the Kaiser had decided to abdicate, despite the fact that Wilhelm II had said nothing of the sort. It didn't matter. The German empire was unraveling.

Suddenly thrust into the spotlight, Friedrich Ebert had to act quickly if he was going to avert anarchy in the streets. Known as a "conformist" with "a rigid mind,"[37] Ebert had earned his political stripes as an effective SPD organizer who expanded the party's institutions. With droopy eyelids that gave him a car-toonish look, the forty-eight-year-old Social Democrat had been co-chairman of the national organization since 1913. A pragmatist who looked down on the antiwar radicals, Ebert was determined to avert revolution at all costs and told Baden that he hated it "like sin."[38] With postwar stability in mind, he imme-diately solicited the support of the military. In a secret phone call to the High Command at Spa, he coyly asked Erich Ludendorff's replacement, Wilhelm Groener, what the military expected of the new government. Groener replied that it must fight against the revolution, and promised the officer corps would place itself "at the disposal of the government for such a purpose."[39] The interim chancellor received the message he was hoping for.

The most pressing threat to Ebert's new-found authority in Berlin seemed to be the unpredictable Spartacists (Marxist revolutionaries) and their leader, Karl Liebknecht. The rebellious progeny of Wilhelm Liebknecht, cofounder of the SPD, wasn't some random agitator who could be quietly arrested. Recently released from his highly publicized stint in prison, Liebknecht had won respect as an elected official in the Reichstag who spoke out against the war. As the pub-lisher of *Die Rote Fahne* (The Red Flag), an incendiary opposition newspaper, Liebknecht commanded a powerful following, and it was rumored he was about to undermine Ebert by declaring Germany a free Socialist Republic.[40] To beat him to the punch, Ebert's SPD colleague Philipp Scheidemann gave an impromptu speech outside the Reichstag to assure the public that a new government was being formed and that the "old and rotten" monarchy had collapsed. Apparently trying to please the crowd, Scheidemann concluded his remarks with "Long live the German Republic."[41] When Ebert found out, he was furious with his colleague for describing the new regime as a republic before parliament had a chance to confer on the matter. Two hours later, Liebknecht made his own declaration by anointing Germany a free Socialist Republic from a balcony at Berlin's city palace. The struggle for power and legitimacy in the capital had begun.

Meanwhile, in a rented flat on Kurfürstenstraße, Erich Ludendorff sat alone, staring into space. After his dismissal on October 26, the former First Quartermaster General had retreated to his wife's apartment in Berlin where he spent his days at a writing table, pale and motionless.[42] Ludendorff brooded over the circumstances that had brought about his demise. Vexed that Field Marshal Hindenburg had failed to protect him, he locked himself in the apartment for days, ignoring the advice of friends who told him that it was no longer safe to stay in the capital.

In late October, Berlin cinemagoers had burst into applause when Ludendorff's dismissal was announced in theaters.[43] Then, in early November, an angry mob had roamed the streets of the city shouting out his name.[44] Time seemed to be running out for the disgraced general. But it wasn't until his landlady urged him to leave that Ludendorff finally agreed. Donning "a fake beard and blue spectacles,"[45] he boarded a train under cover of darkness and headed to Potsdam to stay with his brother. He wasn't the only leader on the run. In the predawn hours of November 10, the Kaiser stepped onto his royal train at Spa and sped away for Holland to begin what would become his permanent exile.[46] News of his abdication would trigger a mass exodus of royalty across Germany.[47]

Just as all these developments were unfolding, far away on the western front, a German peace delegation had slipped across no-man's land and placed itself in the custody of French officials. Whisked to Compiegne, a forest eighty-two kilometers northeast of Paris, the delegation came face-to-face with Marshal Ferdinand Foch, commander-in-chief of the Entente armies. Leading the Germans was Secretary of State Matthias Erzberger, a Reichstag deputy from the Catholic Center Party and outspoken critic of his nation's unrestricted submarine warfare campaign. Baden had wagered that Foch might be more lenient with Erzberger, a civilian politician, than a delegation from the officer corps. In the end, however, the French had no intention of negotiating. When the terms were read aloud in Marshal Foch's train car, Erzberger could hardly believe his ears.

The Entente was demanding, among other things, the removal of all German troops from foreign soil, the creation of an Allied-occupied buffer zone west of the Rhine River, and the internment of the German navy. Everything the Germans had gained was to be taken away. The treaty of Brest-Litovsk would be canceled, nullifying the advances the Germans had made in the east and forcing them to retreat behind the territorial boundaries of 1914.[48] Additionally, tens of thousands of weapons, including aircraft, artillery, and machine guns, were to be handed over. Finally, Erzberger learned that Britain's naval blockade would remain in effect until a formal peace treaty could be signed. This was particularly worrisome, as the famine in Germany had reached dire proportions. In recent weeks, hunger had compelled people to scrounge through refuse bins "full of potato peelings, and scraps, moldy bread and bones, [digging] their hands into the festering stinking heaps and [cramming] their mouths full."[49] Foch gave the Germans seventy-two hours to accept the terms.

When Erzberger pled for the British naval blockade to be lifted, and for the army to retain some measure of its weapons to prevent Communist revolutionaries from overtaking the country, Foch flatly refused.[50] As the clock started ticking down, Erzberger wired the Entente's terms to interim chancellor Ebert in Berlin and Field Marshal Hindenburg in Spa. With Germany teetering on the brink of revolution, news of Foch's demands was likely to send the country over the edge. As much as he hoped to avert an uprising, Hindenburg knew the army couldn't go on any longer. As the deadline approached, he urged Erzberger to accept. From Berlin, Ebert's instructions were similar: sign the document. At 5:00 a.m. on November 11, 1918, Erzberger and his delegation, together with their Allied counterparts, affixed their names to the armistice papers.[51] Six hours later, Paris time, the guns stopped. The First World War was over.

On his way home to Germany, Matthias Erzberger could hardly have realized the full implications of what had just occurred. By signing the armistice in place of Germany's defeated military leadership, he had not only acknowledged his country's culpability for the war and officially recognized the Entente's right to seek reparations, he'd naively played a role that would allow Ludendorff and Hindenburg to escape scrutiny and shift the blame for defeat onto the civilian leadership. This would haunt Germany for the next quarter century. Twenty-two years later, when the Nazis swept through France in 1940, Adolf Hitler ordered the defeated French leadership to enter the same train car at Compiegne and surrender in a humiliating reenactment of the armistice of 1918. Afterward, the train car was shipped to Berlin where it was put on display, and the French victory monument at Compiegne was reduced to rubble.[52]

Where were Adolf Hitler and Ernst Toller during these extraordinary days? Both were sick and out of commission. Toller, who'd been gravely ill over the summer—so sick that he was released from jail—found himself stricken again with a high fever and battling influenza in early November. Hitler was also ill, still hospitalized for "war hysteria" in Pasewalk. It mattered little that the pair had not participated in the events of early November. Each would return to Munich in plenty of time to witness Kurt Eisner's revolutionary experiment.

CHAPTER FOUR

THE OPPOSITION STIRS

"DECLARE THE JEW TO BE OUR MORTAL ENEMY"

Long before the still-obscure future Nazi dictator took power in Germany, a handful of far-right extremists began stirring up a fanatical brand of nationalism in Bavaria. Among them was Hitler's future mentor, Dietrich Eckart. Known as a thinker, a writer, and a cheerful drunk who expressed himself bluntly, the bald-headed Eckart had sought employment during the war as a combat correspondent but was turned down because of his advanced age, alcoholism, and morphine addiction.[1] The key to understanding his appeal to Hitler was his commitment to anti-Semitism, a pervasive and long-standing influence in the country.

Dietrich Eckart was born in 1868 and grew up in Neumarkt, a country town southeast of Nuremberg. Frequently at odds with his father, he was sent away to boarding school after his mother died when he was

Dietrich Eckart.

ten. Years later, after qualifying for university, he was accepted at his father's alma mater in Erlangen, where he intended to study medicine. However, his studies were suddenly interrupted in 1891 when he was stricken with a mysterious illness and sent to convalesce in a clinic that prescribed him morphine. The two-year episode marked the beginning of a life-long addiction to the drug and ongoing health problems. When Eckart was well enough to leave the clinic, he abandoned his studies and took up poetry.[2]

At the outset of his literary career, Eckart did not appear to be anti-Semitic. In fact, his favorite writer was the controversial Jewish-born poet, Heinrich Heine, who was attacked and forced into exile by German xenophobes. Identifying with the poet's struggle and his cosmopolitan ideals, Eckart published two volumes of poetry in 1893, the first of which he devoted to Heine. It's not clear exactly what inspired Eckart's later obsession with Jews: perhaps it was the dueling fraternity he attended in college, which excluded Jews and foreigners;[3] maybe it was the pseudoscientific racial theories that he came into contact with in Bayreuth when he covered the Wagner Opera Festival in 1894;[4] or perhaps his early poem titled *Jordansblume* (Jordan Flower), about a young man's unrequited love for a Jewish girl, was based on real life.[5] What seems most likely is that Eckart started hating Jews when he couldn't get his plays staged.

In 1899, four years after his father died and left him a sizeable inheritance, Eckart relocated to Berlin where he hoped to become an influential playwright. At the time, the pernicious rumor that Jews controlled the media was floating about the German capital.[6] Soon, Eckart joined that chorus. In an arts journal published in 1902, he attacked the Berlin theater scene for selling out to commerce, and accused the Jews of pulling the strings.[7] He even denounced his former literary hero, Heinrich Heine. Then in 1903, Eckart was discouraged when theaters in Berlin declined to stage his first published play.[8] After this disappointing episode, he wrote *Familienväter* (Family Fathers), a disturbing drama about the struggles of a newspaperman who commits suicide while working for a corrupt Jewish publisher. *Familienväter*, which reflected Eckart's increasing paranoia about Jews sabotaging his career, was staged in multiple cities but not Berlin. Later in 1905, when Eckart's romantic comedy *Froschkönig* (Frog King) debuted in Berlin's Königliche Schauspiele (the royal court theater), it was panned by critics and closed after only four performances.[9]

The humiliating experience marked the beginning of a six-year period of inactivity. Down on his luck and feeling sorry for himself, Eckart drowned his sorrows in alcohol. In his gloom and isolation, he fixated on the problems of modernity and began to read about the Jews. There was plenty of extremist literature to choose from: anti-Semitic publications were a cottage industry in Europe. Guido von List, an Austrian occultist, had suggested that non-Aryans be enslaved as manual laborers.[10] Lanz von Liebenfals, a racial theorist, advocated for Jewish removal to Madagascar.[11] Less interested in racial theories, Eckart gravitated toward the writings of Otto Weiniger, a Jewish-born, Protestant convert who defined Jewry not as a race or creed but as a state of mind. Weiniger's approach resonated with Eckart, and he was prompted to investigate the works of celebrated Norwegian playwright Henrik Ibsen, and in particular his least understood play, *Peer Gynt*.[12]

For four years, Eckart translated a version of Ibsen's drama into German. Then, in 1914, his adaptation was staged at the Königliche Schauspiele in Berlin and became a breakout hit. The play enjoyed a successful four-year run in numerous German cities and provided Eckart with royalties for the rest of his life. Even Kaiser Wilhelm II came to see the play twice.[13] Critics, however, some of whom were Jewish, accused Eckart of straying from Ibsen's intent and injecting the play with German nationalism. In a tedious rebuttal, roughly one hundred pages in length, Eckart referred to his critics as the "Jewish literary mafia."[14]

In 1915, Eckart relocated to Munich. Hoping to find new life as a playwright in the arts district of Schwabing, he caught the attention of a well-known critic and writer named Michael Georg Conrad. Lavishly praising Eckart's devotion to race and country in the *Deutsches Volkstum*, Conrad questioned why critics in Berlin had failed to notice him. For the first time in his career, Eckart received the acclaim he'd been longing for. Inspired by Conrad's praise, he began to see himself as a defender of German culture, and took an interest in politics. Through his subsequent friendship with a well-connected, right-wing publicist, he started to think that politics might offer a more direct route to influencing people than theater. During the Ludendorff offensives of 1918, he launched a series of articles in which he blamed the Jews for causing the chaos that had enveloped Europe.[15] The material reflected Eckart's newfound commitment to anti-Semitic, political activism. Later that year, he became a guest member of the Thule Society, a racist community organization in Bavaria.[16] Through Thule and its affiliates, Eckart would eventually discover Adolf Hitler.

A forerunner of the Nazi Party, the Thule Society was created by Rudolf Glauer, a German-born charlatan and occultist who had traveled the high seas running shady investment schemes. Adopted by a wealthy Austrian nobleman living in Turkey, Glauer changed his name to "Rudolf von Sebottendorff," and told people he was a baron.[17] Settling in Bavaria, he decided to promote pan-Germanism by establishing the Thule Society in July of 1918. "Remember that you are a German! Keep your blood pure!" was Thule's motto.[18] The society's name referred to the northernmost region of the ancient world, the mythological homeland of the German race. With its chosen symbol, the swastika, Thule required applicants to demonstrate three generations of racial purity in order to be admitted. On the surface, the society sponsored lectures on themes like Nordic heritage and looked like a benign cultural club. Behind the scenes, its leadership was bent on fostering a nationalist movement dedicated to the defeat of the Bolsheviks and the Jews. Its members included judges, police officials, doctors, and academics.[19]

For the Thule Society, Kurt Eisner's revolution was a nightmare come true. Not only had an alien and a Jew assumed power in Bavaria, the new minister-president was popular with workers in a way that Thule wasn't. On November 9, two days after Eisner seized power, Sebottendorff issued a chilling statement: "In place of our prince of Germanic blood rules our deadly enemy: Judah. . . . Now we shall declare the Jew to be our mortal enemy . . . and from today we will begin to act."[20] Dietrich Eckart had been making similar statements at wine bars and cafés in Schwabing. For years he'd been dreaming of starting a newspaper to spread his anti-Semitic ideology to the masses. As a guest member of Thule, he hoped the society's network might help him with this undertaking.

On the night of Germany's surrender, when Eckart learned of the armistice, he was so angry he couldn't sleep. Tossing and turning in bed, he decided to launch a publication that would provide the Germans with mass education, revitalize their patriotic spirits, and expose the Jewish menace for what he thought it was. Thinking of a title for his paper, Eckart was struck by the simple phrase *Auf Gut Deutsch* (*In Good German*).[21] Sitting up in bed, he roused his wife from slumber, and she asked groggily what time it was. One can imagine Eckart's face as he smiled at her. It was time to wake up.

A TRIP TO BERLIN

Dietrich Eckart wasn't alone in his outrage over the armistice. For those on the opposite side of the political spectrum, as well as those occupying the center, the terms of the truce were deeply disturbing. Germany's representatives had capitulated to what seemed a set of unfair and excessively harsh Allied demands. Now that a ceasefire had been achieved, they would be forced to negotiate a formal peace treaty from a position of weakness, or risk the resumption of combat operations. The final price tag of peace was yet to be determined.

In Bavaria, Kurt Eisner wasn't prepared to sit around and watch the politicians in Berlin bungle the negotiations. As far as he was concerned, the nation would have been better served if politicians like interim chancellor Friedrich Ebert and Secretary of State Matthias Erzberger had followed the Kaiser into exile. Believing that his antiwar background gave him credibility, Eisner decided to personally intervene in the peace process to secure a better deal. Like Max von Baden before him, he presumed that winning over Woodrow Wilson was the key to softening the peace terms. President Wilson had, after all, advocated for the League of Nations and pledged to make the world safe for democracy. It didn't make sense that the US president would hobble the fledgling League of Nations, "which has become the common ideal of humanity," by destroying Bavaria, "the youngest member of democratic culture."[22]

Eisner's conviction was reinforced by correspondence with George D. Herron, an influential American living in Switzerland. Herron had written a well-known book entitled *Woodrow Wilson and the World's Peace*, and was said to have a personal friendship with the US president.[23] When the terms of the armistice became headline news, Eisner released a statement, which read, "Led by men who since 1914 have passionately opposed the wicked policy of the German government and princes, the Bavarian people have swept away all those guilty of the war."[24] A few days later, Herron agreed to cable the minister-president's statement directly to the US president. "You can be sure beyond a shadow of a doubt," Herron assured Eisner, "that if you succeed in establishing at once a real democratic regime in Bavaria and the other German states, the President will be the first one to bring you all possible sympathy and help."[25]

However encouraging this assurance may have been, it was made irresponsibly. Though he had facilitated back-channel communications with the US State Department, Herron had never actually made the president's acquaintance.[26] But Eisner didn't know that. When Herron later suggested that the minister-president should try to obtain a full and open confession of Germany's war guilt, Eisner assumed he was given sage advice based on the US president's expectations. Seeming to corroborate Herron's guidance was the counsel of Dr. Friedrich Muckle, Eisner's Bavarian representative in Berlin, who had advised the minister-president to publish "secret documents" that demonstrated Germany's war guilt.[27] Based on what seemed to be sound intelligence, Eisner prepared to take bold action.

The minister-president knew politicians in Berlin were unlikely to include him in the peace process, let alone concede their guilt, unless they came under intense pressure. Traveling to Berlin to attend a German states conference, he planned to leak top-secret ambassadorial reports from 1914, which proved "conclusively that Germany and Austria forced the war and that England tried to prevent it."[28] However, when these reports were published in newspapers on November 24, the Germans didn't react the way Eisner had expected. In fact, many accused Bavaria's minister-president of committing treason and condemned him for sabotaging the country when the terms of peace were still being negotiated with the Allies. Miscalculating the public mood, Eisner had aroused deep hostility and committed a terrible political faux pas.

At the German states conference, Eisner tried to win allies by convincing his fellow governors that the national government was tainted by politicians who had supported the war. But Berlin's political heavyweights lined up to repudiate him. When he reasoned that the Entente would only deal fairly with those who "enjoy the confidence of the people,"[29] he was accused of impugning Germany's Social Democratic leadership. In the end, a majority of participants voted to adopt a resolution reaffirming their confidence in interim chancellor Ebert's central government. Kurt Eisner's trip to Berlin had backfired. Not only had he failed to ignite mass atonement for Germany's war guilt, he'd been unable to attract the support of Woodrow Wilson. Though he and former chancellor Max von Baden had both tried to win favor with the US president, Eisner's strategy, which played itself out in public, had deeply offended people. Back in Munich, Social Democrats in his cabinet were outraged to hear how he'd attacked their colleagues in Berlin and taken unilateral action without consulting them.[30] But their anger was nothing compared to the fury of far-right nationalists. For the first time since coming to power, Kurt Eisner stood on shaky ground.

DICTATORSHIP

No sooner had the minister-president returned to Munich in late November than Erhard Auer and the Social Democrats tried to subvert his authority by placing limits on the powers of Bavaria's council system. During the revolution, councils had formed in nearly every town and city to provide a forum for peasants, workers, and soldiers to express their will. Intimately connected to the Marxist ideal of class struggle, the councils appeared to emulate those formed during the Russian Revolution. But Eisner had no intention of using them to redistribute land, seize property, or nationalize industry. He saw the councils as serving a democratic purpose to ensure that the voice of the people would continue to be heard.

However, when council duties began to overlap with the civil service, Social Democrats in Eisner's cabinet started pushing to reduce their number and limit their authority. Minister of Interior Auer posted six hundred letters informing council leaders that they had no executive powers.[31] As far as Auer was concerned, the councils' purpose had been to ensure law and order during the initial phase of the revolution, and since that period was over it was time for their dissolution. Lobbying to preserve the councils as a permanent feature of the government, Eisner implored his cabinet, "You must have confidence in me."[32] But the Social Democrats didn't, and they began to press for statewide elections in order to reconstitute the idle Bavarian parliament and unseat the minister-president.

Eisner didn't believe elections were necessary and resisted their authorization. For him, the more pressing task was convincing the US president that Germany rejected the old empire. Preserving the revolutionary councils was part of his strategy. "We don't want a formal electoral democracy where slips are dropped into ballot boxes every four years, and everything else is left to leaders and representatives," he told Bavarians at a political rally. "The people should be continuously and directly involved."[33] But Eisner's reluctance to support elections gave the Social Democrats ammunition to make him look like a tyrant. After the SPD accused Eisner of "dictatorship,"[34] the union of transportation workers threatened to withdraw their support for the government, and Erhard Auer resigned his post. Eisner could ill afford to interrupt food shipments to the Bavarian capital or jeopardize his coalition with the SPD. Making a concession, he declared that new state elections would be held on January 12, 1919. In return, the union of transportation workers went back to work and Auer resumed his post as minister of interior. Though the Social Democrats got what they wanted, the extreme Left was not happy.

Munich's leading Communists and anarchists had been observing the Eisner-Auer coalition with great disappointment. They saw the revolution through a different lens and considered the elections to be a capitulation to the ruling class.[35] In order to be successful, a Marxist revolution needed to show its teeth, and, so far, Eisner's lacked bite. Galvanized into action, they formed a Munich chapter of the Spartacist League, under the Russian-born Communist Max Levien. On December 6, Levien announced plans for the formation of a Bavarian Red Army.

That same night, three hundred armed radicals surrounded Erhard Auer's house in Munich, burst inside, and took the minister of interior hostage.

At gunpoint, Auer was forced to write a letter of resignation. Hearing the news, Eisner rushed to the scene to liberate the SPD leader. Arriving at Auer's home, he praised the radicals as "certainly well intended" men who took action "out of love for me"[36] but firmly rebuked their illegal activity. Eventually convincing them to give up the minister and depart peacefully, Eisner diffused the crisis with nonviolent dialogue and personal bravery. Though frightened by his abduction, Auer was unharmed and tore up his letter of resignation.

Only a few days earlier, the minister-president had narrowly escaped a kidnapping attempt on his own life. During a campaign stop in Bad Aibling, a spa town sixty kilometers southeast of Munich, Eisner was nearly arrested by a group of right-wing extremists.[37] Rudolf von Sebottendorff and supporters of the Thule Society had planned to force the minister-president into a getaway car and steal him away into the mountains, where he would be held hostage.[38] Afterward, they planned to install Auer as the next minister-president. Sebottendorff wagered that the Social Democrats would welcome their assistance in getting rid of Eisner.[39] But the Thulists were denied when cheering crowds prevented them from reaching the minister-president at Bad Aibling.[40]

As early as November 10, militant members of the Thule Society had been discussing ways to destroy the Socialist revolution. Two days after Kurt Eisner's rule began, the society's organizers had formed a secret paramilitary organization dubbed Thule Kampfbund (Thule Fighting League).[41] Acquiring weapons from various armories and hiding them in Thule's rented rooms at Munich's Hotel Vierjahreszeiten (Four Seasons), the Fighting League prepared for armed insurrection. In the coming months, Thule would renew its attempts to overturn the revolution and rid Bavaria of Kurt Eisner.

THE CHRISTMAS CRISIS

For the Germans, the approach of Christmas and the holiday season seemed a welcome respite from war and revolution. Desperate for merriment after four years of deprivation, demobilized soldiers and unemployed workers flocked to Munich's dance halls to party their troubles away.[42] Despite a relative calm in Bavaria, political tensions threatened to boil over in other parts of Germany. In the capital, interim chancellor Ebert faced a myriad of troubles. Day after day, strikes and riots paralyzed Berlin, and leftist politicians pushed for radical change. To stabilize the country, Ebert, too, pressed for democratic elections.

In the German capital, Spartacist leader Rosa Luxemburg and other German Communists believed Ebert's rush to the ballot was simply an attempt to bring the revolution to its end and reestablish the old order. The petite, frail intellectual giant of Germany's left wing concluded that if Socialism were to survive, the revolutionaries had to arm themselves. Calling for the formation of a Red Guard and a workers' militia, Luxemburg was anticipating the possibility of armed conflict.[43]

Ebert was in a tight spot. He couldn't just ignore the Spartacists and the growing numbers of protesters in Berlin pressing their grievances in the streets. In desperation, he renewed contact with General Groener, Ludendorff's successor in the High Command, and arranged for "ten divisions"[44] to be sent to Berlin and placed at the disposal of the government. On December 6, government soldiers opened fire on a Spartacist demonstration in Berlin, killing fourteen unarmed leftists. Two days later, one hundred and fifty thousand protesters marched in Berlin, and the soldiers withdrew.[45] Then on December 11, at the Brandenburg Gate, Ebert presided over a parade of officers who declared their loyalty to the interim chancellor and promised to protect his provisional government, excluding the revolutionary councils. When radical sailors seeking recompense for lost wages seized Berlin's military governor, Ebert's forces went on the attack, and Berlin was poised at the brink of civil war. However, during a break in the fighting civilians intervened and convinced the interim chancellor's men to put down their weapons.[46]

The episode, later dubbed the "Christmas Crisis," exposed the weakness of Ebert's defenses. Many feared that Karl Liebknecht and the Spartacists would exploit the situation and instigate a bloody purge. But five days after the crisis, the interim chancellor received a late Christmas present when USPD cabinet members resigned from his government. Filling their seats with SPD colleagues, Ebert consolidated his power and launched secret plans with Germany's new defense minister, Gustav Noske, for the creation of the Freikorps. A paramilitary force comprised of former officers, soldiers, and mercenaries, the Freikorps was intended to protect Ebert's government and fight against the revolutionaries. Noske assured Ebert that these battle-hardened warriors weren't the type to lose heart in street fighting.

Just as Ebert and Noske were forming their secret army, Liebknecht and Luxemburg announced the formation of the German Communist Party (KPD). Its platform was unambiguous: the KPD was committed to revolution.

Berlin was poised for a showdown like never before.

CONSPIRACY

In the final weeks of 1918, Bavaria's political parties were busy campaigning for the state elections slated for January 12. The frontrunner was the Bavarian People's Party (BVP), which commanded the backing of Bavaria's Catholic majority. The BVP's electoral slogan was "Bavaria for Bavarians,"[47] which played on longstanding regional animosities and discredited Kurt Eisner as a Jew and an outsider. Though not as radical as the Thule Society, the BVP was unafraid to use anti-Semitism to get votes. "The Bavarian People's Party values every honest Jew," read the party newspaper. "But what must be fought are the numerous atheistic elements of a certain international Jewry with predominantly Russian coloring."[48] Floating about Munich at the time was the false rumor that Kurt Eisner was from Russia and intended to unleash Bolshevik terror.

Competing with the BVP were Auer's Social Democrats. To increase their chances for victory, the SPD had allied itself with the third most powerful party in Bavaria, the German Democratic Party (DDP). Founded by former progressives and liberals, the left-of-center Bavarian DDP condemned Kurt Eisner for trying to insert himself into Germany's foreign affairs. "Oh, what an illusion," remarked DDP spokesman Ludwig Quidde, "to be able from here in Bavaria to bring peace to the German Reich!"[49] In contrast, Eisner's USPD relied on the minister-president's antiwar record as a calling card to bolster its election chances. Entering into partnership with the Bavarian Peasants' League, Eisner crisscrossed the state encouraging citizens to "allow those who started the revolution to see it through to the end."[50] Rejecting parliamentarianism, Bavaria's Communists refused to field candidates in the January elections.

During the Christmas holidays, Erhard Auer was still rattled by the incident weeks earlier, when hundreds of radicals took him hostage in his own home. After evacuating his family from the city, Auer accepted a Christmas Eve dinner invitation at a place he knew he'd be safe: Munich's Türken barracks, the headquarters of his old regiment, the Life Guards.[51] On December 5, the Life Guards and their fierce commander, Franz Ritter von Epp, had returned to Munich and received a heroes' welcome. The festivities had been so jubilant that they gave the impression the city had forgotten Germany was defeated. Now, at the Christmas Eve dinner in the officer's mess, Auer was seated at the head table. Like interim chancellor Ebert in Berlin, he understood the importance of forging alliances with military commanders who shared his desire to rid the streets of radicals. The regiment was full of people hostile toward the revolution.

Among those gathered that night at the Türken barracks was Count Anton Arco-Valley, the commander of the 5th company, an Austrian nobleman, and a monarchist.[52] The revelation that Erhard Auer sat down for dinner with Arco-Valley is a bit like finding out that US vice president Lyndon Johnson broke bread with Lee Harvey Oswald. While the episode between Johnson and Oswald never took place, the one between Auer and Arco-Valley did. Unfortunately, no record of their conversation exists.

Auer's courtship of the military had actually begun weeks before Christmas, when the minister of interior had procured arms and authorized the formation of antiradical militia groups, known as Bürgerwehr, in communities outside the Bavarian capital. Then, news of the bloody skirmishes in Berlin between Spartacists and progovernment forces prompted him and a fellow Social Democrat, Johannes Timm, to form an auxiliary security force in Munich.[53] They also chose to not inform Eisner.

Picked to command Munich's antiradical Bürgerwehr was Rudolf Buttmann, a determined opponent of the councils and the Far Left.[54] When Buttmann went looking for a location to stage the militia's first meeting, he made contact with Sebottendorff, the Thule Society founder, through a subordinate. Sebottendorff agreed to allow Buttmann to conduct the meeting at Thule's offices in the Hotel Vierjahreszeiten.[55] This was more than just a favor. Buttmann and Sebottendorff were conspiring to use the Bürgerwehr to recruit right-wing counterrevolutionaries. This went beyond the scope of what the minister of interior intended.

Or did it?

Erhard Auer was absent from the inaugural meeting of Munich's Bürgerwehr on December 27. So were Minister-President Eisner and Munich's chief of police: They'd been left in the dark. At the meeting, a speaker told the assembly that the militia's purpose was to shield the Bavarian capital "against a revolt from within."[56] In order to fill its ranks, an office had already been rented to serve as a recruiting center, which Sebottendorff had graciously offered to manage. Though both Auer and Timm were avowed public supporters of the revolution, the meeting gave the impression that the two Social Democrats were conspiring with right-wing elements to bring about a counterrevolution.

The following day, hundreds of eager Bürgerwehr volunteers reportedly signed up at the recruiting office. Pleased with these early results, Sebottendorff headed for his office in the Hotel Vierjahreszeiten. When he arrived, a doorman tipped him off that a detachment of police loyal to Eisner had just ransacked Thule's offices upstairs and taken thirty-five Bürgerwehr volunteers into custody. Unbeknownst to Sebottendorff, Timm, and Auer, the minister-president had been briefed on the previous night's meeting by an informant. Rudolf Buttmann had saved himself by slipping out an exit just before the arrests were made.[57] Sebottendorff later claimed that he met with Eisner and personally arranged for the release of the men in custody. Whether that was true or not, many of the volunteers would go on to join Thule Kampfbund. Among those who had signed up were three future members of Adolf Hitler's inner circle: Hermann Esser, Rudolf Hess, and the Estonian immigrant Alfred Rosenberg.[58]

When Munich's revolutionary councils caught wind of the Bürgerwehr controversy, they accused Auer and Timm of conspiring with counterrevolutionaries and called for their resignation.[59] On December 30, the pair was summoned to a closed-door meeting with cabinet and council representatives to learn their fate. Leading the attack on Auer was none other than Ernst Toller. Though he had missed the November revolution due to illness, Toller had returned to Munich in its aftermath, pledged his support to Eisner, and become the deputy chairman of Bavaria's councils. Convinced like Eisner that the councils were indispensable to grassroots democracy, he was dubious of politicians like Auer who belonged to the old government and accused him of being "either naïve or dumb."[60] Denying that he had any counterrevolutionary intentions, Auer was booed when he called the whole thing a misunderstanding. Then, Eisner suggested a compromise: Auer would renounce the Bürgerwehr, admit that he and Timm had made an error in judgment, promise to protect the revolution, and work to prevent any further distribution of arms. In exchange, they would be allowed to continue, respectively, as minister of interior and minister of justice. Three days later, Eisner's measure was passed by a vote of 112 to 11.

The Bürgerwehr controversy exposed the Thule Society as a counterrevolutionary organization. Shortly after the incident, a Munich newspaper specifically mentioned Thule's offices at the Hotel Vierjahreszeiten as a gathering place for right-wing activists.[61] As author David Luhrssen observed, the fact that Sebottendorff didn't close down the location and move Thule Kampfbund's headquarters somewhere else suggests that he may have had assurances that he would be allowed to continue his work without obstruction. The failure to hold Sebottendorff, Thule, and others accountable was, at the very least, a terrible oversight. Eisner and

Toller's chance to stop Bavaria's far-right movement before it gained momentum, discovered Hitler, and started grooming him had been missed.

As for Auer and Timm, with their strong prospects for victory in the upcoming elections, it seems unlikely that the two Social Democrats willfully took an unnecessary risk by launching a counterrevolutionary plot at the end of 1918. Nevertheless, the Bürgerwehr incident suggests that Auer and Timm were actively trying to rid Bavaria of Kurt Eisner and his revolution. The consequences of that would be devastating.

CHAPTER FIVE

THE DEATH OF IDEALISM

"NO HUMAN FATE HAS BEEN AS HARD AS MINE"

F ar away from Munich, in the Swedish backcountry, Erich Ludendorff was living in exile and writing his memoirs during the Christmas holidays. In late November, he had disguised his appearance, entered a second-class train compartment in Berlin, and fled Germany with a fake passport. Bemoaning his fall from grace, the general had sent a letter to his wife, Margarethe: "I never counted on being thanked, but this ingratitude on the part of my country hurts me deeply. . . . No human fate has been as hard as mine."[1] The commander who had needlessly prolonged the war was now writing a book to defend his honor. "To assert that we could have had peace earlier on some condition or other," Ludendorff wrote, "is a scandalous piece of frivolity and a willful misleading of the German people."[2] But it was Ludendorff who was doing the misleading.

After four years of war and famine, many Germans hoped the New Year would bring an end to their troubles. However, interim chancellor Ebert knew that things were going to get much worse before they got better. His provisional government in Berlin still had to negotiate a treaty with the Entente, keep the population fed, and transition the economy to peacetime. To deal with radicals in the capital, Ebert had asked his defense minister, Gustav Noske, for help. "Of course!" the minister had replied. "Somebody will have to be the bloodhound— I won't shirk the responsibility."[3] Noske solicited the Freikorps—volunteer para-military units comprised of demobilized officers, mercenaries, and loyalists—to defend Ebert's government.[4] Filling its ranks would not be difficult.

Many soldiers in Germany were eager to extend their service. Among them were men who'd been transformed by the war into cold-hearted killers.[5] "People told us that the war was over. That made us laugh," wrote Friedrich Heinz, a war veteran who would later join the Nazi Brown Shirts. "We ourselves are the war."[6] Joining the Freikorps gave men like Heinz a chance to delay their return to civilian life and the anxieties of work, family, and their own thoughts. In the Freikorps, they could reunite with their brethren and continue to fight for Germany.

On January 4, 1919, Noske and Ebert slipped out of the capital to watch four thousand freshly assembled Freikorps troops march at a military encampment.[7] The sight of such a well-disciplined paramilitary force brought smiles to their faces. "Now you can rest easy," Noske said to Ebert as he slapped him on the back.[8] But the defense minister's jubilation was premature. That same day, Berlin erupted in anger when the city's police chief from the USPD was ordered to step down. News of his dismissal prompted demonstrators to take to the streets. Stretching nearly five kilometers, the crowd was described as "an army of two hundred thousand, such as none [that even] Ludendorff had ever seen."[9]

Hoping to capitalize on the demonstrations, USPD and Communist leaders, including Karl Liebknecht, formed a committee to overthrow Ebert's provisional government. But the heady group lost itself in ideological arguments. When frustrated workers grew sick of waiting for direction, they seized control of various locations inside the capital, including the newspaper quarter and the offices of the SPD newspaper, *Vorwärts*.[10] While Liebknecht and his committee tried to negotiate with Ebert's government, Freikorps and army units started quietly slipping into position.

Beginning on January 9, the Freikorps launched a three-day attack on the occupiers. Authorized by a note endorsed with the names "Ebert-Scheidemann"[11] they used machine guns, howitzers, and mortars to bombard the workers. When the assault concluded on January 11, a white flag was raised, and the survivors stepped out to offer a truce.[12] But Noske's Freikorps weren't interested in taking prisoners. Instead, they rounded up the workers and, with no one to restrain them, shot them on the spot. In all, several hundred workers perished in the melee and its aftermath.[13] In the pages of *Die Rote Fahne*, Rosa Luxemburg cried out, "Victory will flower from the soil of this defeat."[14] But Berlin was no longer safe for the Communist heroine and her compatriots. The Freikorps were determined hunt them down and kill them too.

BIRTH OF THE PARTY

In the first days of 1919, the revolution looked decidedly different in Munich than Berlin. At the head of a coalition government, Kurt Eisner was attempting to secure Bavarian democracy through peaceful means. He wasn't rounding up, jailing, or killing his adversaries like the Freikorps in Berlin. The contrast created the impression that Munich was secure. But a sinister movement was brewing in the Bavarian capital.

On Sunday, January 5, 1919, in a tavern just southwest of the Marienplatz, an ordinary railway man gathered with around two dozen guests.[15] His name was Anton Drexler, and this was the inaugural meeting of the German Workers' Party (DAP). The bespectacled and thinly mustached Drexler had little reason to believe that the DAP would amount to much.[16] There were already numerous right-wing parties well established in Germany, and new ones were popping up all the time. But the DAP had a novel mandate, and Drexler had been encouraged to achieve a specific objective: to steal Germany's working class from the Communist and Socialist movements that attracted them in such large numbers. Though its initial prospects seemed doubtful, in the next thirteen months the DAP would discover Adolf Hitler and morph into the Nazi Party.

Anton Drexler seemed ideal for the role of DAP chairman. Born in Munich in 1884, he grew up the son of devoted Social Democrats who filled his head with Marxist idealism. In his teens, Drexler became an apprentice locksmith, then traveled to various German cities to become a master of the trade.[17] However, a conflict with union officials in Berlin brought an end to his employment and left him feeling bitter.[18] Drifting for a while, he worked on a farm to make ends meet. But the experience turned sour when his boss, a Jewish cattle dealer, started treating him poorly.[19] Drexler quit his job and returned home.

Unemployed and depressed, he began to suspect that sinister forces were manipulating the German economy. Introduced to the extreme ideology that Jews and Freemasons controlled international markets, he turned his back on Socialism. Eventually gaining employment in Munich's railyard as a toolmaker, he became a crusader, urging his coworkers to beware of the Jews, Freemasons, and Socialists.[20] Always sickly, Drexler was denied admittance into the army and remained at the railyard throughout the war. One night, he claimed a Jewish man from Antwerp had spiked his wine with a sedative after an argument and he blacked out. For Drexler, it was more proof that Jews were nefarious.[21]

Seated in the tavern, Drexler was joined by Karl Harrer, a popular sports-writer for a local evening paper. What linked the club-footed, twenty-nine-year-old journalist to the railway worker? Harrer was a member of Rudolf von Sebottendorff's Thule Society.[22] When Harrer had attended an impassioned speech against Bolshevism by Drexler the previous year, he judged him someone who could reach workers and communicate the nationalist, racist, and anti-Semitic platform of Thule.[23] Though the exact connection between the DAP and the Thule Society remains mysterious, evidence suggests that Karl Harrer's influence emboldened Anton Drexler to form the DAP.[24]

Speaking to his guests, Drexler disparaged wealthy Jews who "rule us with their money" and envisioned a Germany governed "only by Germans."[25] Denouncing the Marxist view of class warfare, he proposed that Germans unite across socioeconomic lines to fight against Bolshevism and the Jews. Seated among his listeners was a self-proclaimed economist named Gottfried Feder, who in the very near future would have the chance to tutor Adolf Hitler. Well-known among Bavarian nationalists, Feder's presence at the inaugural meeting suggested that powerful forces were guiding the fledgling party. When the meeting concluded, a handful of attendees decided to join. The DAP had taken its first step.

THE ELECTION OF JANUARY 12

In the days before Bavaria's state elections, tempers began to flare in Munich, as postwar unemployment and overcrowding put a strain on the population. Since November, the Bavarian capital had served as a processing center for troops coming home from the front, and the authorities were billeting over fifty thou-sand soldiers in temporary facilities around the city. Adolf Hitler was one of the soldiers who had come and gone. After his release from a hospital in November, Hitler had returned to Munich in the hopes of reuniting with his old regiment. The Austrian immigrant wanted to stay in the German army for as long as pos-sible. A few weeks after his arrival, he was dispatched to a prisoner-of-war camp at Traunstein near Austria, where he performed various jobs under the super-vision of a pro-revolutionary soldiers' council.[26] Back in Munich, conditions were deteriorating so rapidly that some feared the Bavarian capital was heading toward anarchy.

On January 7, three people were killed at a demonstration of unemployed workers and soldiers.[27] When the police arrested ten radical council members suspected of stirring up trouble, an angry crowd marched on Kurt Eisner's office. Rudolf Egelhofer, a veteran of the sailor's mutiny in Kiel, climbed up the side of the building and compelled the minister-president to sign the radicals' release papers. Just days earlier, chanting crowds had stood in the same position, taunting Eisner with the slogan, "We want a Bavarian! We want a Bavarian!"[28] When one of his advisors suggested that he retaliate, Eisner shrugged: "Let them insult me as much as they want."[29]

On Sunday, January 12, 1919, nearly four million Bavarians went to the polls to determine their political future.[30] The scene at voting stations across the state was unlike any in the region's history. Eisner had managed to deliver women's suffrage to Bavaria, and an estimated two million women came out to vote. Women in the United States would have to wait another nineteen months to gain their voting rights with the ratification of the nineteenth amendment to the US Constitution. The minister-president also lowered the voting age from twenty-five to twenty-one. But he would not be rewarded for his efforts.

When the ballots were counted, the Catholic-backed Bavarian People's Party received the most votes, while Erhard Auer's Social Democrats came in second. Running third was the left-of-center German Democratic Party (DDP). By forming a coalition with the DDP, the Social Democrats were assured of a parliamentary majority and control over Bavarian politics. The election delivered a stunning defeat to the Independent Socialists, who received less than three percent of the vote.[31] When the results were announced, many expected Kurt Eisner to resign. But existing laws stipulated that his term would extend until parliament resumed session and held its first full meeting.[32] That meeting was still several weeks off. Until that time, the minister-president vowed to stay.

Above all, Eisner wanted to remain in office to salvage the council system. But Auer and the Social Democrats were ready to junk it, and they believed the election gave them the authority to do so. Opposing them were Communists, anarchists, and workers, who warned that they would summon all their strength to protect the council system.[33] Instead of creating political stability, as the SPD had hoped, the elections provoked further dissent and agitation.

MURDER IN BERLIN

Following the violence of January 11, when the Freikorps swept through Berlin's newspaper district, took prisoners, and summarily executed them, Communist Party leaders Karl Liebknecht and Rosa Luxemburg went into hiding. Four days later, their location was discovered. That evening, the pair was apprehended. Delivered to Berlin's Eden Hotel where German officers had set up a command center,[34] the two Communist leaders must have wondered why they hadn't been driven to a police station, arrested, and processed in accordance with German law. Both were prepared to return to jail if necessary. But the men at the Eden Hotel had something else in mind.

After separate interrogations, Liebknecht and Luxemburg were informed that they would be driven individually to Moabit Prison for further questioning.[35] But it was a lie. Outside the hotel, a loyalist soldier named Otto Runge was waiting to assault them. When Liebknecht stepped from the hotel entrance and into a waiting car, Runge cracked him in the face with his rifle butt. Two blows were enough to render Liebknecht incapacitated, and the car sped off with him in the back. Arriving at a wooded location inside Berlin's Tiergarten Park, Liebknecht was forced to his feet and shot to death, execution style. Later, a cover story was leaked that he had been killed while attempting to escape. His female compatriot didn't fare any better.

Outside the Eden Hotel, Runge likewise smashed the diminutive Rosa Luxemburg in the face with his rifle butt, and she was dragged, barely alive, to a waiting car.[36] As she lay there motionless, dripping in blood, an officer casually removed his pistol and put a bullet in her brain. Driven to a bridge over the Landwehr Canal, Luxemburg's body was weighted down and thrown in the water. When her abductors arrived back at the Eden Hotel, they proudly displayed her petite shoe as a memento of their struggle against Bolshevism. Hidden in the frigid waters of the canal, Luxemburg's body would not be discovered for several months.

The abduction and murder of Liebknecht and Luxemburg was stunning news to the Left. Interim chancellor Ebert and Defense Minister Noske had set a dangerous precedent. By looking the other way when military forces performed summary executions of their political rivals, the Social Democrats had sidestepped the judicial system and legitimized state-sponsored murder. This practice would be repeated on a larger scale in the coming months. Fifteen years into the future, the Nazis would start killing their enemies without due process. Hitler's murder of his political adversaries during the "Night of the Long Knives" would become infamous around the world as an example of Nazi brutality. Few would remember how the executions of Luxemburg and Liebknecht had precipitated these terrible crimes.

"THE DUTY OF THE GERMANS"

In January, Munich's Communist leadership decided it was time to take bold action in defense of the councils. Believing that Kurt Eisner had been living under a "dangerous illusion"[37] when he formed a coalition with the Social Democrats, the Communists concluded that Erhard Auer would eventually use violence to suppress the revolution and dissolve the councils. At a council meeting on January 11, Communist leader Max Levien proposed incendiary measures, including a demand for the resignation of Ebert, Noske, and Philipp Scheidemann in Berlin. Overwhelmingly approved by a vote of 84 to 5, these resolutions sounded the alarm to the SPD that Munich's councils had become radicalized.

On February 7, Levien was arrested on trumped up charges and brought to Stadelheim Prison. Released four days later due to a lack of evidence, he was whisked back to the city center, where a council meeting was "fortuitously" in progress.[38] When Levien's colleagues proposed that a massive demonstration in support of the councils be held on February 16, Social Democrats stormed out of the meeting in protest, leaving those that remained to approve the date. State elections had decisively shown the public's preference for parliamentary rule, but the struggle for political control in Bavaria was far from over.

Private Adolf Hitler returned to Munich from sentry duty along the Austrian border in late January or early February 1919.[39] A few weeks later, he accepted an assignment guarding the city's central train station. Given his later views, it is hard to imagine that Hitler was ever sympathetic to Kurt Eisner or his government. Yet, soon after his return, he was elected to the soldier's council of his regiment. The future Nazi dictator had a front row seat to the second half of the German revolution, and it would leave an indelible mark on his thinking.

Around the time of Hitler's arrival, Eisner boarded a train at Munich's central station and headed out of the city. He had a lot on his mind. Two weeks earlier, 80 percent of the German population had participated in national elections. Receiving a majority of votes, the SPD, led by Ebert, Scheidemann, and

Noske, had enough seats in the Reichstag to retain power at the head of a coalition government. In contrast, the USPD received less than 10 percent of the vote. The results signaled a rejection of revolution and suggested that most people wanted to return to the stability of the prewar years.

In February, Germany was scheduled to hold a national assembly, write a new constitution, and select a new government. Concerned by recent unrest in the capital, organizers and political authorities decided to move the convocation from Berlin to Weimar, a city associated with Goethe and Schiller, giving rise, accordingly, to what became known as the Weimar Republic in the interim between the First World War and the Third Reich. At Weimar, the central government was threatening to infringe on state's rights. Earlier, Eisner had tried to defend Bavaria's autonomy, which included an independent transportation system, postal service, and diplomatic corps. A trip to Weimar now seemed his last chance to fight for these rights and services. But the lame duck Eisner was headed elsewhere.

Since January 18, the Entente had been deliberating over the postwar treaty terms at the Paris Peace Conference. Representatives from twenty-seven nations, including President Wilson, had assembled to deliberate Germany's fate. If Eisner hoped to influence better treaty terms, a diplomatic trip to Paris might have been fruitful. But Eisner wasn't headed there either. Instead, his train was bound for the Swiss capital of Bern, where 102 Socialist delegates from twenty-six countries were gathering in a glittery, art deco building to attend the first postwar meeting of the Second International.[40] Accompanying him from Bavaria was Ernst Toller.

At one time, the Second International had been among the most exciting conferences in Europe. To Communists and Socialists, it provided direction for the international movement. But the First World War had divided its participants, and when the Russian Revolution succeeded, the International was considered obsolete. Still, participants in Bern were ready to give it another go in 1919, even without such past notable figures as Vladimir Lenin and Rosa Luxemburg.[41] Despite a lack of prewar luster, representatives gathered for five days in a "dingy"[42] room, discussing disarmament, the League of Nations, and the international solidarity of workers. After a litany of forgettable speeches, it was the address of Kurt Eisner that had everyone talking.

Admitting that he belonged "to a beaten people" with a "heavy guilt," Eisner announced that a great transformation had taken place in Germany. The revolution, he said, "was a moral revolution."[43] Condemning Germany's wartime leadership, Eisner begged delegates to stop thinking of the Germans as "unteachable." Claiming that many Germans had protested the war and gone to prison for it, he urged the delegates to think beyond "revenge and punishment."[44]

Praised for representing the "good" Germany, Eisner's admission of war guilt scored points with French and English delegates.[45] Encouraged by the feedback, he proposed that all prisoners of war, regardless of nationality, be immediately released. Admitting that it was "the duty of the Germans" to help rebuild war-torn France and Belgium, he urged German students to embrace the spirit of volunteerism and go there to "lay the foundation stone of the new age."[46] Eisner's ideas were met with rousing cheers.[47]

Historian Allan Mitchell believed that Eisner's attempt to "strike a moral tone in Bern," was a deliberate effort to revitalize his popularity at home and "force" Auer and the Social Democrats "to accede to the continuation of his leadership."[48] Others have suggested his goal was to "modify"[49] anti-German attitudes and lessen war reparations. While both of these theories appear reasonable, Eisner's statements at the Second International also seemed to demonstrate profound ignorance of the hatreds harbored by nationalists and anti-Semites back home. Before returning to Munich, the minister-president had shown some awareness of the risk he was taking when he picked up a newspaper and joked, "I must find out if I haven't been deposed yet."[50] But this was a reference to his political rivals in the SPD who were anxious to replace him. In *Mein Kampf*, Hitler would later make his position clear about politicians who tried to win over their adversaries with the promise of peace: "Only children could believe that sweet and unctuous expressions of goodness and persistent avowals of peaceful intentions could get them their bananas . . . with the prospect of never having to fight for them."[51]

WRITING ON THE WALL

Back in Munich, a public relations nightmare was waiting for Eisner. Munich's press coverage of his activities were deliberately distorted.[52] His appeal for student volunteerism was described not as a gesture to help rebuild Europe's war-ravaged cities, but an offer to the victors of German POWs as a slave labor force. Before he had even returned, his cabinet, led by Erhard Auer, held a closed-door meeting and decided to reconvene parliament on February 21 to bring an end to Eisner's rule.

Across the city, right-wing groups distributed leaflets calling for Eisner's head.[53] At Ludwig-Maximilians-Universität, "Circles of students and military officers openly demanded his assassination."[54] In the city's central train station, among crowds of hurried commuters, Dietrich Eckart was selling copies of his sixteen-page anti-Semitic broadsheet, *Auf Gut Deutsch*. With a chewed cigar between his lips, the man who had tossed and turned on the night of the armistice had found financing for his anti-Semitic publication, which was now selling for 50 Pfennig a copy.[55] In the pages of *Auf Gut Deutsch*, Eckart castigated Eisner's speeches and blamed Bavaria's woes on the minister-president's Jewishness.[56] The early response among right-wing readers was exceptionally positive, though he did receive at least one letter criticizing the paper's blatant anti-Semitism. "Now let's take up the Jewish question," was his defiant reply in the second edition of *Auf Gut Deutsch*. "There are numerous Germans who go out of their way to avoid it as if it doesn't exist. And yet it is the question of mankind, which envelops all other problems."[57]

Among those contributing articles to *Auf Gut Deutsch* was Gottfried Feder. Joining him on Eckart's team was an Estonian immigrant named Alfred Rosenberg. In his tract *The Russian Jewish Revolution*, Rosenberg suggested that Europe's tolerance for Jews, though seemingly "a highly humanitarian achievement,"[58] was terribly naive. The proof, the immigrant asserted, was the Russian Revolution. According to Rosenberg, after promising the masses peace and freedom the Bolsheviks had systematically murdered their enemies.[59] Peddling the lie that Jews had instigated the Bolshevik terror, Rosenberg hinted that the same thing was likely to happen in Bavaria. Since January, Thule Society members had been busy collecting intelligence on the minister-president's regime. By February, Thule sympathizers had infiltrated Eisner's government and were reporting back to the society's leadership in the offices of Munich's Hotel Vierjahreszeiten. Eisner's hour of reckoning was fast approaching, though he failed to perceive that it was at hand.

THE CONFUSING CAVALCADE

On Sunday morning, February 16, crowds assembled on the Theresienwiese for the scheduled demonstration in support of Bavaria's council system. Organizers, who believed the councils were an absolute necessity, were determined to revive the spirit of revolution. Along the scheduled route into the city, large red flags and banners were already up in strategic locations. But unlike the unseasonably warm day that launched Eisner's revolution from this same location, a cold drizzle fell from the skies, melting snow banks and forming icy puddles.

Braving the wet and cold, demonstrators in hats and overcoats carried signs, which cried out, "Remember Karl Liebknecht and Rosa Luxemburg!" and "All Power to the Councils."[60] Crashing the demonstration to support the Bavarian parliament, Social Democrats brought signs that read, "Against Bolshevism," and "For the Parliament."[61] The combination of demonstrators in support of the councils assembled peacefully with those who favored parliament presented a confusing picture. Arriving in an open vehicle to lead this contradictory cavalcade into the city was Kurt Eisner. And the minister-president was in a defiant mood.

In a report issued in the *Frankfurter Zeitung*, Eisner had suggested that if parliament demanded his resignation, he would call on the people to decide his fate through a referendum.[62] With the top down in his car, the minister-president led the procession as it snaked its way through the city's canyon-like corridors. The number of participants was estimated to be somewhere between 9,000 and 150,000, depending on which politically affiliated newspaper was doing the reporting.[63] There were no incidents of violence, except for a few altercations in which revolutionaries forced officers to remove the epaulets of rank and colors of the old empire from their uniforms.[64]

Observing one of these episodes during the parade was Anton Arco-Valley of the Life Guard's regiment, who'd sat at the head table with Erhard Auer on Christmas Eve.[65] Beneath his calm exterior, the twenty-two-year-old boiled with rage over the disrespect shown his fellow officers. The minister-president had also passed by. Dressed in black and seated next to his pretty, fair-skinned wife, Eisner had looked nothing like an ethnic German. Toying with his revolver inside his overcoat, Arco-Valley had a murderous epiphany. "I shall be Bavaria's Wilhelm Tell," he told himself.[66] When he returned to his barracks later that day, Arco-Valley committed these murderous thoughts to his diary. But would he act on them?

Count Anton Arco-Valley.

The day after the demonstration, Eisner joined Auer and his fellow ministers for a closed-door cabinet meeting. Safe from the ears of the general public, Auer declared that he would disband the councils once his new government was formed. Eisner protested, but the minister of interior was immovable. Auer knew that as soon as parliament was reconstituted, public support for the Social Democrats would solidify like concrete. Until that time, the most important thing was to avoid taking an either/or public position about the councils.

On February 20, the eve of parliament's convocation, Kurt Eisner had to concede that political realities in Bavaria had changed. In what would be his final cabinet meeting, he gave the minister of interior his word that he would resign.[67] By the time the sun reached its midpoint the following day, Auer and the Social Democrats would assume power.

"THE MOST UNSULLIED IDEALISM"

On the morning of February 21, in his office at the foreign ministry, Eisner prepared a speech for his appearance at the opening of the new parliament: "In the name of the cabinet, I declare that all the ministers will resign from their offices and place themselves at the disposal of the parliament."[68]

On this day, the Bavarian parliament would begin the process of appointing his successor. Eisner considered it immoral to try and stop these lawful proceedings. Although resolute in his support of the council system, he refused to stand with radicals who sought to undermine parliament. Guided by the wish to remain relevant in Bavarian politics, Eisner crafted his speech to remind the assembly of what he'd accomplished during three short months of rule. "Just as the revolution itself was achieved without bloodshed," Eisner wrote in his speech, "so has Bavaria until now been preserved from serious and lasting internal convulsions."[69]

After saying goodbye to his staff, Eisner grabbed his floppy hat and departed for the parliament building just before 10:00 a.m. Out on the street, he was led by two security officers and walked with his colleagues Felix Fechenbach and Benno Merkle.[70] As the sun shone brightly in a sky free of clouds, it almost felt like spring. Given recent death threats against the minister-president, Fechenbach suggested that Eisner take a less familiar route to parliament, but Eisner shrugged him off.

In the chamber where they were headed, excited delegates were just taking their seats. Above them in the hall's public galleries, large crowds had gathered in anticipation of the historic proceedings. Below, Erhard Auer, the man likely presumed to become the next minister-president, sat down with his fellow Social Democrats. No doubt, the minister of interior was feeling good that Eisner's revolution would finally end. Just down the street, Eisner and his colleagues were lost in conversation as they continued toward the parliament building. But waiting for them in the shadows of a doorway stood an armed assailant. With a revolver in his overcoat, Arco-Valley was prepared to make good on his promise.[71]

The assassin presented a tidy appearance: starched uniform, slicked-back blonde hair, and clean-shaven. An unstable right-wing monarchist from Austria, and guided by what he believed were patriotic feelings for his adopted Bavarian homeland, Arco-Valley claimed he "despised and hated him [Eisner] from my heart."[72]

The assassin's crime was premeditated: After bathing on the morning of February 21, he had joked with an attendant that he was going to shoot the minister-president.[73] He wasn't taken seriously. Calling the parliament building by telephone, Arco-Valley learned that Eisner was expected at 10:00 a.m. Arriving fifteen minutes early, he settled into a doorway just down the street, released the safety on the revolver in his pocket, and waited. Arco-Valley had no way of knowing that the minister-president was about to resign. Neither did it appear that he had really thought through the political ramifications of going through with the murder. Eisner was already defeated, politically speaking; his assassination would serve no civic purpose.

When the minister-president's group walked past where Arco-Valley stood, tragically they weren't paying attention. With murderous intent pulsing through his veins, Arco-Valley stepped up behind Eisner, raised his barrel, and fired two shots in his head and back. One bullet punctured a lung, the other cracked his skull and entered his brain.[74] Eisner fell on the sidewalk in a pool of blood. Having accomplished his deed, Arco-Valley turned to depart, only to be shot in the leg by the security detail. Unloading four more rounds into his body, they stood menacingly over the assassin. According to one author, Arco-Valley's wounds were in the "neck, mouth and chest."[75] Having watched the assassination take place in front of them, several bystanders rushed over and violently kicked Arco-Valley's prostrate body.

Despite the assault and his life-threatening wounds, the killer was not dead. Later, when a detail of soldiers placed him on a stretcher and delivered him to a nearby hospital where Germany's top surgeon was waiting, the assassin's life would be saved.[76] Eisner's condition was altogether different. Slumped over the minister-president's body, Felix Fechenbach wept as he scanned Eisner's bloodied head for some sign of life. But it was too late. When two guards placed him on a stretcher and carried him to the porter's lodge at the foreign ministry, he was already dead.

Covered in blood, a dazed Fechenbach realized that someone needed to inform parliament, so he headed there on foot. Meanwhile, a crowd of bystanders assembled at the site where Kurt Eisner's body had lain. Crying women pressed their handkerchiefs in the fresh pool of blood.[77] One onlooker speculated that Erhard Auer had orchestrated the murder. Another accused the Bavarian People's Party (BVP) of hiring a gunman to brutalize the minister-president. Arriving in the chamber where parliament was just about to be called to order, Fechenbach rushed down an aisle in his bloodied clothes and spread word to the delegates of Eisner's murder. The news quickly reached the minister-president's young wife. Frau Eisner fainted and was carried from the chamber.

Up in the galleries, angry spectators shouted, "Revenge for Eisner" and "Down with Auer!"[78] Pandemonium in the chamber forced the deputies to postpone the session for one hour. Out on the street, delegates visited the site of Eisner's murder and watched soldiers pour sawdust to soak up the remaining pools of blood. When the delegates returned to parliament, the galleries overflowed with spectators eager to see what would happen next. Auer stepped up to the rostrum and delivered an impromptu eulogy, saying that Eisner was "a man of the most unsullied idealism."[79] Concluding his remarks with a plea for calm, Auer returned to his seat. He and his fellow SPD delegates were determined to get on with the parliament's business. But before they could do so, a new individual entered the chamber.

Unlike Fechenbach, this person was not delivering news. No sooner had Auer sat down than a man in an overcoat stopped in front of him, produced a rifle from beneath his coat, steadied it on a bannister, and shot him at point-blank range. Struck in the chest, the minister of interior was literally blown from his chair.[80] His attacker was Alois Lindner, an ordinary butcher, ardent supporter of Eisner, and a member of the Workers' Council. Lindner had hurried to the parliament building in a murderous rage, determined to strike down the man he felt was responsible for the minister-president's killing. Having completed his self-appointed mission, Lindner began his exit down the aisle, but not before unloading a few more rounds at delegates from the BVP. No sooner had he departed the chamber than another man, seated in the galleries, produced his own weapon and started firing on the politicians below. Scrambling for cover, the delegates cowered beneath their benches, while others stampeded toward the doorways. Shot in the head, one BVP delegate was fatally wounded. On his way to the main entrance, Linder was attacked by a porter, but the butcher shot him dead before escaping into the sunlight. Gravely wounded, Eisner's anointed successor Erhard Auer was rushed to a hospital, where the same surgeon who'd saved Anton Arco-Valley's life would attempt to save his. The assembly of the new parliament was indefinitely postponed. A violent Right had emerged, radicals prepared to arm themselves, and Munich was gripped by dread.

CHAPTER SIX

THE SOVIET REPUBLIC

Ernst Toller was away from Munich on the morning that Eisner was killed. After accompanying the minister-president to the Second International, the playwright had stayed on in Switzerland to visit friends. Returning by rail, he heard the grim report of Eisner's murder when his train was stopped outside the city. It was difficult news to accept. Eisner and Toller weren't casual friends who simply liked each other's company. Based on a shared commitment to nonviolence, democracy, and equal rights, the pair had thrown themselves into politics without regard for personal safety. "He [Eisner] did not fear death," wrote Toller in his memoirs. "The people felt this, and believed in him because of it. Talents are given to many, but the masses will follow only those whom they know have overcome the fear of death."[1]

Later that day, Toller's train was permitted to continue to its final destination. Across Munich, people were reacting to the news of Eisner's murder in different ways. While revolutionaries in trucks crisscrossed the capital shouting, "Revenge for Eisner,"[2] students at Ludwig-Maximilians-Universität appeared to celebrate his assassination.[3] At the Theresienwiese, Toller joined a group of mourners and consoled them by reading poetry he had written.[4] More than a few people believed that Arco-Valley had assassinated Eisner as part of a conspiracy. "The assassination was not an independent act," wrote the anarchist Erich Mühsam.[5]

Anton Arco-Valley had been consorting with Eisner's enemies in the months before the assassination. Evidence suggests that he tried to join the anti-Semitic Thule Society but was denied admittance on account of being half Jewish. Thule's founder, Rudolf von Sebottendorff, later claimed that Arco-Valley had killed Eisner to prove his worth to Thule. No one could say for certain what his motives really were. Arco-Valley's confession in court—whether or not we believe it—explained, "I told myself that if Eisner were removed, the fight [against the Communists] would require less blood, and be less dangerous to the government."[6] For now, the assailant was confined to a hospital bed, recovering from life-threatening wounds.

"THE SECOND REVOLUTION MIGHT BE DELAYED, BUT NOT SUBDUED FOREVER"

After Eisner's murder, the appointment of a new minister-president and the resumption of parliament were indefinitely postponed. Though a surgeon had succeeded in saving Erhard Auer's life, the SPD leader was too weak to assume power. Political parties remained deeply divided, and the spread of violence seemed likely. The Communist Party (KPD), which had until now been "practically impotent, with little or no influence,"[7] spiked in popularity. To prevent civil war, the leaders of the Social Democrats, the USPD, and the KPD formed a committee called the Zentralrat (Central Council), comprised of eleven delegates, to act as a temporary government. Deploying armed revolutionaries in the capital, the Zentralrat announced a curfew and declared a three-day strike. Fearing a right-wing counterrevolution, it also ordered Munich's privileged classes to hand over their firearms and took fifty hostages from wealthy organizations as insurance.[8] These measures and others left many residents questioning if the Zentralrat intended to overturn the election results of January 12. Clarifying its position, the committee promised to recall parliament when conditions allowed for it. If the Zentralrat had been composed entirely of Social Democrats, there likely would have been no delays. But after Eisner's murder, the KPD and the USPD had been allowed into the decision-making process.

On February 25, talks were initiated in Bavaria's council congress on the issue of parliamentary versus council systems. Participants felt the pressure to come up with a coherent solution as quickly as possible. Though the Social Democrats said they would be willing to include the councils in some form of future government, they remained distinctly opposed to the inclusion of the Communists and the dictatorship of the proletariat.[9] In response, KPD leader Max Levien defended Russian Bolshevism and warned that "the second revolution might be delayed, but not subdued forever."[10] Then news arrived that five thousand radicals and workers gathered in the Wagnerbräu beer hall had issued demands to close parliament permanently, proclaim a Soviet Republic, and open diplomatic channels with Soviet Russia. Leading the group was Rudolf Egelhofer, the same man who had climbed the walls of the foreign ministry back in January to convince Eisner to rescind the arrest warrants of radical council members.[11] These developments required serious attention, but talks in the council congress were suspended as Munich prepared to say goodbye to its slain minister-president.

"LIKE JESUS"

On February 26, Kurt Eisner was laid to rest in Munich. The revolutionary leader who had deposed Bavaria's monarch was given a funeral befitting a king.[12] Since early morning, church bells had been ringing across the city, though some reluctant priests had been forced to do so at gunpoint.[13] Red flags symbolizing support for the revolution and black banners mourning Eisner hung from municipal buildings and churches. Along a parade route from the Theresienwiese to Munich's Ostfriedhof (East Cemetery), Eisner's coffin was carried in a royal coach flanked by somber politicians, state officials, and close friends. Marching to the cadence of drums, a detail of former Russian POWs carried a wreath and held aloft a framed portrait of the minister-president. Dressed in heavy overcoats, troops of Bavaria's soldiers' council joined the procession behind Eisner's cortege. Curiously, among the parading troops captured on film and motion picture that day was a man who bears the striking resemblance of Adolf Hitler.[14]

While little is known of his life during this period, evidence suggests that Hitler probably marched in Eisner's funeral procession and was caught on camera. Housed in barracks near the future site of Munich's Olympic Park, he had recently been chosen to serve in the soldiers' council of his regiment.[15] Does this mean he inwardly supported the slain minister-president? Were Hitler's political positions still at this time in flux? Years later, he would ascribe sinister intentions to Eisner, and accuse him of trying to dismember the German Reich so that it would fall to the Bolsheviks. "Kurt Eisner was not acting in the slightest degree from the standpoint of Bavarian interests," he wrote in *Mein Kampf*, "but merely as the commissioned representative of Jewry."[16] What could have been going through Hitler's mind as he walked in the cortege? In the casket ahead of him, the man reviled for admitting Germany's war guilt was being canonized as a saint. Hitler's mysterious sighting prompts more questions than it answers. Like a ghost, no sooner had he appeared than he quickly vanished again.

One hundred thousand people participated in Eisner's funeral procession.

Gustav Landauer, the antiwar Socialist who had inspired Ernst Toller, eulogized Eisner by saying, "He was one like Jesus, like [Jan] Huss . . . who were executed by stupidity and greed."[17]

As Bavaria's minister-president received his royal send-off, his killer, Anton Arco-Valley, and his rival, wounded SPD leader Erhard Auer, found themselves convalescing in the same ward of a Munich hospital. For reasons that remain a mystery, Auer chose this occasion to send a bouquet of red roses to Arco-Valley.[18] Was the minister of interior thanking Arco-Valley for murdering his political rival? Auer's gesture certainly seemed like a political statement. When news of the flowers was leaked in the press, Social Democrats were outraged that their colleague had given their opponents the ammunition to suggest collusion. Subsequently, the minister of interior's daughter was blamed for sending the flowers out of naiveté.[19]

In the days after Eisner's funeral, talks resumed in the council congress on the subject of parliamentary versus council systems. When the matter was finally brought to ballot, delegates repudiated a motion to declare Bavaria a "Soviet Republic" and voted in favor of parliamentarianism, 234 to 70.[20] The election results of January 12 would be upheld.[21] However, some council members, refusing to accept the outcome, called for demonstrations. In response, several thousand protesters gathered on the Theresienwiese the following morning to express their defiance. This time, when a security detail appeared and started firing on the demonstrators, the crowd dispersed, leaving three dead. Though news of the attack threatened to delay the council congress from completing its business, delegates pressed forward and selected nominees for a new Bavarian cabinet.[22] The only thing left to do, apart from setting a date to reopen parliament, was to achieve party approval for the nominees.

In early March, party meetings were held outside Munich in cities like Nuremberg and Fürth, where a protracted and complicated series of interparty negotiations ensued. The SPD was insisting that only elected parliamentary delegates could approve a new cabinet. On that basis, the nominees proposed in the council congress had to be scrapped. When the Social Democrats got their way, parliament was reopened on March 15.

Before a packed house, Johannes Hoffmann of the SPD was elected Bavaria's new minister-president. Hoffmann, who had served in Eisner's cabinet as minister of education, believed he could take the middle road and lead Bavaria away from danger by excluding extremists from both the Right and the Left. Neither Communists nor members of the Catholic-backed BVP were selected to serve in his cabinet. Standing below a portrait of Eisner, Hoffmann invoked his predecessor's memory, stating, "The political act which Minister-President Eisner wanted to undertake on February 21 is now accomplished."[23] Though delayed by three weeks, the Social Democrats were finally in control of the government. But the struggle for power was far from over.

CONSPIRATORS IN THE QUEEN'S CHAMBERS

Since early 1919, the KPD in Berlin had been observing developments in Munich with growing concern. The killings of Karl Liebknecht and Rosa Luxemburg in the German capital had taught them that it was better to avoid violence until conditions ripened for a true Marxist revolution. While the KPD's popularity was growing in Munich, due in no small measure to massive postwar unemployment, there was still need for caution. To guide their comrades in the south, Communists in Berlin decided to send Eugen Leviné to take leadership in Bavaria. An educated Russian Jew with a high-pitched, nasal voice, Leviné had been captured and tortured by the tsar's secret police during the Russian Revolution of 1905 and later served in the German army during the First World War. He was both resilient and shrewd. Arriving in Munich, Leviné took charge of the movement by demoting the party's existing leadership, including Max Levien, terminating the KPD's alliance with Erich Mühsam and his fellow anarchists, and organizing Communist cells in Bavaria's factories.[24]

Meanwhile, at engagements in five Munich beer halls, Minister-President Hoffmann whipped up public support for his new government by making personal appearances with his cabinet members.

Eugen Leviné.

In his early fifties, Hoffmann possessed the kind of charisma and self-assurance that put many residents at ease. Asking for calm in the city, he appeared to be winning support by promising to "get Bavaria moving" again.[25] But each of his appearances ended in sabotage when Communists showed up and drowned out his speeches with demands for a Soviet Republic.[26] Compounding Hoffmann's troubles was news from Weimar that the German National Assembly had decided to reduce Bavaria's autonomy, making it "subordinate to the Reich."[27] Despite the past efforts of Eisner and other diplomats, Bavaria would lose important revenue streams, including its post office, rail system, diplomatic corps, and state tax administration. The decisions of the National Assembly renewed Bavarian hostilities toward Prussia and politicians in Berlin.

Whispers of secession began to float about Bavaria. When Hoffmann lobbied for German unity, saying, "Bavaria outside the Reich is a thing of impossibility,"[28] some began to question his loyalties. Back in February, German voters had elected Friedrich Ebert to a seven-year term as the nation's Reich president. Was Hoffmann betraying Bavaria to cozy up to the president, his Social Democratic colleague? As president, Ebert had been given the power to appoint and dismiss Germany's chancellor, direct foreign affairs, command the military, set up special courts, and dissolve the Reichstag if necessary. He even had the authority to crush revolutionary activity. Was Hoffmann going to be Ebert's lackey? Critics suggested that even Eisner had done more to protect Bavarian rights than the current minister-president.

In late March, news arrived that red revolutionaries in nearby Hungary had formed a Soviet Republic, lifting the morale of Munich's Communists. Frustrated by food shortages, inflation, and unemployment, Hungarians under Béla Kun had answered the clarion call "Workers of the World, Unite!" and proved that Communist revolution was more than a Russian commodity. "Next to those of Lenin and Trotsky," wrote Erich Mühsam, "the name of Béla Kun was now on every proletarian's lips."[29] With only Austria separating Bavaria from Hungary, Communists began dreaming of a Soviet corridor extending through central Europe. To head off trouble, Minister-President Hoffmann scheduled an emergency recall of Bavaria's parliament for early April and, ignoring rumblings in the streets, departed for Berlin to speak with the newly appointed German chancellor, Philipp Scheidemann of the SPD.[30] In his absence, large numbers of Communists gathered at Munich's Löwenbräukeller beer hall and issued demands for a Soviet Republic in solidarity with Russia and Hungary. Once again, Munich was on the precipice of leftist revolution.

When Hoffmann departed for Berlin, members of his cabinet in Munich decided to hold a top-secret meeting with delegates from the USPD and the KPD behind his back. The summit, held at the Ministry for Military Affairs, was so sensitive that stenographers were barred from the proceedings. As the meeting unfolded after midnight on April 5, Bavaria's new war minister, Ernst Schneppenhorst, an SPD politician known for his staunch opposition to Communism, suddenly announced his support for a Bavarian Soviet Republic. The assembly was shocked. Could the minister be trusted? What precipitated his 180-degree turn? In Hoffmann's absence, Schneppenhorst was proposing to kick out the minister-president, his cabinet, and parliament. Communists and Independents in the councils would form the new government. Historians would later speculate that Schneppenhorst thought he could tame the Communists by giving them the burden of government responsibility.[31] Regardless of his reasoning, when he made his proposal, all eyes fell upon Eugen Leviné, the KPD leader from Berlin with the nasal voice.

Leviné regarded political collaboration as a fallacy. In the heated silence, he tested Schneppenhorst's sincerity by dismissing his proposal as a "pseudo-putsch from a smoke-filled room."[32] Stung by his rebuff, the war minister began to smolder. Continuing, Leviné asserted that only the Communists could declare a Soviet Republic.[33] Unable to control his rage, Schneppenhorst sneered that Leviné was a "Jewish goblin."[34] The minister had revealed his true colors. Together with his fellow Communists, Leviné got up and walked out. To let tempers settle and allow party representatives to confer with their constituents, the assembly decided to postpone their decision for forty-eight hours, and the meeting adjourned. Back among his SPD fellows, Schneppenhorst was encouraged to retract his proposal as soon as possible.

On April 6, a bitter chill and twenty inches of snow besieged Munich.[35] That evening, the assembly of Socialists and Communists reconvened for their second secret meeting in the queen's chamber of the former Wittelsbach palace, known as the Residenz. For the leaders of the proletariat, the queen's royal bedroom was a meeting place rich in irony. Joining them was Ernst Toller. Having been away during the first conference, Toller had rushed back to the Bavarian capital to attend the second. Describing the scene, he later wrote, "The great rooms where once maids-in-waiting and powdered lackeys had fawned attendance on their royal masters now rang with the heavy tread of workmen, farmers, and soldiers."[36] After a stirring speech by Gustav Landauer, the attendees made up their minds to overthrow Minister-President Hoffmann and create a new government, with or without the support of the KPD. Bavaria, they declared, was now a Soviet Republic. Only Ernst Niekisch, an influential Social Democrat, voted against the decision.[37]

To Toller, the coup seemed half-baked. Without the support of the Communists and Social Democrats, he doubted that the fledgling regime could survive. But the playwright kept his mouth shut.[38] In the opulent bedchamber, the group began feverishly nominating cabinet ministers. Niekisch begrudgingly accepted the top post as head of state. Supporting him was a cast including Landauer as minister of education and enlightenment and Dr. Franz Lipp as minister of foreign affairs. Hardly anyone knew who Lipp was. Looking distinguished in his impeccable suit and neatly trimmed goatee, the new foreign minister was possibly approved simply because the group believed he was a better choice than the anarchist Mühsam. After filling the cabinet in the predawn hours, the assembly was suddenly interrupted by the arrival of Eugen Leviné, who had returned to denounce the creation of a Soviet Republic that joined forces with tainted leaders from the old regime. Though he aroused considerable doubt, Leviné was unable to change their minds. Later that morning, in Munich and cities across Bavaria, residents discovered that their state was now a Soviet Republic.

On his first day in office, Ernst Niekisch found himself haunted by the looming burdens of government bureaucracy. Institutions including banks, courts, factories, and the military were all going to press for answers about how the Soviet Republic intended to rule. Though Niekisch and his fellow conspirators had established control over Munich, Minister-President Hoffmann would eventually return and enlist the support of his fellow Social Democrats to regain power. Would the Soviet Republic be strong enough to fight them off? Within hours of assuming his role as head of state, Niekisch resigned, concluding that the new government had little chance of success. As his replacement, he nominated Ernst Toller, whose only experience in office was a brief stint as deputy chairman of Bavaria's councils. The young patriot who had fought in the trenches of Verdun only to return to Germany and take up the antiwar cause was now Bavaria's head of state. Consumed by his own doubts, Toller reportedly took the job against his better judgment because he felt obliged to stand with the workers.[39]

Like Niekisch before him, Toller received no support from the KPD. Planning to spark a Communist revolution in the Russian model, Leviné was indifferent to democracy and nonviolence and unwilling to support the playwright. And Leviné wouldn't be Toller's only opponent. From Bamburg came news that the ousted minister-president, Johannes Hoffmann, was setting up a government-in-exile to oppose the Soviet Republic. In reality, only a portion of Bavaria—from Augsburg in the north, to Garmisch in the south, and Rosenheim in the east—was under Soviet control. The rest of the state refused to recognize Toller's regime. Bavaria's new head of state was surrounded by enemies.

"THE COFFEE HOUSE ANARCHISTS"

Ernst Toller at the time was twenty-six years old. Asking himself what the new regime could achieve and how long it would last, he worried that his government might be nothing more than a madcap attempt "to salvage the lost German Revolution."[40] On his first day in office, Toller was besieged by a long line of visitors all wanting to speak with him. "Each one of them believed that the Soviet Republic had been expressly created to satisfy his own private desires," he later wrote. "Unappreciated cranks submitted their programs for the betterment of humanity, believing that at last their much-scorned ideas would have a chance to turn earth into paradise."[41] Toller was deluged by concerns, not the least of which were the strange cables being sent abroad by Dr. Franz Lipp.

The newly appointed foreign minister had reportedly expressed his unequivocal devotion to the pope in Rome and cabled Vladimir Lenin with a bizarre complaint that the outgoing regime had stolen "the keys to my ministry toilet."[42] Observing Lipp's unhinged manner, Erich Mühsam later wrote, "His post had obviously gotten to his head. . . . His work ranged from highly compromising to unbelievably ridiculous."[43] Launching a probe into Lipp's background, colleagues discovered that, among other things, the foreign minister had twice been institutionalized for mental illness.[44] To resolve the situation, Toller took it upon himself to present Dr. Lipp with resignation papers. After running a comb neatly through his perfectly trimmed goatee, Lipp reportedly read the document, affixed his name to it, and sighed, "The things I do for the revolution."[45]

The Lipp scandal lent credence to the doubts many citizens had about the Soviet Republic. Names like Toller, Landauer, and Mühsam conjured the impression that Bavaria's fate rested with inexperienced bohemian intellectuals, and the leadership was dubbed "the coffee house anarchists."[46] But a representative of Munich's Orthodox Jewish community, Sigmund Fraenkel, had a much more prescient concern. Names like Toller, Landauer, and Mühsam were also Jewish, and they were being associated directly with Bolshevism. Foreseeing danger, Fraenkel penned an open letter to Toller and his cabinet, which communicated a dire warning. It read in part:

> We Jews in Munich have remained silent during the last hard, woebegone weeks during which you and other non-Bavarian romancers and dreamers, ignorant of the Bavarian national character, have exploited our misery and mental depression, in order to recruit believers in your well-intentioned but flawed plans of future order of economics and society, which run counter to human nature. We remained silent because we were afraid of harming our religious community by chastising you in public, and because we hoped every day ... that you would realize the chaos of destruction and desolation in which your chosen [political] path must surely end. Today, when thousands and thousands of inflammatory anti-Semitic pamphlets have been distributed in the streets of Munich [it is clear to me], that not only members of our religious community, but Judaism itself [is] endangered if the mass of Munich's working population connects the tenets and beliefs of the Jewish religion with the false Bolshevik and Communist doctrines [that you have been preaching to the mass of people who have become] demoralized and confused during the [last] four and a half years of war.[47]

If the Jews were linked to a failed Bolshevik experiment, the entire Jewish community might pay the price when the anti-Semites came to exact their revenge. Sigmund Fraenkel had foreseen what others, but not Hitler, would miss.

Toller and his cabinet had no time to respond to Fraenkel's warning. The Soviet Republic had more immediate concerns. From Bamberg, exiled leader Hoffmann declared the new regime illegal and started gathering support for an armed attack on Munich. At the Mathäserbräu beer hall, Leviné was stirring up his own rebellion. The KPD leader openly lobbied for regime change before a large audience. "You allow a handful of confused men [including Toller] to take charge of your destinies," Leviné informed the packed crowd, "We [the KPD] mean to convert the pseudo Soviet republic into a genuine one."[48] Tipped off about the meeting, Toller rushed to the scene.

Arriving at the beer hall, Bavaria's head of state interrupted Leviné by crying out to the workers: "If you have revised your political opinion and really believe now that the present confusion is due solely to the incompetence of the government, then it is up to you to cooperate in saving the revolution. If you overthrow us and set up a new government without the support of the peasants, where will you be? How will you feed the city?"[49] Toller was reminding the workers that

Bavaria's rural farmers did not support the KPD. Leviné brashly countered that he would follow the Russian example and threaten violence to make the peasant farmers give up their food. "The Bavarian peasant is utterly different than the Russian peasant," Toller retorted. "He is armed, and he would put up a strong fight. Do you want to go to war about every gallon of milk?"[50] When their verbal sparring ended, Toller was taken hostage, and the Communists started drawing up a proclamation to announce their new government. But later, as dawn approached, armed men loyal to Toller suddenly arrived at the beer hall and, with guns drawn, liberated their leader. Just like that, Leviné's coup fizzled.

Three days later, on April 12, Toller received news that forces loyal to Hoffmann were planning a putsch. The playwright had been trying to negotiate with Hoffmann's government for several days but came up empty-handed.[51] Reich president Friedrich Ebert had sent orders to the Hoffmann government-in-exile to attack. "I consider it necessary that the restoration of the former conditions in Bavaria be accomplished as soon as possible," read Ebert's cable. "Experience in other places has taught that the quicker and more thoroughly this is accomplished, the less resistance and bloodshed are to be expected."[52] Though the Reich president and the minister-president-in-exile were Social Democratic colleagues, Hoffmann recognized that Ebert's message contained a threat: If he didn't clean up the mess in Bavaria, Prussian forces would be deployed to do it for him. If that happened, Hoffmann understood his political future would be ruined.

Though he needed more time to prepare his forces, with Ebert breathing down his neck Hoffman decided to take immediate action. In the absence of seasoned military units ready to attack the capital, Hoffmann leaned on supporters from the extreme-right Thule Society. These were the kind of anti-Semites Fraenkel had referred to in his letter to Toller. Thule was among those responsible for the leaflets that had called for Eisner's murder after his trip to the Second International in Bern, Switzerland. On April 10, Hoffmann received a message from Sebottendorff assuring him that thousands of people in Munich were ready to rise up "as soon as loyal troops have reached the gates of the city." Sebottendorff also promised that Thule Kampfbund was prepared to play its part in a counterrevolution and asked for weapons. The message concluded with the salute, "We regard you, minister-president, with the utmost respect and confidence."[53]

On Sunday April 13, Johannes Hoffmann unleashed his attack. Dubbed the Palm Sunday Putsch, the plan had called for an expeditionary force of a few hundred men led by Thule supporter Alfred Seiffertitz to make a surprise attack and take government hostages. Then, a larger force of six hundred men, led by the war minister, Ernst Schneppenhorst, would be signaled from Ingol-stadt to move in and liberate the city. But the putsch didn't work out the way they had planned. Though Seiffertitz's forces succeeded in taking hostages at the Wittelsbach palace, and initiated skirmishes at the Marienplatz and the central train station, the message for reinforcements never reached Schneppenhorst. Consequently, Seiffertitz's forces were pinned down. Rudolf von Sebottendorff apparently called off his supporters when he realized that the war minister's forces weren't coming.[54] Seiffertitz's men were forced to flee.[55] The putschists had wagered that soldiers in Munich's garrisons would switch allegiances and rush into the streets to join their cause, but it never happened.[56] When the Palm Sunday Putsch was over, twenty men were dead and a hundred more injured.[57]

Toller's forces had outlasted a poorly conceived assault on the Bavarian capital. Now the head of state of the Soviet Republic would face adversaries from the Far Left. That evening, Communist leaders convinced council members meeting in Munich's famous Hofbräuhaus to declare a second Soviet Republic,[58] appoint Eugen Leviné as their leader, and assume control of the city. Leviné had finally secured enough support in Socialist circles to replace Toller and his cabinet with a "true" Soviet regime. The playwright was arrested.[59] But it was hardly necessary. This time, neither Toller nor his supporters intended to oppose the Communists. Leviné quickly chose Tobias Axelrod, a fellow Russian Jew, and Max Levien, a Russian believed to be Jewish, as his adjutants.[60] Both men were known to have had direct contact with Vladimir Lenin in the past, and this gave the second Soviet Republic a certain panache in revolutionary circles. Their commitment to Marxist ideals would be uncompromising. "The sun of world revolution has risen!" read an announcement for the new regime. "Long live the world revolution! Long live the Bavarian Soviet Republic!"[61] Ernst Toller's regime had lasted only six days.[62]

CHAPTER SEVEN

THE COUNTERREVOLUTION

"FIGHTING FOR A BETTER WORLD"

The second Soviet Republic, under the direction of Eugen Leviné, intended to make Bavaria the driving force for the Bolshevization of Europe.[1] They knew their chances of success were remote. Johannes Hoffmann's counterrevolutionary forces were defeated on Palm Sunday, but they would come back. With limited time and resources, the regime took extreme measures to ensure its survival. Following the proclamation on the night of April 13, Communists in Munich declared a general strike. Trains stopped running, factories were emptied, and work ground to a halt. A curfew was declared.[2] Food stocks were confiscated.[3] Red Guards replaced the police.[4] Residents were ordered to turn over their weapons.[5]

Rudolf Egelhofer, the sailor from the Kiel mutiny who had been drumming up support for a Soviet Republic in Munich's beer halls, was appointed to recruit a Red Army of twenty thousand soldiers.[6] To entice volunteers, he promised to supply every man with a rifle and ten-day's advance pay.[7] It didn't take long for the new outfit to develop a bad reputation. Reports of Red Army soldiers going on drunken benders and looting became commonplace.[8] In the Wittelsbach palace, the soldiers were rumored to be holding wild orgies[9] with prostitutes. The regime had also released inmates from local jails without determining which ones were actually dangerous. A feeling of lawlessness enveloped the city. As distasteful as the situation was, at least the Communists were not murdering people.

Though his government had been deposed, Ernst Toller had no intention of leaving Bavaria. The playwright had built alliances with workers in the Bavarian councils and wouldn't abandon them. Nor were they willing to quit him: When the new regime placed him under arrest, it was they who had demanded his freedom.[10] Now workers insisted that he be named to a command in the Red Army under Egelhofer.[11] The appointment presented a dilemma: When Toller was arrested for promoting labor strikes back in 1918, he had pledged himself to nonviolence. "Was I to break this vow now that the revolution had come?" Toller asked himself. "I had to break it. The workers had put their trust in me and made me their leader, and I was responsible to them. If I refused to defend them now, if I called on them to renounce force of arms, would I not be betraying that trust?"[12] Toller accepted the post, and his command was quickly put to the test.

On April 16, counterrevolutionary forces seized the town of Dachau, just outside the Bavarian capital. Leading a patrol of armed revolutionary workers into the area, Toller received orders from Egelhofer to pound Dachau with artillery and storm it. The tactic was reminiscent of General Falkenhayn's strategy at Verdun, and the playwright couldn't stomach it. "I hesitated to carry out this order," he later wrote, "for the peasants and farmers round Dachau were on our side, and it was up to us to avoid all unnecessary destruction."[13] Ignoring Egelhofer's order, Toller tried to negotiate with his adversaries. In a face-to-face meeting with an officer and a soldier from the other side, he quickly deduced that the latter had been deceived by right-wing propaganda, which portrayed the Soviets in the capital as murderers. "Very well then," Toller encouraged him, "go to Munich and see for yourself. I'll give you a safe-conduct and nobody will touch you. Go and see for yourself what liars the newspapers are."[14] The playwright's impudence irritated the soldier's superior, who stormed off in a huff.

Later, when the two sides started exchanging fire, Toller stormed Dachau on foot. Supported by workers from a nearby factory, he succeeded in taking back the town and secured thirty-six prisoners. Learning of his victory, Egelhofer ordered the playwright to execute the officers in his custody. "I tore up the order," Toller later wrote, "believing that generosity to the conquered should be an axiom of revolutionary conduct. . . . I knew that in Berlin the counter-revolutionaries had murdered Red prisoners in cold blood; but we were fighting for a better world; we were demanding humanity, and we had to show humanity ourselves."[15]

In Munich, Egelhofer agreed with a colleague who joked that Toller was turning his forces into "a Salvation Army."[16] The Red Army commander, who had once remarked that it saddened him "to come to Munich and not see an old capitalist or officer hanging from every lamp post in the city,"[17] doubted that the playwright had the proper commitment to class warfare. At Dachau, Toller's army had stopped drilling, dropped formality, and blurred the distinctions between ranks. The playwright had reportedly told his men, "We are not making a Russian or Berliner revolution of bloodshed, but a Bavarian revolution of love."[18] Back in Munich, Eugen Leviné wanted to relieve Toller of his command but was preoccupied with bigger problems.

Johannes Hoffmann's forces were blocking food shipments to the Bavarian capital. With the economy crippled and residents starving, conditions in Munich began deteriorating rapidly. Red Army soldiers broke into the homes of wealthy residents to search for hidden food stocks. Fresh out of cash, the regime started printing emergency bills.[19] Fearing that their children's health was being jeopardized by the city's plummeting supply of fresh milk, residents demanded that Leviné negotiate with Hoffmann's government-in-exile. "What does it matter if for a few weeks less milk reaches Munich," the Communist leader fired back at them. "Most of it goes to the children of the bourgeoisie anyway. We are not interested in keeping them alive."[20]

"THE STRAIGHTEST BOSS I EVER HAD"

On April 22, nine days after seizing power, Leviné and his cohorts decided to hold a parade in Munich. Twelve to fifteen thousand armed men marched in a demonstration of power down Ludwigstraße.[21] Among a crowd of onlookers was a thirty-three-year-old photographer named Heinrich Hoffmann. Unrelated to the exiled minister-president in Bamburg, Hoffmann was "intent on photographing a bit of history in the making."[22] With piercing eyes and a robust sense of humor, Hoffmann had a knack for insinuating himself into situations. And, in a few short years, he would become Adolf Hitler's trusted friend and personal photographer.

Before being drafted by the German army in 1917, Hoffmann had enjoyed a lucrative career as one of Munich's top portrait and press photographers.[23] The son of a royal court photographer, he had opened a studio in Schwabing where he took portraits of actors and celebrities. At the time, photo publishing was a new and profitable enterprise, and Hoffmann had the resources and talent to make a name for himself. During the war he joined an elite cadre of photographers allowed access to the western front, but he never filmed combat.[24] Then, in August 1917, he received a conscription notice and was ordered to the front in France. Hoffmann wasn't cut out for combat. Heart and stomach ailments eventually allowed him to retreat to a military hospital.[25] Later, he was transferred to a base north of Munich, where he served out the remainder of his duty.

On November 7, 1918, Hoffmann was stuck at his post in Schleißheim and missed Kurt Eisner's revolution. When he finally did make it home, he began documenting the revolution in pictures. Over the next few months, Hoffmann managed to photograph some of the revolution's best-known figures, including Eisner, Gustav Landauer, and Erich Mühsam. Unbeknownst to anyone at the time, he'd also captured Adolf Hitler through his lens. On August 2, 1914, Hoffmann had been snapping shots of a rapturous crowd in Munich's Odeonsplatz on the eve of the First World War.[26] Years later, he would discuss the event with Hitler and discover the Nazi dictator's face among the masses in one of his pictures. Later, on February 26, 1919, Hoffmann caught Hitler on film a second time, at Eisner's funeral procession. Now, standing in the crowd on Ludwigstraße, Hoffmann hoped to record a picture of his latest target: Rudolf Egelhofer. As he positioned himself to snap the Red Army commander, he failed to notice a group of men closing in on him.

Since November, revolutionary soldiers wearing red armbands had been seen standing guard at various locations inside the capital. Hoffmann wore his own red armband when he filmed in the streets,[27] and until now he'd been left alone. But according to his memoirs, on this day he was apprehended by Red Army soldiers and escorted away for interrogation.

Hoffmann was brought to a Munich prep school called the Luitpold Gymnasium,[28] where the First Infantry Regiment of the Red Army was housing prisoners. The cameraman had no idea why he was detained. As a photojournalist, he would always claim to be apolitical.[29] What did the Red Army soldiers want with him? Hoffmann was led into the office of Egelhofer's deputy commander, Alois Dufter.[30] When the deputy turned to address him, the photographer was greatly relieved to be looking into the face of his former apprentice: Dufter was apparently surprised too. According to Hoffmann's memoirs, Dufter explained to the soldiers that the photographer was his "very good friend" and "the straightest boss I ever had!"[31] Not only did Hoffmann get his camera back, he "received a written pass" authorizing him to take photographs "when and where" he liked.[32]

Many of Munich's press corps cameramen had refused to film the revolution because they didn't want to be associated with it.[33] Hoffmann didn't share their fears. With his new pass, he felt he could corner the market. "My permit removed all obstacles from my path," he later wrote. "I was [now] the officially authorized photographer of the Soldiers' and Workers' Republic!"[34] It was a strange twist of fortune. Had Hoffmann's interrogator been someone else, the photographer might have been taken hostage, thrown into a jail cell beneath the gymnasium, and suffered another fate, making it impossible for him to produce Hitler's most famous propaganda stills.

"THE MUNICH DISGRACE MUST BE WIPED OUT"

The failed Palm Sunday Putsch and the military defeat at Dachau were regrettable outcomes for Johannes Hoffmann's government-in-exile. Though he had hoped to take back Munich with Bavarian troops, the exiled minister-president was now forced to accept assistance from Berlin. Hoffmann knew the decision would infuriate his fellow Bavarians, but he didn't have a choice. Germany's war minister, Noske, had offered to send 20,000 troops.[35] He also insisted that Prussian general Ernst von Oven lead the operation. As part of preparations for an assault on Munich, the decision was made to utilize the assistance of Freikorps. Among the paramilitary groups already available was Freikorps Epp, a regiment named after the leader of Bavaria's Life Guards regiment, Colonel Ritter von Epp.[36] Its operational planner was Ernst Röhm.

One of the key militarists supporting Hitler in the early years of the Nazi movement, Röhm had fancied soldiery and dreamed of a military career since childhood. Though he would later become famous for his homosexuality, Röhm was likely closeted before, during, and immediately after the war.[37] All his passions were rather channeled into soldiering.

During the First World War, Röhm participated in some of the bloodiest battles on the western front. Wounded fourteen times, he nearly had his face blown off while fighting the French. Yet each time he returned to the front eager to rejoin his men. In 1917, Röhm was promoted as a general staff officer. Then, while recuperating in Brussels from an illness in the fall of 1918, he learned of the Kaiser's abdication, the

Ernst Röhm.

revolution in Munich, and the armistice. Röhm believed the people back home had gone insane.[38] Having seen so much death and sacrifice, he couldn't fathom why the politicians capitulated and he had no idea that the armistice had been instigated by General Ludendorff. Returning to Munich, he concluded that Eisner's success had hinged entirely on the fact that all of Bavaria's fighting men had been away at war. Believing the best thing he could do was return to his division, Röhm left Bavaria to join the 12th Infantry in Westphalia, in northwestern Germany. Then in January, he transferred to Ingolstadt in central Bavaria where he served as a brigade major in the 11th Infantry.[39]

After Eisner's assassination, Röhm had resigned from his unit and slipped across the state border to join the Freikorps in Thuringia, where he ingratiated himself as one of Epp's most trusted aides. Enlisted to find adequate housing, weapons, and food for volunteers, Röhm became the glue that enabled the militia to function while it trained for an assault on Munich.

To complement Epp's regiment, Hoffmann requested the assembly of additional Freikorps militia on April 19: "Bavarians! Countrymen! In Munich rages a Russian terror, unleashed by foreign elements. This insult to Bavaria cannot be allowed to last another day.... Step forward! The Munich disgrace must be wiped out."[40] Between Reichswehr (German Army) troops under General von Oven, the Freikorps, and the Volkswehr (Bavarian People's Army), the exiled minister-president would eventually have 35,000 men at his disposal. But the number of volunteers that wished to see his return at the head of a Social Democratic government was decidedly less. The counterrevolution was predominately fueled by anti-Marxist passions and not by loyalties to Hoffmann and the center-left SPD.

Far-right propaganda accused the second Soviet Republic of shooting civilians in the streets and desecrating churches.[41] Young Bavarians, like Hitler's future deputy Rudolf Hess, were rushing in droves to join the Freikorps because they perceived Bolshevism as an existential threat to the state.[42] Service in the militia also provided the opportunity to realize the romanticized, boyhood fantasy of defending the homeland against an alien intruder. Mercenary activity was legendary in Bavaria and dated back to the seventeenth century.[43] The image of rough-and-ready fighting men serving under a single commander roaming about the countryside, completely detached from operational oversight, was intensely attractive to young Bavarians; particularly those who wanted to prove something because they had reached the age of conscription after the First World War ended. However, some garrisoned soldiers in Munich refused to attach themselves to the Freikorps or serve in the Red Army. Among them was Private Hitler. Given the later direction of his life and his pronounced anti-Bolshevik and anti-Semitic hatreds, Hitler's neutrality during the reign of the second Soviet Republic is a mystery. In 1933, Nazi propaganda would try to cover up Hitler's neutrality by claiming that he had joined Freikorps Epp, but the story was false.[44]

Unlike Hitler, supporters of the Thule Society were quite clear about their roles. To support the counterrevolution, Thulists incited their fellow Bavarians against the second Soviet Republic by linking the Jews with the Communists. In the pages of Sebottendorff's far-right newspaper, the *Beobachter*, an advertisement attacking the Soviet Republic's Jewish leadership read, "Arrest the Jews, then there will be peace in the land! Jews incite Spartacism! . . . Jews prevent Germans from understanding each other! Therefore, let's get rid of the Jewish troublemakers and instigators."[45] The advertisement was a clear example of what Sigmund Fraenkel had been trying to communicate to Toller and his associates.

Spreading propaganda that linked the Jews with Bolshevism wasn't the only task anti-Semitic nationalists would undertake. The Jews were also accused of conspiring to control the world of international finance through capitalism. Earlier in April, Dietrich Eckart and his Estonian colleague Alfred Rosenberg had distributed copies of a counterrevolutionary pamphlet entitled *An alle Werktätigen* (*To All Working People*) from a car, as they raced through the streets of Munich. The two-pager introduced Gottfried Feder's economic theory of "interest slavery" and suggested that hardworking Bavarians were undermined by a Jewish economic system that allowed capitalists to collect interest and increase their wealth without doing any work.[46] In response, an organization of patriotic Bavarian Jews published a rebuttal in the *Münchener Post*.[47] Though the regime failed to identify Eckart and Rosenberg as the culprits, it released a statement condemning the pair as "anti-Semitic agitators" that endangered public safety by throwing "flyers from speeding automobiles."[48]

Not only were Thule supporters spreading propaganda, Sebottendorff and Thule Kampfbund were establishing a Freikorps militia near Ingolstadt at Treuchtlingen[49] and aiding and abetting the counterrevolution from their offices in the Hotel Vierjahreszeiten. When military police raided Thule's offices on April 26, they found a cache of weapons, forged signatures and documents, and Thule's membership roster.[50] This last item held great significance. It included the names of some of Hitler's future supporters, including Alfred Rosenberg and Anton Drexler. But no one could have known at the time what role these individuals would play, and again the opportunity to arrest history slipped through their fingers.

However, during the raid seven Thulists were netted, most notably the countess Heila von Westarp and an aristocrat named Prince Gustav Franz Maria von Thurn und Taxis. When news of the arrests spread across the city, and people heard that the detainees included two royals, the public was more interested in knowing their fate. Brought to the Luitpold Gymnasium, the same Red Army jail where Heinrich Hoffmann had been briefly detained, the prisoners had no idea how long their confinement would last. In the coming days, as the Red Army prepared to defend the city against the counterrevolutionaries, their survival would depend on the good graces of Rudolf Egelhofer.

"A DISASTER FOR THE WORKING PEOPLE OF BAVARIA"

On the same day that the Thule Society's offices were raided in the Hotel Vierjahreszeiten, Ernst Toller announced his resignation from the Red Army. Referring to the Communist leadership of Eugen Leviné as "a disaster for the working people of Bavaria,"[51] the playwright could no longer deny the certainty of defeat. Joined by other dissenting voices, he accused the regime's Russian leadership of blindly conforming to Bolshevik ideology while ignoring the facts on the ground. When a rumor circulated that Leviné was secretly preparing to flee the city with his top lieutenants, the KPD leader and his immediate subordinates received a vote of no confidence and were compelled to resign from leadership.[52] Toller and his supporters immediately tried to reach out to Hoffmann's government-in-exile to start peace talks. But the hour was too late: Berlin had already informed the exiled minister-president that only unconditional surrender could prevent a military assault. Since Egelhofer was determined to fight to the bitter end, military confrontation was now a foregone conclusion. Counterrevolutionary forces were moving into position for an armed assault on the Bavarian capital.

On April 30, 1919, Egelhofer was informed that his Red Army had no hope of defending the city.[53] In the suburb of Starnberg, southwest of the city,[54] counterrevolutionaries advanced with brutal efficiency. When news arrived that the Freikorps had murdered twenty innocent medical orderlies,[55] Egelhofer and his lieutenants in the First Infantry Regiment vowed to retaliate. Their decision would reverberate throughout Germany for the next quarter century. At the Luitpold Gymnasium, ten hostages were lined up in pairs in the school's courtyard and shot to death. According to eyewitness accounts, a crowd of onlookers taunted the prisoners before they were killed.[56] Six of the Thulists rounded up at the Hotel Vierjahreszeiten, including Countess Heila von Westarp and

Prince von Thurn und Taxis, were among the dead. Toller tried to prevent the executions but failed to persuade Egelhofer to rescind the order before they were carried out. Rushing to the scene, he released six hostages who had been left behind in the gymnasium's cellar. Brought to a shed where the dead were stored, he paused to gaze at their lifeless faces. "As I stood looking down at these corpses," Toller later wrote, "I thought of the war . . . of the countless millions murdered throughout the length and breadth of Europe."[57]

Perceiving that news of the executions would incite a savage bloodletting, Toller hastily contacted a surgeon's clinic and asked that the bodies be removed to a mortuary. But the clinicians never arrived.[58] As he had feared, reports of the killings spread like wildfire. Sordid exaggerations accompanied the story, including the rumor that Communists had hacked off the prisoners' genitals and thrown them in waste bins. Macabre autopsy photos of their naked, abused bodies were later circulated. Anti-Semites quickly painted the massacre as a Jewish plot, despite the fact that one of its victims had been Jewish, a detail deliberately hidden from the public. Toller's attempt to save the hostages didn't fit the skewed narrative either; nor did his little-known intervention to save another hostage, the twice-lucky Count Anton Arco-Valley, the assassin of Kurt Eisner.[59] It mattered little. In the shed of the school, the Far Right had their first martyrs.

"IT IS A LOT BETTER TO KILL INNOCENT PEOPLE"

When news of the Luitpold Gymnasium massacre surfaced, it was immediately relayed to the counterrevolutionary forces surrounding Munich. Though Gustav Noske and Johannes Hoffmann had hoped to delay the assault on the city until after International Workers' Day, the Freikorps were already impatient. On May 1, in trucks, by locomotive, on horseback, and on foot, they advanced on Munich. Some wore steel helmets with swastikas—a symbol used by paramilitary groups before it became the emblem of the Nazi Party—and heavy trench coats. Others were dressed in traditional lederhosen, with thick socks and felt hats. To distinguish themselves from the enemy, they painted skulls and crossbones on their vehicles. From the west came Freikorps from Württemberg; from the south, the men of Freikorps Epp; advancing out of the north were Freikorps under Hermann Ehrhardt; and closing the circle from the east were more volunteers. Indignant over reports of the hostage massacre, men like Ernst Röhm wanted to teach the Reds a lesson and give them "a thorough cleansing."[60]

Inside the capital, members of Thule Kampfbund and other right-wing rebels seized the Wittelsbach palace and other key buildings. From their hastily constructed barricades, Red Army soldiers attempted to mount a defense. But their numbers were severely reduced by last minute desertions. The Freikorps showed no remorse in shelling their positions. With grenades and flamethrowers, they stormed the Stachus (Karlsplatz Square) and assaulted the Mathäserbräu beer hall. Though the Reds fought them off in sporadic gun battles, the counter-revolutionaries would not be denied. In the end, the death toll from battle was relatively low when compared to the number of shootings and executions the Freikorps perpetrated on civilians.

The infamous directive of a Freikorps major named Schulz appeared to sum up the policy of the counterrevolutionaries: "Anyone . . . whose conscience bothers him, had better get out. It is a lot better to kill innocent people than to let one guilty person escape. . . . You know how to handle the problem: shoot them first and then report that they attacked you or tried to escape!"[61] Freikorps soldiers in Pucheim summarily executed fifty-two Russian POWs in a stone quarry.[62] At Perlach, they murdered twelve unarmed workers. Days later they marched twenty-one Catholic theater enthusiasts into a cellar and bayonetted them to death because someone mistook them for Communists.[63] In all, the Freikorps murdered nearly a thousand people during the six-day assault. One hundred and forty-two were shot without trial. One hundred and eighty-six were court-martialed and executed.[64] The Soviet Republic's leadership didn't fare much better.

At Stadelheim Prison, Freikorps soldiers slowly beat to death the rabbinical-looking Socialist philosopher Gustav Landauer. Gasping for his final breaths, the Jewish leader was silenced with bullets and kicks to the body.[65] Rudolf Egelhofer was simply hauled from his getaway car and shot. Eugen Leviné was discovered hiding in Heidelberg, arrested, and thrown in jail. Max Levien fled Munich for Austria and wouldn't be killed until years later. Influenced by xenophobia, anti-Semitism, and propaganda, many Bavarians believed that Communist brutality at Luitpold was far greater than anything perpetrated by the Freikorps. Ernst Toller went into hiding. As Bavaria's best-known fugitive, the former soldier and head of state quickly became public enemy number one.

By May 5, the counterrevolutionaries had assumed control of the Bavarian capital. The second Soviet Republic had been defeated, and the councils, which Kurt Eisner had desperately tried to make permanent, ceased to exist. With Munich's boulevards teeming with counterrevolutionary soldiers, General Ernst von Oven informed his superiors that it was now safe for Hoffmann's government to come back to the city.[66] But another three months would pass before the exiled minister-president, his cabinet, and parliament would return to the capital and resume civilian control of the government.[67] Until then, the military under General von Oven would act as an ad hoc governing authority.

No longer fearing for their safety, Munich's residents returned to the streets. Among them was the photographer Heinrich Hoffmann. In the final moments before the assault on the city, the future photographer of Adolf Hitler had removed his red armband, switched sides, and started filming the counterrevolution. Just as he had ingratiated himself with the Communists, the photographer was now playing the Freikorps and the Reichswehr. According to artist and author Rudolf Herz, Hoffmann's images of the counterrevolution demonstrated sympathy for the nationalist cause and reflected his true feelings.[68] Hoffmann had already amassed enough photos of the revolution to fill the pages of a photo publication. Now he could complete the work by documenting the victors on the other side. This may have been his objective all along.

A year later, Hoffmann would release an enormously successful picture magazine entitled *Ein Jahr bayerische Revolution im Bilde* (*One Year of Bavarian Revolution in Pictures*). Hiring the writer Emil Herold to pen the text that accompanied his photos, Hoffmann crafted a skewed depiction of the postwar revolution that appealed to the Far Right.[69] To stir xenophobic passions, Hoffmann selected and arranged picture portraits of the revolution's Jewish leadership to bring attention to the physical differences between Europe's Hebrews and Germany's Aryans. The tactic foreshadowed the work of Nazi propagandists who later depicted Jews as an alien race in homogenous Germany. The publication also suggested that Kurt Eisner had made himself an impediment to the revolution by insisting on taking leadership in a society that already hated Jews. "Would a German of German blood have been capable of such Jewishness?" the magazine asked.[70] The publication also expressed sympathy for Count Anton Arco-Valley and suggested that if the timing had been different Eisner's murderer might have been hailed as a "liberator" instead of a "political assassin."[71] But the embellished editorial of the Luitpold Gymnasium massacre was the most damning.

Hoffmann's magazine charged that the victims at Luitpold had suffered brutal interrogations and beatings. When the prisoners were separated into pairs for their execution, Herold, the writer, suggested that the group's only Jewish victim, who did not belong to Thule, volunteered to be shot because he mistakenly assumed that he was lining up to be interrogated. "You do not belong [with the others]!" he was purportedly told.[72] But the man insisted on joining the condemned and was executed. In this way, Hoffmann's publication invented a clever story to justify why a Jew had been inadvertently murdered in a Jewish-Bolshevik plot.

Next to photos of the crime scene, the victims, and the perpetrators, Herold described the atmosphere with particular flare. When the prisoners were led into the Luitpold courtyard where "the beast" would "drink blood,"[73] Herold claimed that six to eight hundred onlookers had assembled to watch the firing squad. From windows above the scene, women purportedly laughed and danced as someone played an accordion. As she begged for mercy, Countess Westarp was cruelly mocked as a "whore."[74] When the killings were finished, witnesses joined a post-execution party where participants performed "a cheerful dance-trot."[75]

One Year of Bavarian Revolution in Pictures sold more than 200,000 copies and spawned a second print edition.[76] Thirteen years before the Nazis gained power, it concretized the image of Bolshevik cruelty in the minds of many Germans and promoted the lie that Jewish conspirators were behind the failed revolution. The publication also offered evidence of the hidden network that would later serve Hitler. On the back cover of the magazine's second printing, an advertisement appeared for one of Dietrich Eckart's anti-Semitic publications. The blurb instructed readers to send their orders to the address of Hoffmann's photo studio in Schwabing.[77] Eckart and Hoffmann had apparently been meeting as early as April 1919, during the failed Soviet Republic.[78] Their alliance indicated that Hoffmann's alleged support for the revolution had been little more than economic opportunism. It was the kind of duplicity that would typify his later effort to mislead Allied interrogators after the defeat of the Nazis in 1945. In the 1950s, Hoffmann would defend his photo magazine by claiming that the text could not be considered anti-Semitic.[79] Regardless, the publication, the activities of the Thule Society, and the formation of the DAP in 1919 underscored the fact that a network of organized anti-Semites was taking deliberate action in Bavaria long before Adolf Hitler became the Führer. Active though they were, these nationalists had no guarantee that the Communists wouldn't reorganize and rally Bavaria's workers to rise up again. Nor could they count on the Social Democrats to provide the kind of leadership they desired. Bavaria's Far Right needed to foster a legitimate party if it was going to be successful in mainstream politics. To do that, it would require a spokesman.

CHAPTER EIGHT

HITLER IN AUSTRIA

"STABBED IN THE BACK"

Weighty though it was, the defeat of the second Soviet Republic in Munich was quickly overshadowed by an announcement of great consequence. On May 7, 1919, the terms of the Treaty of Versailles were made public. The punishing conditions set forth by the Allies went far beyond curbing Germany's ability to wage war on its neighbors. Forced to accept responsibility for starting the First World War, Germany was ordered to pay staggering reparations. The price tag of defeat was destined to paralyze the economy. All of Germany's colonies were seized. Significant territories along its borders with France, Belgium, and Poland were confiscated. But perhaps most crippling in the immediate sense was the restructuring of the German military. Under the treaty, Germany's High Command was to be dismantled, its cadet schools shut down, and the army reduced to one hundred thousand soldiers and officers.[1] This was going to put a lot of men out of work. To ensure compliance, the Allies announced their intention to occupy German territory west of the Rhine River for a ten-year period and create a demilitarized zone.

The humiliating terms of the treaty compelled Ludendorff to further advance the theory that civilian politicians had betrayed the nation.[2] In an infamous conversation with a British diplomat, Sir Neil Malcolm, the former First Quartermaster General blamed Germany's defeat on corrupt politicians and the postwar revolution:[3] "You mean that you were stabbed in the back?" Malcolm inquired. "That's it exactly!" Ludendorff replied. "We were stabbed in the back!"[4] The phrase would become the rallying cry of Hitler and German nationalists.

News of the treaty was particularly unwelcome in Munich, where months of postwar political upheaval had only just ended. Despite the ongoing food crisis and rampant unemployment, people were finally enjoying sunny skies, children went back to school, and plans were underway for the resumption of traditional market festivals.[5] But newspaper articles describing the harsh reparations reminded the people that their troubles were far from over. Hitler would later echo the discontent that millions felt when he called the Treaty of Versailles "an act of highway robbery against our people."[6]

In the weeks following the counterrevolution, Munich's military occupiers maintained tight control over the capital. For every day that SPD leader Johannes Hoffmann and his deputies remained in Bamberg, military administrators in Munich increased their power and influence. Without a civilian cabinet to restrain them, they began injecting right-wing politics into city governance.[7] Press censorship prevented opposition newspapers from speaking out.[8] To supplement Munich's police and ensure law and order, an armed resident's militia called the Einwohnerwehr (Civic Guards) was formed. The militia was expected to defend the state regardless of party politics. But it excluded members of the USPD and the KPD.[9]

Bavarian officers in the German army, recently renamed the Reichswehr, were deeply concerned that Communist sympathies still lingered in Munich's garrisons. Since November 1918, soldiers stationed in the Bavarian capital had been unwilling to topple Eisner or the successive Soviet Republics. Now, to keep an eye on the troops and prevent Communist subversion, Reichswehr leaders established a military intelligence bureau. Leading the effort was Captain Karl Mayr, a general staff officer who recruited agents to provide political education for the troops and to monitor the growing number of political groups that had formed in Munich following the war. Mayr claimed his men were selected because of their "exemplary war records."[10] Among these recruits was Private Hitler.

Describing him as "a stray dog looking for a master," Mayr claimed that Hitler at that time was "ready to throw in his lot with anyone who would show him kindness ... [and someone who] would have worked for a Jewish or a French employer as readily as for an Aryan."[11] Mayr's description and the Hitler of Nazi infamy seem entirely dissimilar. If anything, Mayr's observation appears to support an inference of Hitler's public political ambivalence during the regimes of Eisner, Toller, and the second Soviet Republic. To make sense of the discrepancy, we must explore Hitler's trajectory from his childhood in Austria in the 1890s to his recruitment by the intelligence bureau in 1919, the year he emerged from total obscurity.

"WHY COULDN'T I HAVE BEEN BORN A HUNDRED YEARS EARLIER?"

Adolf Hitler was born in Braunau am Inn—a little known border town between the German Reich and the Austro-Hungarian Empire, some forty kilometers north of Salzburg, on April 20, 1889.[12] Hitler's father, Alois—an Austro-Hungarian customs official—had married Klara, Alois's first cousin once removed. It was his third marriage. Twenty-three-years his junior, Klara was seduced by Alois while she attended to his second wife as a live-in nurse before her death.[13]

At the time of Adolf's birth, Europe's German-speaking peoples were divided into two separate states: the German Reich (Empire) and the Austro-Hungarian Empire, led by the House of Habsburg in Vienna. Whereas the population of the Reich was almost entirely ethnic German, in the Austro-Hungarian Empire, Germans lived side by side with Czechs, Slavs, Poles, Italians, and Hungarians. Many Germans in the Austro-Hungarian Empire envied their brethren living on the other side of the border. While Austro-Hungary was approaching its twilight, the German Empire was a rising nation state that had recently triumphed in the 1870 Franco-Prussian war. During Adolf's childhood, German nationalism was becoming popular in Austria. But Alois Hitler did not count himself among those Austrians swept up by the movement. With little promise or education, he'd managed to rise through the ranks and gain respect as a mid-level customs official in the Austro-Hungarian empire, and he wasn't the type to rock the boat.

Much is unknown about Hitler's early life. When he was three, his family moved to Passau, a border town to the north of Salzburg.[14] There, they lived on the German side of the border, where young Adolf acquired a Bavarian accent. Two years later, Alois was re-stationed to the outskirts of Linz—the most "German" city in the empire.[15] Shortly thereafter, he retired from the customs office, and the family settled to the south of Linz at Hafeld, where he started a farm and pursued his hobby of beekeeping. Alois was reputed to be an ill-tempered man, and retirement proved to be difficult.[16] Missing his drinking pals and his daily routine at the customs office, he became increasingly irritated with the chaotic atmosphere in his cramped household.

After Adolf, Klara had given birth to two more children, Edmund and Paula. At Hafeld, Alois and Klara, Adolf, Edmund, and Paula all lived under the same roof with two children from Alois's previous marriage, Alois Jr. and Angela, as well as Klara's sister Johanna and a maid and a cook.[17] Efforts to make the farm productive failed. Alois allegedly started drinking more, and took out his frustrations on his eldest son.[18] In 1896, when Adolf was seven, his half-brother, Alois Jr., ran away from home. Alois had been grooming the fourteen-year-old to follow his career path, and the youngster apparently wanted no part of it.[19] Adolf was next in line. According to his sister, Paula, he received a "sound thrashing every day."[20] It seems he also endured scenes of his father abusing his mother. "Those who are not familiar with such conditions," Hitler recalled in *Mein Kampf*, "can hardly imagine the form of brutal attacks on the part of the father toward the mother or to assaults due to drunkenness."[21]

In 1897, Alois gave up the farm and moved the family to the nearby town of Lambach, where Adolf attended elementary school, received good grades, and took singing lessons at a Benedictine monastery.[22] Like many boys his age, Adolf liked to play war after school. He later wrote in *Mein Kampf*, "The fields and the woods were then the terrain on which all disputes were fought out."[23] Playing war provided Hitler with a sense of adventure that he felt was lacking in the adult world that surrounded him: "During the boisterous years of my youth nothing used to damp my wild spirits so much as to think that I was born at a time when the world had manifestly decided not to erect any more temples of fame except in honor of business people and state officials."[24] When Adolf was nine, his family moved to Leonding on the outskirts of Linz. At his new elementary school, Adolf became a leader of boys, continued to do well in his studies, and kept playing war after school.

One day while at home in his father's library, Hitler said he came across an illustrated book about the Franco-Prussian war. The book depicted war as glorious: German soldiers were pictured defeating the French on the battlefield, and parades showed the conquering heroes as they returned home to cheering crowds. "From that time onward," he wrote, "I became more and more enthusiastic about everything that was in any way connected with war or military affairs."[25] But Europe was enjoying peacetime, and the nine-year-old concluded that his future prospects for adventure were dim. He lamented, "Why couldn't I have been born a hundred years earlier?"[26]

"HIS FAILURE"

The first year of the new century brought disappointment and heartache to Hitler. Tragedy struck the family when his younger brother, Edmund, died of the measles, leaving him the only male child in the household. The family loss seemed to ratchet up the tension between father and son. As a proud civil servant, Alois wanted Adolf to follow in his footsteps. Hitler thought the profession was dull: "It nauseated me to think that one day I might be fettered to an office stool, that I could not dispose of my own time but would be forced to spend the whole of my life filling out forms."[27] Adolf was dreaming of becoming a painter, and mustered the courage to tell his father. "A painter? An artist-painter?" Alois replied, "Not as long as I live, never."[28]

Adolf had turned eleven, the age when German parents made a crucial decision about high school placement for their children. Having taken an interest in painting and shown promise in drawing, Adolf had hoped to attend Gymnasium, the most advanced school in the system and one that offered classes in fine art. But Hitler's father dismissed his son's ambition and insisted he attend Realschule (secondary school), which prepared students for future employment in such midlevel professions as the civil service. By forcing Adolf to go to Realschule, Alois cut his son off from the only recognizable path to becoming an artist. Adolf was placed at Realschule in downtown Linz, roughly an hour's walk from his home in Leonding. At the new school, he struggled to make friends, and his city-born classmates treated him like a village peasant.[29] Adolf was no longer a leader of boys, and it didn't take long for his grades to slip. Denied access to Gymnasium and reduced in stature, young Adolf took solace in the popular writings of Karl May.

Best known for his fictional characters Winnetou and Old Shatterhand—prototypes for Tonto and the Lone Ranger—Karl May wrote adventure stories set in the old American West, though he'd never been there himself. His books were so popular among German-speaking boys, that they reportedly outsold the works of Goethe. Hitler loved May's stories and identified with his romanticized heroes. By the end of his first year at Realschule, his marks were so poor that school administrators decided to hold him back to repeat his entry-level courses. Years later, Realschule principal Eduard Huemer commented on his poor performance: "Hitler seemed to have been led astray by the stories of Karl May and tales of Red Indians, and no doubt an over-indulgence in such reading combined with the time wasted on drifting back and forth from home and school which was some distance apart, was mostly responsible for his failure."[30]

In *Mein Kampf*, Hitler claimed that his poor performance was a deliberate attempt to force his father to take him out of Realschule so that he could pursue art.[31] If so, the tactic failed. Outraged by his son's insolence, Alois apparently increased his use of corporal punishment. The physical abuse that Hitler endured has led some to speculate about a causal relationship between his tortured childhood and the later role he played as the leader of Nazi genocide. But the argument is thin. As author Ron Rosenbaum has pointed out, many children sadly suffer abuse, but only one of them became Adolf Hitler. "Theories of Hitler as a victim of bad parenting are extensions of the common, careless attempt to explain Hitler as a victim of a mental disease, dysfunction, or syndrome," Rosenbaum wrote in *Explaining Hitler*, "all of which tend to exculpate if not excuse the crimes he perpetrated on the grounds of what the courts call 'diminished capacity,' an inability to know right from wrong."[32] Indeed, no exploration of Hitler's human experiences will ever exonerate, excuse, or explain away his crimes or the Nazi genocide. They do teach us something, however, about the commonality of evil, its recurrence, and ourselves.

Despite the gloom Hitler felt while attending Realschule, there was one subject he liked. Under the tutelage of Dr. Leopold Poetsch, Hitler became fascinated by history and was drawn to German nationalism. A fiery pan-German, Poetsch openly yearned for the collapse of the Habsburg Empire, so that Austria might be joined with Germany. "When we listened to him," Hitler later wrote, "we became afire with enthusiasm and we were sometimes moved even to tears."[33] Poetsch was not only a convincing speaker, Hitler found him to be kind.

On January 3, 1903, tragedy struck the Hitler family again when Adolf's father suddenly collapsed and died while drinking his morning wine.[34] Shortly thereafter, Hitler's mother, Klara, moved them all to an apartment in Linz so that Adolf wouldn't have to walk so far to school. However, school administrators soon informed her that her son would only be allowed to continue if he attended classes at a provincial campus eighty kilometers away. At the time, it was not uncommon for subpar students to be shipped out to less prestigious schools in Austria. Thereafter, Adolf was enrolled at Realschule in Steyr, where he was forced to rent a room.[35] It was during this period that he befriended his only teenage confident, August Kubizek.[36] The son of an upholsterer, Kubizek was a would-be composer and a good listener.[37]

In 1905, when Hitler was sixteen, he contracted a severe infection that convinced his mother to withdraw him from school. Some have speculated that his illness was faked.[38] Whatever the case, for the next two years, he lived like a teenage dandy in a state of what biographer Ian Kershaw called "parasitic idleness."[39] Free from work or responsibility, Hitler was isolated from the inevitable friction that comes with having a job, going to school, or even doing chores.

Wishing to become a famous architect or painter, he roamed the streets of Linz sketching buildings and redesigning the city. Presenting his elaborate architectural drawings to Kubizek, Hitler seemed to believe he was destined for greatness. But the day was soon to come when reality would interrupt his fantasies.

"A BOLT FROM THE SKIES"

In 1906, Hitler made his first trip to the Habsburg capital of Vienna. Like many young men who migrate to capital cities, seventeen-year-old Adolf dreamed of conquering it. On this brief trip, he reportedly staked out the Academy of Fine Arts, where he hoped to apply as an arts student in the near future. Shortly after returning home, he learned that his mother had breast cancer. During her convalescence from surgery in a local hospital, Hitler attended to Klara every day. Her physician, Dr. Bloch, later recounted, "Outwardly, his love for his mother was the most striking feature. . . . I have never witnessed a closer attachment."[40] Appearing to recover quickly, Klara was soon back at home running the household.

With his mother's blessing, Adolf returned to Vienna to seek admission to the academy as an arts student. But he could not count himself among the twenty-eight pupils who were accepted. His failure was a terrible shock. "I was so convinced of my success," Hitler later wrote, "that when the news that I had failed to pass was brought to me, it struck me like a bolt from the skies."[41] The rejection assaulted Hitler's sense of personal grandeur. Adolf was told that his talents were better suited for architecture. But he'd been excluded from taking the compulsory classes required for admittance to the architecture school when he was denied access to Gymnasium. Unable to bear his humiliation, Hitler concealed his rejection from his mother, Kubizek, and everyone else.

His mother's condition worsened. Returning to Linz, he nursed Klara until she died on December 21, 1907. Pale with grief and sleep deprived at dinner with the Kubizek family, Hitler was near collapse. After sending his younger sister, Paula, to live with their half-sister, Angela, Adolf returned to Vienna with an orphan's pension and a monthly allowance from his father's humble estate. Though his elder siblings and family friends tried to encourage him to take up a trade, Hitler refused to give up his dream: "With an indomitable resolution in my heart, I left for Vienna. . . . I was determined to become 'something'—but certainly not a civil servant."[42] Convincing Kubizek's parents to allow their son to leave Linz too, and to seek placement at the music conservatory in Vienna,[43] Hitler was soon reunited with his composer-friend, and the pair became roommates in the Habsburg capital.[44]

In Vienna, Kubizek and Hitler occupied a flat in a gloomy neighborhood of ill-lit tenements. The would-be composer was astonished by the work that preoccupied his friend. Hitler spent hours with his eyes buried in books, writing notes and sketching. Settling into his own routine at the music conservatory, Kubizek assumed that Hitler's curriculum came from the academy. Eventually, however, his roommate's activities aroused suspicion, and though Kubizek tiptoed around the subject, Hitler finally confessed that he'd been rejected by the academy. "His face was livid," the composer later wrote, "the mouth quite small, the lips almost white. But the eyes glittered. There was something sinister about them. As if all the hate of which he was capable lay in those glowing eyes!"[45]

At the time, Kubizek was likely Hitler's only friend. The future Nazi dictator had cut himself off from family members and had no schoolmates or coworkers to talk to. There were no elders to whom he would confide his feelings; no adults to challenge his most basic assumptions; no one to guide his passions. Isolation was Hitler's worst enemy. It allowed him to build up his self-importance and diminished his ability to self-reflect, if such a facility was active to begin with.

In 1908, Kubizek returned home to Linz for the summer after completing his first year of studies. That September, Hitler made a second attempt to gain admission to the academy but was again denied. When Kubizek returned to Vienna, he discovered that Hitler had paid his last share of rent, moved out, and left no forwarding address. Unbeknownst to his roommate, Hitler was staying only a short distance away, but when his funds ran out the following year, he became a drifter, sleeping in parks and doorways. In desperation, Hitler sought employment as a day laborer at a construction site.[46]

Forced to work in close proximity to others, Hitler claimed he was introduced to city politics. Among the political parties seeking support in the Habsburg capital were Austria's Social Democrats. According to his recollections in *Mein Kampf*, Hitler was pressured at a job site to join one of the trade unions popular with the party or risk being "flung down from the scaffolding."[47] Intimidated, he walked off the job. To restore his injured pride and repudiate his coworkers—without actually confronting them—Hitler said he started reading SPD party literature and concluded that it was poisonous propaganda "intended for the masses."[48] It's hard to believe that the episode was factual, considering Hitler's political objectives when he wrote *Mein Kampf* in 1924. Yet it attests to the conflict that would recur again and again when reality didn't conform to Hitler's thinking.

In the fall of 1909, Adolf resigned himself to joining the ranks of the homeless living in a shelter for the destitute on the edge of town. At the Asyl für Obdachlose (Asylum for the Homeless), he bunked in an open dormitory. When an acquaintance noticed that he had a talent for drawing and suggested that he sketch picture postcards for money, Hitler agreed to draw the cards if the man would sell them. Relocating to the Männerheim (Men's Home), a hostel for five hundred men on the other side of town, he busied himself with sketching and reading about politics. In February 1910, his postcards started selling. Buoyed by his success, the twenty-one-year-old reportedly started using his free time to engage in political discussions and attend sessions of parliament. According to *Mein Kampf*, two of the subjects that began to preoccupy his mind were "Marxism and Judaism."[49]

Hitler claimed he was initially against attacking Jews and considered Vienna's anti-Semitic press to be "unworthy of the cultural traditions of a great people."[50] In the pages of *Ostara*, Austro-Hungary's most vile anti-Semitic broadsheet, Jews were portrayed as rich, powerful, and fearsome creatures who preyed upon fair-skinned German women. Hitler said he didn't start reading *Ostara* until he stumbled across a Hasidic Jew in Vienna's inner city: "I suddenly encountered a phenomenon in a long caftan and wearing black side-locks. My first thought was: Is this a Jew? They certainly did not have this appearance in Linz. I watched the man stealthily and cautiously: but the longer I gazed at the strange countenance and examined it feature by feature, the more the question shaped itself in my brain: Is this a German?"[51]

According to *Mein Kampf*, the encounter made such an impression that Hitler started studying the Jews. After investigating Jewish influence in the press and the arts, he concluded that Jews were infecting the public with "a moral pestilence."[52] He also concluded that Jews controlled the Social Democrats and that Marxism was an evil "Jewish doctrine."[53] Few experts consider his depiction in *Mein Kampf* to be credible. Hitler's run-in with the Hasidic Jew was undoubtedly a literary invention. There simply is no evidence to support Hitler's contention that his anti-Semitic ideology was developed in Vienna. That transformation occurred later.

In the fall of 1911, Hitler made a final attempt to enroll in the arts academy but was rejected for a third time. Increasingly disenchanted with Vienna and hoping to avoid compulsory military service in the Austro-Hungarian army, he decided to emigrate to the German Reich.[54] Having received a payout from his father's estate, he set out for Bavaria where he could evade Austria's draft board.[55] In the artist's colony of Schwabing, he rented a room in May 1913. The unformed Austrian immigrant was twenty-four-years-old.

CHAPTER NINE

THE RIGHT-WING TALENT SEARCH

"I SANK DOWN UPON MY KNEES"

At his new flat in Schwabing, Hitler presented himself to his landlords, Joseph and Anna Popp, as an architectural painter from Vienna. The couple learned that their courteous tenant intended to sell enough paintings so that he could begin studying architecture.[1] But it didn't come to pass. Hitler never had enough money to pay for tuition. Perhaps he never intended to take classes to begin with. Down on his luck, he spent many afternoons at the library and in local coffeehouses contemplating his future. During this time, he made no effort to investigate Munich's Far Right. This fact undermines his claim in *Mein Kampf* that he left Vienna as a dedicated anti-Semite. Then, as if on cue, world events conspired to fulfill Hitler's boyhood longing for adventure.

Fourteen months after his arrival in Munich, news arrived of the assassination of the Habsburg heir, Franz Ferdinand, and the outbreak of the First World War. Hitler could not have been more enthusiastic: "I am not ashamed to acknowledge today that I was carried away by the enthusiasm of the moment and that I sank down upon my knees and thanked heaven out of the fullness of my heart for the favor of having been permitted to live in such a time."[2] As quickly as he could, he volunteered and was admitted into the Bavarian infantry, where he ended up in the First Company of the List Regiment, named after its first commander, Colonel Julius von List. Contrary to Nazi propaganda, Hitler's regiment was a haphazard assembly of untrained recruits and conscripts, hastily formed by the military to bulk up its forces.[3] Divided into three battalions, it consisted of three thousand men, mostly farmers and craftsmen, and included fifty-nine Jews.[4]

After nearly two months of training, the List Regiment departed Germany for Belgium on October 21. Shortly thereafter, along the French border, Private Hitler[5] participated in the first battle of Ypres, charging British positions as a frontline soldier with his regiment. The assault was hampered by enemy artillery, and inexperience soon led to confusion. Forced to retreat, Hitler's regiment continued fighting for three more days. But the engagement ended in stalemate. When it was over, three-quarters of Hitler's regiment had perished.[6] For the survivors, the battle eviscerated any notion that war was glorious. A chaplain assigned to Hitler's unit reported that the battle had "shattered the hearts"[7] of the survivors. Even Hitler claimed that he started looking at life differently. But the future Nazi dictator was about to receive an assignment that would take him some distance away from the dangers of the front. In the aftermath of Ypres, Hitler was reassigned as a dispatch runner to regimental headquarters. Contrary to Nazi propaganda, which portrayed Hitler as facing down death and braving enemy machine gun fire as he carried messages to the front, his actual assignment was to bring communiqués from regimental headquarters to battalion headquarters in the rear.[8] For the majority of his service, Hitler was spared the front line, its muddy trenches, and the nauseating smell of rotting human entrails, like Ernst Toller had endured. Instead, he was billeted behind the lines in relative comfort, received better meals than frontline soldiers, and rarely was required to brave enemy fire.[9]

Hitler's colleagues in the support staff thought he was a loner who lost himself in books.[10] The gap between the Austrian volunteer and his comrades became most apparent during military furloughs. While his compatriots headed for the nearest bar to numb their pain in alcohol, Hitler, a teetotaler, preferred to venture alone through the occupied territories on foot. Like he had in Vienna, Hitler spent an enormous amount of time in the isolation of his own thoughts and gradually became estranged from the war-weary attitudes and grievances that typified his regiment. This separation proved to be significant as it apparently allowed him to believe that his fellows still shared the same patriotic zeal that he did. Hitler's belief in the German cause was uncompromising, and it would prevent him from questioning the war effort. Even a brief human moment at the front, when German and British troops emerged from their trenches to celebrate Christmas together in December 1914, was considered intolerable by the fanatical Hitler.[11]

Though he had good relations with his fellow dispatch runners and the support staff, which was the closest thing he ever had to a family, Hitler lacked empathy for those who questioned the war. He didn't seem to grasp the connection between low morale and the horror of life in the trenches. Not surprisingly, his closest friend for much of the conflict turned out to be a dog. Having wandered away from his British masters, "Foxl" delighted Hitler with his willingness to perform tricks.

"THE TORRENT OF BLOOD"

During interludes between fighting, German soldiers often preoccupied themselves by writing letters to loved ones back home. Having cut himself off from family members, Hitler chose to write instead to his Munich landlords, the Popps, and an acquaintance who'd occasioned to purchase one of his paintings. Some of these letters have survived the war. In one of them, postmarked February 6, 1916, Hitler was strikingly candid about his xenophobia, but didn't mention Jews: "I often think of Munich, and each one of us has only one wish . . . that those of us who are lucky enough to return to the fatherland will find it a purer place, less riddled with foreign influences, so that the daily sacrifices and sufferings of hundreds of thousands of us and the torrent of blood that keeps flowing here day after day against an international world of enemies will not only help to smash Germany's foes outside but that our inner internationalism, too, will collapse. This would be worth much more than any gain in territory."[12]

According to historian Thomas Weber, the letter provided the clearest picture of Hitler's personal ideology during the war.[13] While it was possible that he was using the phrase "foreign influences," to suggest the Jews, it seems unlikely. Hitler's fixation on German homogeneity was more likely derived from his early exposure to German nationalism, his rejection of Austro-Hungary's cosmopolitanism, and his disappointments in the land of his birth. As a failed artist and a private in the infantry, he had no real accomplishments to make him feel good about himself. He also lacked a sound philosophy or religious practice to guide his spiritual development. Instead, Hitler found his esteem in his German identity.

In the aftermath of its engagement at Ypres, Hitler's regiment spent eighteen months along the front in northern France. Then, in July 1916, the Entente powers engaged the Germans in the Battle of the Somme. Men in Hitler's regiment could hear the distant bomb blasts throughout the summer, and it frightened them.[14] Informed in September that they'd be joining the battle, many were terrified. After a short train ride south, they moved into position on October 2. The Battle of the Somme was the largest confrontation of the war and involved more than three million soldiers. Scenes at the front were as hellish as those at Verdun. Working as a dispatch runner behind the lines, Hitler didn't have occasion to see them up close and personal. Three days after joining the battle, he sustained a shrapnel injury to his thigh when an enemy shell exploded near his position behind the lines.[15]

Hitler was taken to a military hospital southwest of Berlin, where he spent the next weeks recovering. In his absence, the List Regiment lost 78 percent of its men. Hitler was not around to experience this horror and see the effects that the gruesome battle had on morale. Neither would he have had an occasion for revelations about the brotherhood of man, as Ernst Toller had.

Back in Germany, Hitler had a hard time understanding why people were losing confidence in the war. In *Mein Kampf*, he groused about his stay at the hospital, where soldiers purportedly mocked the war, showed off their self-inflicted wounds, and bragged about shirking their responsibilities. The contrast between these "loudmouthed agitators"[16] and the "glorious" army at the front irked the Austrian volunteer. "As soon as I was able to walk once again," he wrote, "I obtained leave to visit Berlin."[17] But on the streets of the capital, he had the impression that seditious agitators were everywhere. Transferred to Munich, the situation seemed even worse. "I felt as in some strange town," he later wrote. "Anger, discontent, complaining met one's ears wherever one went!"[18] Though he witnessed the terrible famine gripping the Bavarian capital, Hitler's commitment to German nationalism prevented him from questioning the justness of the war and the High Command.

When Hitler returned to his regiment in March of 1917, he found it stationed behind the front, too depleted to engage in battle. Receiving orders to retreat to Alsace, the regiment made ready to leave for two months of recuperation. But before it could, a British assault at Ypres forced some of the men into battle, and Hitler barely escaped with his life.[19] "Foxl" went missing.[20] Hitler's beloved dog was most likely pilfered by another canine-lover. When Hitler finally made it to Alsace, he was granted leave. Unlike other soldiers who returned home on furlough to see their wives, families, or friends, Hitler set off to travel through parts of Germany he'd never seen before.[21]

In Berlin at the end of his trip, Hitler entertained himself much as he had in Linz and Vienna—enjoying the city's impressive architecture and visiting museums. When he rejoined his fellows at the front in the fall of 1917, he found his regiment deployed to the northeast of Paris. The war dragged on. German spirits on the western front were temporarily lifted when news came that their enemies, Russia and Italy, were nearing defeat. This surge in morale contrasted sharply with the discontent back home, personified by the labor strikes organized by Eisner and others in Bavaria. Then, in the spring of 1918, Hitler's regiment participated in Ludendorff's ill-fated offensives and suffered severe casualties.

Confined to his duties in the support staff, Hitler was spared the carnage. But by mid-July, when freshly arrived American forces joined the French near Rheims, Hitler and his fellows were sent running for their lives across the Marne River. The tragic failures of the Ludendorff offenses were adding up, and death was omnipresent. Rather than question the judgment of the First Quartermaster General or the High Command, Hitler blamed the German press. Claiming in *Mein Kampf* that German newspapers had demoralized soldiers and civilians alike and were responsible for "mass-murder," he suggested that if he'd been in charge of German propaganda the war and its outcome might have been different. "But I was a being without a name," he continued, "one among eight million. Hence it was better for me to keep my mouth shut and do my duty as well as I could in the position to which I had been assigned."[22] Devout readers of *Mein Kampf* likely sympathized with the confession and considered it evidence of Hitler's humility. But the passage betrayed another agenda: Hitler needed to obscure his record during the postwar revolution, and the explanation that "it was better for me to keep my mouth shut" was an all-around, convenient excuse.

Toward the end of July, Hitler's regiment was removed from the front and stationed at the French town of Le Cateau, not far from the border with Belgium. Then, on August 8, the German army suffered a devastating defeat one hundred kilometers to the west, near Amiens. This was the battle that prompted Erich Ludendorff to admit to himself that the war was lost. Four days earlier, Hitler had been awarded the Iron Cross, First Class. It was the second Iron Cross the Austrian immigrant had received during the war. Decades later, Nazi propaganda alleged that the first class medal was given in recognition of his valor when he captured twelve French prisoners in June 1918.[23] In reality, Hitler had done nothing of the sort. He was recommended for the Iron Cross after bringing a dispatch to the front lines at a time of exceptional danger.[24] Ironically, the officer who proposed Hitler for the award, Hugo Gutmann, was Jewish.[25] Not surprisingly, Gutmann's role was later omitted in *Mein Kampf*. As Thomas Weber successfully argued, "If Hitler had really been a fervent, overt, and active anti-Semite by 1918, it seems odd, to say the least, that a Jewish officer would go out of his way to propose him for an Iron Cross."[26] In fact, evidence suggests that Hitler served amicably with Jewish soldiers and Jewish officers throughout the war.

After its tour of duty at Le Cateau, the List Regiment moved west, where it sustained seven hundred casualties in an all-out attack by the British. Having been in Nuremberg to receive signal training, Hitler missed the battle. Then, in late September, Hitler and his regiment moved to a position near Ypres. At his headquarters in Spa, Ludendorff was finally ready to pursue the peace negotiations that would send Hitler and his fellows home. But the war dragged on for another six weeks. In the meantime, Hitler was poisoned by mustard gas on October 14 and left the battlefield for the last time.

"DEPRAVED CRIMINALS!"

When Hitler, at the hospital in Pasewalk, later learned of Germany's surrender, he claimed he was filled with rage. As far as he was concerned, the German army had been "stabbed in the back" by a civilian press back home. "How could we justify this act to future generations?" he asked in *Mein Kampf*. "What a gang of despicable and depraved criminals! The more I tried then to glean some definite information of the terrible events that had happened the more my head became afire with rage and shame."[27] Hitler had no way of knowing that Ludendorff had initiated the pursuit of peace talks before the civilian government took over. "My opinion was that those people [Social Democrats Friedrich Ebert and Philipp Scheidemann] thoroughly deserved to be hanged," he stated in his autobiography, "because they were ready to sacrifice the peace and if necessary allow Germany to be defeated just to serve their own ends."[28]

Following his hospital release, Hitler returned to Munich on November 19. But the Austrian immigrant was not ready to announce himself an opponent of Kurt Eisner's fledgling republic. Obsessed with more immediate concerns, he attempted to reunite with friends from his regiment before demobilization sent everyone their separate ways. Without family, a job, or a home, he decided that prolonging his service in the military was his first priority, and he quickly volunteered with a friend from his regiment for an assignment at a POW camp along the Austrian border. When the camp was later closed and Hitler returned to Munich, he found himself garrisoned in barracks near today's Olympic Park, where he was elected to the soldiers' council of his unit.[29] Eight weeks later, during the reign of the second Soviet Republic, instead of supporting Hoffmann's Social Democratic government-in-exile, Hitler ran for office in the soldiers' council and was elected to the position of deputy battalion representative.[30] Did that mean he supported the Communists? It seems more likely that Hitler was simply doing what was required of him so that he could remain in the military, which was his first priority.

While his participation in the soldier's council seemed to imply a certain willingness to serve the revolutionary agenda, not every council member—even ones like Hitler, photographed at Eisner's funeral procession—was a member of the USPD or a radicalized Communist. More likely, Hitler was just another hungry soldier trying to fit in and keep his job. There's no evidence that Hitler either backed the revolution, fought against it, or joined the Freikorps. In fact, when counterrevolutionary forces entered Munich at the beginning of May, the future Nazi dictator was nowhere to be found.

"Where was Hitler on that day?" asked Otto Strasser, a future opponent of Hitler's in the Nazi Party. "In which corner of Munich did the soldier hide himself, he who should have been fighting in our ranks?"[31] As Strasser's indictment made clear, Hitler's lack of participation in the fight against the Soviet Republic was likely to become a public relations problem in the future. However, in 1919, Hitler could hardly have anticipated this. According to historian Peter Longerich, he had adopted "an indifferent, wait-and-see attitude toward the new political situation."[32] He was adrift and confused—unwilling or unable to fight on either side. But as soon as the Soviet Republic was destroyed, Hitler's indecision vanished like the wind.

"I COULD SPEAK"

In the weeks following the counterrevolution, Hitler worked as an informer to rat out fellow soldiers who had conspired with the second Soviet Republic.[33] Details are scant because the Nazis later destroyed all records of his activities during this period. Nevertheless, as an informer, Hitler came to the attention of Karl Mayr, who notably had described the future Führer at this time as a "stray dog" and who recruited him for the Reichswehr's military intelligence bureau. Shortly thereafter, in July 1919, Hitler and his fellow recruits attended political courses.[34] Funded by the Reichswehr, in classes taught by men including Gottfried Feder, agents were exposed to nationalist ideology and coached on how to present arguments against Germany's so-called war guilt, Bolshevism, and, to a lesser extent, Judaism.[35] Fueling Hitler's passion to absorb his lessons and put them to use was the July 9 announcement that the government had ratified the Treaty of Versailles, which underscored Germany's defeat.

Over the summer, Professor Karl Alexander von Müller took notice of the Austrian immigrant. "The men seemed spellbound by a man in their midst," he later wrote, "who rallied at them uninterruptedly in a strangely guttural yet passionate voice. I had the unsettling feeling that their excitement was his work and simultaneously the source of his own power. I saw a pale, thin face under an unsoldierly shock of hanging hair, and striking large light blue eyes that glittered fanatically."[36] Soon thereafter, Müller informed Captain Mayr of Hitler's skills as a "natural orator,"[37] and the Austrian immigrant was assigned to lecture soldiers at various Munich garrisons. Well-received by his listeners, Hitler's confidence began to grow.

Having committed to memory the popular anti-Bolshevik and anti-Semitic slogans of the day, Hitler was learning how to use propaganda to stir up the passions of his listeners. "[The] thing that I had always presumed from pure feeling without knowing it was now corroborated," he wrote in *Mein Kampf*. "I could speak."[38] Historians are left wondering if this statement is true, or if Hitler had discovered his knack for speech making while serving as a representative in the soldiers' council of the second Soviet Republic. The Austrian immigrant's transformation from a lowly private who followed orders to a persuasive leader of men likely began in the soldier's council. But *Mein Kampf* obscures from view his activities during this period.

The summer of 1919 witnessed profound changes in Hitler's self-esteem. Receiving the mission to inoculate Munich's garrisons from malicious influence and discovering that he had a gift for public speaking gave Hitler a profound sense of purpose. For the first time in his life, the Austrian immigrant was acknowledged for having talent and was encouraged to put it to use. When in the presence of an approving audience, Hitler's insecurities seemed to vanish, and he felt powerful. The experience was intoxicating and left him wanting more.

Later in the summer, Hitler was assigned to reeducate soldiers awaiting discharge at a camp on the outskirts of the city. Reichswehr officials wanted to root out any remaining sympathy for the Soviet Republic, and Hitler's task was to win soldiers over to the nationalist cause. According to eyewitnesses, Hitler "revealed himself to be an excellent and passionate speaker" who "absolutely compel[led] his audience to take note and share his views."[39] In this setting, the future Nazi dictator outshone his fellow agents with a blistering castigation of the Jews.[40] Hitler had found his scapegoat for a lifetime of personal, and collective, national grievances.

Observing his protégé's unusual commitment, Mayr decided to unburden himself of some of the work piling up on his desk. Having received a letter asking him to clarify his position on the so-called Jewish question, Mayr assigned Hitler to respond on his behalf. In his written reply, the thirty-year-old unleashed a torrent of extremist vitriol. Defining "Jewry as a race"[41] and not a religious or cultural community, Hitler argued that Jews were a disease infecting Germany and required "deliberate removal." Doubting that Friedrich Ebert's government would undertake the task, Hitler suggested that the Reich needed a new government with the requisite strength and sense of responsibility to be uncompromising with the Jews. Written fourteen years before he became chancellor of Germany in 1933, the letter provided the earliest written evidence of his anti-Semitic radicalization.

Hitler's new-found zealotry was the opposite of his neutrality during the counterrevolution. Nowhere was his devotion more evident than when he was excoriating the Jews. While not yet articulating plans for extermination, he was calling for their "deliberate removal." Like a radical madrasa that convinces impressionable teens to seek martyrdom, Mayr's education program and teachers like Gottfried Feder had enabled the future Nazi dictator to find his voice and complete the first stage of his radicalization.

THE RIGHT-WING TALENT SEARCH

Ever since the armistice of 1918, Dietrich Eckart had been yearning for a national revival that would restore Germany's honor. As a guest member of the Thule Society, he'd fraternized with Bavaria's ethnic chauvinist community to seek out like-minded fellows. His broadsheet, *Auf Gut Deutsch*, had attempted to awaken readers to the so-called dangerous influence of Jews and Bolsheviks. His leaflet, *To All Working People*, which he had distributed with Alfred Rosenberg back in April, called for a new government that would emancipate Germany from the Entente powers.[42] Throughout the revolutionary period, he kept contact with various right-wing groups and observed their attempts to gain popularity. But Eckart was discontent with the slow pace of advancement. Burning with a desire to increase the number of adherents to the nationalist movement and his personal brand of anti-Semitism,[43] he concluded that the Far Right needed to find an outstanding spokesman.

Though confident in his abilities as a writer, Eckart knew his attractiveness as an orator was limited.[44] This set him apart from other far-right leaders that were too pompous to recognize their own deficiencies. To inspire young Germans, the workers, and soldiers, Eckart reasoned the movement needed someone charismatic and bold: a new type of leader. "We need a fellow at the head who can stand the sound of a machine gun," Eckart had remarked during a night of drinking at the Brennessel Wine Cellar. "We can't use an officer, because the people don't respect them anymore. The best would be a worker who knows how to talk. . . . He doesn't need much brains; politics is the most stupid business in the world, and every market woman in Munich knows more than the people in Weimar. I'd rather have a vain monkey who can give the Reds a juicy answer, and doesn't run away when people start swinging table legs, than a dozen learned professors. He must be a bachelor, then we'll get the women."[45]

Eckart wasn't alone in his discontent over the slow pace of advancement in the nationalist movement. Anton Drexler, who had formed the German Workers' Party (DAP) with Karl Harrer, was frustrated with his own efforts to attract members. Shortly after the counterrevolution, Drexler—an avid reader of *Auf Gut Deutsch*—had introduced himself to Eckart and solicited his help.[46] After putting their heads together, Drexler asked Eckart to speak at a DAP meeting scheduled for August of 1919.[47] Sensing that the DAP leader had limitations inhibiting the growth of his party,[48] Eckart decided to help and accepted the invitation. On August 15, he attended his first DAP meeting and spoke about the dangers of Bolshevism and the Jewish question to three-dozen attendees. Apparently out of a desire to support his new friend, Eckart identified himself as a member when he affixed his name to the meeting's sign-in sheet.[49] Drexler asked Eckart to return as a guest speaker for the next DAP meeting in September.

"SOMEONE WE CAN USE"

Since its formation in May, the Reichswehr's military intelligence bureau had been tracking various political groups in Munich that had emerged during the revolutionary period. In order to ascertain their motives and keep an eye on their activities, the bureau sent undercover agents in plainclothes to monitor their meetings and mingle with members. With this intention, Mayr purportedly sent Hitler to attend a DAP gathering on September 12, 1919. According to his account in *Mein Kampf*, Hitler's assignment was to investigate the party and report back what he found. For several decades, this version was accepted as fact. Later, however, scholars uncovered the fact that Mayr had actually sent Hitler to the meeting with seven other propaganda agents.[50] Contrary to the traditionally accepted narrative, their purpose was not to spy but to lend support to the DAP. In fact, the captain had even considered attending the gathering himself.[51] Based on the evidence, it seems probable now that Mayr was already well informed about the DAP's activities, and that he and Eckart were collaborating in secret to prop it up. Yet even they could not have realized what their efforts would set in motion.

The assembly on September 12, which took place in the back room of the Sterneckerbräu beer cellar, a few hundred meters west of the Isar Gate, turned out to be Hitler's historic introduction to the group that would become the Nazi Party. The future dictator wore a suit and had trimmed his infamous moustache in the style of Charlie Chaplin a few days before the meeting. Eckart, who was to return as the guest speaker for the meeting fell ill, so Gottfried Feder took his place.[52] Hitler was apparently disappointed. Having attended Feder's lectures during his political indoctrination at LMU, he was already familiar with the economist's theories. Enduring Feder's talk, which apparently lasted two hours, Hitler claimed he was ready to get up and walk out when a professor named Baumann started calling for Bavaria to split from the Reich and join with Austria. "In the most self-assured way," Hitler later reported, "this man kept on insisting that German Austria would join Bavaria and that the peace would then function much better."[53] Though he had himself dreamed of a greater German empire that included Austria, Hitler could not accept Baumann's proposal, which suggested a break with Berlin. Unable to restrain himself, he said he took the floor and struck down Baumann's argument with such force that it made the professor look "like a wet poodle."[54] Watching Hitler flatten his opponent, Anton Drexler, DAP's cofounder, was electrified and remarked to a colleague, "He's got a gift! He's someone we can use!"[55]

According to historian Volker Ullrich, Hitler's story about Baumann is likely an invention because the professor's name didn't appear on DAP attendance sheets until months later.[56] Be that as it may, before Hitler could leave, Drexler introduced himself and slipped a copy of his own short book, *My Political Awakening*, into Hitler's hands. Later that night, during a fit of insomnia, Hitler claimed he cracked open Drexler's book and started reading about the railyard worker, his rejection of Socialism and trade unions, and he was reminded of his own experiences in Vienna before the war.[57] But just as quickly as he had picked it up, Hitler said he forgot the book and thought nothing more of the DAP. However, a week later he received a postcard from Drexler inviting him to the next meeting and announcing that he'd been accepted into the party. The DAP chairman had recognized Hitler's talent and wanted to make use of it. Captain Mayr may have intended for this to happen all along.

Karl Mayr had worked as a military contact for the Thule Society during the second Soviet Republic. Later, when selecting reading materials for his intelligence recruits in the bureau, Mayr's syllabus had included copies of Dietrich Eckart's *Auf Gut Deutsch*.[58] In fact, Mayr wrote cordial notes to Eckart in the weeks before sending Hitler to the September 1919 meeting.[59] The captain had even been seen at Eckart's home in the days following the demise of the Soviet Republic.[60] Therefore, it seems likely that Eckart would have briefed Mayr about the German Workers' Party after he attended his first DAP meeting on August 15.

In *Mein Kampf*, Hitler wanted his readers to believe that he saved the German Workers' Party from obscurity. In reality, a network of far-right nationalists had delivered him to the DAP with instructions to support it. Whether or not the Austrian immigrant would accept their tutelage and work with them to lift the party up, remained to be seen.

CHAPTER TEN

LAUNCH OF THE NSDAP

"KILL HIM!"

In a lonely cell, on a bed made of wood planks and tattered blankets, Ernst Toller sat staring out a dingy prison window. Captured in Schwabing on June 4, 1919,[1] after five weeks of evading capture, Bavaria's former head of state and public enemy number one was brought to Stadelheim Prison and placed in a maximum-security ward. Isolated in his tiny cell, Toller's only company was the oppressive smell of a stinking chamber pot that sat in the corner. Sometimes he would read the prison regulations to pass the time, or he would scan the walls for graffiti left by previous inhabitants. In one corner, he discovered a particularly haunting message: "They're coming for me now to shoot me. I am innocent."[2] The note was dated "May 2, 1919." Toller concluded that its author must have been a member of the second Soviet Republic. But who? Had they been killed? Was he destined to suffer a similar fate? Slumping back onto his dilapidated bed, Toller may well have reflected on the events that led to his capture.

Ten days after counterrevolutionaries had defeated the Red Army in Munich, an arrest warrant was issued for Toller and wanted posters were pasted up all over Bavaria. Accompanied by an old photograph, the poster described Toller as a "student of law and philosophy"[3] and offered a ten-thousand-mark reward for any information leading to his capture. Whenever they could, sympathetic colleagues tried to deface his photo in order to conceal what he looked like. But the authorities were determined to bring him to justice even if they had to seek his extradition from abroad.[4] Spreading out across the countryside, they received tips, stopped trains, threatened relatives, and even searched obscure castles. It was all in vain; Toller never left the Munich area.

In the first days of May, the playwright had gone into hiding at a friend's flat in Schwabing. Though his host didn't agree with his politics, he couldn't stomach the idea of Toller being killed and took great personal risk to hide him. But the playwright didn't stay long. Toller relocated to the home of a local artist. To disguise his looks, he dyed his hair red with peroxide. In the event that the authorities came to the artist's home, he intended to hide behind a secret door on the ground floor that was covered up with papers.

Three weeks passed without incident, and Toller was going stir crazy. Hiding in isolation with no one to talk to and constantly thinking about the moment when the police might arrive made him extremely anxious. Only after dusk could he go outside into his host's private garden and breathe in a little spring air. One night, Toller received a visitor who offered to arrange passage out of Munich. Trusting the woman, Toller gave her a tour of the premises, including his secret hiding place. The following morning around 4:00 a.m., the authorities arrived. Clad only in a nightshirt, Toller retreated behind the hidden door. When the police discovered his hiding place, the playwright opened the door and presented himself. "I'm Toller," he announced with his arms raised over his head. "If you shoot me now, it won't be while attempting to escape."[5]

After ordering Toller to the ground at gunpoint, the police allowed him to dress and then handcuffed him before leading him through the streets at the center of an armed detail. Despite the playwright's effort to protect his host, the artist was also arrested and spent several months in prison. On their way to the police station, Toller and his escort happened upon an elderly woman heading to mass. Clutching her rosary beads in her trembling fingers, she seemed to recognize the fugitive and screeched, "Kill him!"[6] The woman's hatred reflected the attitude of many city dwellers, some of whom considered Toller's Socialist experiment for "the happiness of humanity" horribly naïve.[7] The failures of the leftist regimes of Eisner, Toller, and Leviné's second Soviet Republic had helped create an audience receptive to someone like Hitler.

When the elderly church lady called for his death, did the playwright remember the letter he had received from Jewish leader Sigmund Fraenkel? "My belief in showing solidarity with all Jews urges me to inform you about all this in your own best interest," Fraenkel had warned, "because the same mass that is today cheering you at your speeches will be cursing you as soon as they realize that you brought empty promises instead of bread and mutual hate instead of the desired inner peace. Furthermore, my inner voice urges me to guard my community of faith from the hatred, which says that traditional Judaism has something to do with the destructive tendencies of ambitious, revolutionary politicians."[8]

A few days later, Toller was driven in an armed police motorcade to Stadelheim Prison. Pausing at the front gates he spied out a message board, which read, "This is where we make sausages of Spartacists. Reds executed free of charge."[9] Processed into the prison, Toller endured taunts and jeers before being deposited into his cell in the maximum-security ward. Now, sitting on his bed in isolation, his mind returned to the haunting graffiti he'd discovered in the corner of his cell. Who could have written it? The most probable candidate was Eugen Leviné, who had been captured during the counterrevolution. Imprisoned at Stadelheim, Leviné likely hoped that members of the USPD and the Peasant's Federation serving in Johannes Hoffmann's cabinet would intervene and commute his sentence. But when it was announced that Hoffmann had replaced these representatives with officials from the Bavarian People's Party (BVP) and the German Democratic Party (DDP), that possibility evaporated.

On June 3, one day before Toller's arrest, Hoffmann's new cabinet sanctioned a court's decision to level the death penalty. Leviné was shot by a firing squad two days later. Alone in his cell, Toller couldn't escape the thought that a similar fate awaited him. When a prison warden informed the playwright that Leviné had been the previous occupant of his cell, Toller's heart sank. There was no escaping the thought of imminent death.

In July, Toller was brought before a Munich court[10] presided over by the same judge who had sentenced Eugen Leviné to death.[11] Despite the easing of tensions in the city, Toller remained an object of hate for extremists. Right-wing Bavarians despised him as a cunning Jewish agitator who had undermined the war effort by promoting antiwar labor strikes. Left-wing radicals loathed him for his eleventh-hour resignation from the Red Army and attempt to negotiate with the Hoffmann government-in-exile. Ideologues were incapable of understanding his faith in humanity. Since he was the most notable revolutionary leader left alive, and something of a celebrity in Munich, his trial became a popular curiosity.

Accusing him of high treason for his role in the overthrow of Hoffmann's government, Toller's prosecutor made it a point to tell the court that the playwright was Jewish.[12] Later in the trial, a number of notable figures, including Thomas Mann, Romain Rolland, and Max Weber, submitted testimony praising the playwright's moral character.[13] Toller also received the support of a fellow frontline soldier[14] and a Prussian politician who suggested he was not responsible for the violence of the Soviet Republic.[15] These testimonials, along with evidence that Toller had intervened on behalf of the hostages at the Luitpold Gymnasium, made an impression on the court.

Speaking in his own defense, Toller said, "Everything I have done, I have done soberly and deliberately, and I must ask you to regard me as fully responsible for all my actions.... We revolutionaries recognize the right to revolution only when conditions as a whole have become permanently and utterly intolerable. Then, and only then, do we believe we have the right to overthrow them.... Gentlemen, I am convinced that the sentence you will pass upon me will be entirely in accordance with the dictates of your conscience and your conception of justice. But I should make it clear that, as I see it, your judgment, whatever it is, will be the judgment of might, not of right."[16] When his sentence was later announced, Toller escaped the death penalty, receiving instead five years' imprisonment without parole. Though declaring him guilty of treason, the court concluded that the playwright had acted with "honorable intent."[17]

The decision was highly unusual considering the prominent role Toller had played in the revolution and the court's appetite for punishing radicals. Following the defeat of the second Soviet Republic, over 1,800 prison sentences were meted out to persons associated with the revolution.[18] All six people brought to trial for the Luitpold Gymnasium murders were executed. On the other hand, none of the Freikorps, Reichswehr, or Volkswehr forces responsible for murdering hundreds of suspected Communists in the streets of Munich were brought to justice.[19] For many Bavarians, nothing compared to the brutality of the Soviet Republic. In their eyes, those leftists responsible for the terrible suffering and deprivation of the revolutionary period deserved no quarter. When prejudiced courts, the army, and the police targeted the revolutionaries selectively, many citizens were satisfied that justice had been served.

In this atmosphere, right-wing nationalism found legitimacy in the political mainstream, and anti-Semitic scapegoating became more blatant. "Our misery is due entirely to the Jews who have infested our fatherland," read a leaflet distributed by factory workers. "They should be summarily expelled."[20] Racism and nationalism were conflated, and both were on the rise in Germany. Since November of 1918, the number of far-right groups in Germany had grown to seventy-three, with nearly a dozen located in Munich.[21] Which party would rise above the others and win the public's support remained to be seen.

"NOT EVEN A PARTY STAMP"

It's hard to know what Hitler's initial response was to the German Workers' Party. Five years after he attended his first meeting, when he wrote *Mein Kampf* in 1924, he claimed he thought it was "just another one of these many new societies which were being formed at that time."[22] He dismissed its leadership for not having "the slightest idea of what it means to bring together a number of people for the foundations of a party or a movement."[23] But Hitler had an agenda when he wrote those things; he wanted people to believe that he saved the party. The reality in 1919 was somewhat different.

ADOLF HITLER
FÜHRER DER N.S.D.A.P.
PHOT. H. HOFFMAN.
MCH.

Adolf Hitler.

Hitler had been sent to the DAP because Captain Mayr wanted him to support it. After becoming a member, he was given a weekly stipend of around twenty gold marks to prop it up.[24] The arrangement was quite nice for a thirty-year-old veteran without prospects for other employment. The Austrian immigrant must have been thrilled. First, he kept his job in the army during a time of intense economic instability. Second, he was being rewarded with an assignment that made him feel important. And third, the DAP "had not yet hardened" into a bureaucratic organization, and there was room for him to make his mark.[25]

When Hitler attended his second DAP meeting, he was invited to sit down with the party's core leadership, including national chairman Karl Harrer. Under the dim light of a flickering gas lamp in the Alte Rosenbad tavern, he concluded that despite their "good faith and good intentions,"[26] the party leadership was completely disorganized. "I found that, apart from a few general principles," he wrote in *Mein Kampf*, "there was nothing—no program, no pamphlet, nothing at all in print, no cards of membership, not even a party stamp."[27] Once again, Hitler was portraying the DAP as a hopeless political club and concealing its strengths. While it may not have had an attractive party program, the German Workers' Party was backed by key figures in the military and the Far Right. The support of Mayr, Feder, and Eckart is evident. But the DAP also enjoyed the patronage of a prominent city commander, the head of a publishing house, and a number of Reichswehr officers, including Captain Ernst Röhm.

Hitler claimed he joined the DAP only after "careful brooding and reflection."[28] It seems more likely that he jumped at the opportunity. The Austrian immigrant wanted to establish himself as a leader and was eager to transform the party into a popular political movement. One of his earliest innovations came in the area of advertising. For a DAP meeting scheduled on October 16 at the Hofbräukeller, Hitler convinced the leadership to allow him to place an advertisement in the *Münchener Beobachter*, a weekly newspaper affiliated with the Thule Society and owned by Rudolf von Sebottendorff.[29] Though he had never run an advertising campaign, Hitler had confidence that his strategy would work. On the night of meeting, one hundred and eleven participants showed up—the largest attendance in the party's history.[30] The breakthrough engendered confidence that Hitler knew what he was doing, and he was given the title of advertising chairman.[31]

Eager to build on his success, Hitler started attending DAP leaders' meetings every Wednesday. Observing Drexler and Harrer at their regular table at the Café Gasteig, he concluded that neither man possessed the essential qualities to lead the party into the mainstream. Harrer, in particular, seemed apprehensive about Hitler's emphasis on recruitment. Whereas the Austrian immigrant was envisioning a mass movement that would attract "those who were suffering from profound anxiety and could find no peace," Chairman Harrer seemed to want to keep the party small.[32] Making up for his lack of experience with raw political instinct, Hitler focused on what he seemed to do best: public speaking.

On November 13, Hitler gave a speech at a DAP meeting at the Eberlbräu beer cellar. Describing how the German people had been forced to accept the "shameful" Treaty of Versailles, he aroused intense indignation. Local police described his performance as "masterful."[33] Among the crowd that evening was the publisher of *Auf Gut Deutsch*, Dietrich Eckart.[34] The occasion marked the beginning of their close collaboration.[35]

"THE RIGHT MAN FOR THE YOUNG MOVEMENT"

When Eckart left the arts for politics and began publishing *Auf Gut Deutsch*, he had been reluctant to endorse a particular political party. While supporting the Thule Society, he also remained in good standing with the leadership of the Bavarian People's Party (BVP).[36] Keeping his options open, and accepting various speaking engagements, he commanded considerable respect in Bavaria's right-wing circles. According to Sebottendorff's colleague Georg Grassinger, "Eckart had much influence and no enemies in the national movement."[37] But few politicians were willing to go as far as he did when it came to anti-Semitism.

Throughout the winter of 1919–1920, Hitler frequented Eckart's home in Munich and his cousin's house in the suburb of Giesing,[38] where the publisher lectured on the so-called Jewish question. Eckart, who liked young people and always had a kind word of encouragement, treated Hitler with respect. "I felt drawn to his whole manner," he later wrote of young Adolf, "and saw very quickly that he was the right man for the young movement."[39] Hitler, in turn, responded favorably to Eckart's tutelage. Later, he would dedicate the second volume of *Mein Kampf* to the anti-Semitic publisher. Bound by common interests, the pair appeared like mentor and disciple and enjoyed an unusual kinship.

Hitler and Eckart had both been fathered by ill-tempered officials who mocked their artistic aspirations, suffered the early deaths of their mothers, escaped into fantasy and megalomania as teenagers, tasted the bitter pill of rejection in the arts, developed a persecution complex, worshipped Richard Wagner, found an object of hate in the Jews, and entered politics to vent to their frustrations. Eckart clearly saw a bit of himself in Hitler, and he hoped that the young man's burgeoning powers of persuasion could be harnessed to fulfill his anti-Semitic agenda.

Toward the end of 1919, Karl Harrer abruptly resigned his position as DAP chairman. The future Nazi dictator was not sorry to see Harrer go. Since November, Hitler and Drexler had been working on a party platform, reportedly with the help of Eckart and Feder, which they intended to unveil in the coming year at a mass meeting.[40] The leadership was determined to produce a cohesive party credo that could be disseminated widely—apparently an activity to which Harrer had objected.[41] Under the leadership of Drexler, who now had assumed the position of chairman, the platform was later completed, and plans were set in motion for its unveiling in February 1920. This event would change the party forever.

"I LOVE THE REAL PEOPLE OF BAVARIA"

Ever since his return from exile in August of 1919, Bavaria's Minister-President Hoffmann had been engaged in a power struggle with army leaders in Munich. While the Reichswehr was trying to build up the state's citizen militias,[42] Hoffmann was preparing to shut them down in compliance with the Treaty of Versailles. Like his Social Democratic colleagues in Berlin, the minister-president was in a difficult position: Defying the treaty meant offending the Entente; enforcing it guaranteed public condemnation. Right-wing nationalists were already taking advantage of the situation and accusing SPD politicians of stabbing the army in the back. It seemed only a matter of time before they invented some pretext to justify Hoffmann's removal from power.

In January of 1920, public sympathies for nationalism were heightened during the trial of Kurt Eisner's assassin. In a Munich court, Count Anton Arco-Valley was charged with first-degree murder. The officer pled guilty with the knowledge that he could receive the death penalty. Unlike the Freikorps soldiers who escaped prosecution after the counterrevolution, he seemed prepared to pay his debt. But much of Munich was unprepared to see him die. Despite public affection for his victim, Arco-Valley's popularity had increased during the interim between his crime and his trial. Many on the right came to see him as a patriot who tried to save Munich from the evils of leftist radicalism. Nevertheless, on January 16, Arco-Valley was sentenced to death.

"I hate Bolshevism. . . . I hate the Jews!" the Austrian nobleman had said in his defense. "I love the real people of Bavaria. . . . I am a true Catholic!"[43] Arco-Valley had said all the right things in court. After his trial, his prosecutor remarked, "If the whole German youth were imbued with such a glowing enthusiasm, we could face the future with confidence."[44] Students at Munich's Ludwig-Maximilians-Universität demanded his pardon. As they marched down Ludwigstraße past the war ministry, soldiers waved at them in solidarity. The following morning, the court announced that it was commuting Arco-Valley's sentence to life in prison. Further reductions would eventually reduce his sentence to five years of incarceration. The authorities sent Arco-Valley to Landsberg Prison to serve out his sentence. Unlike Toller and other former revolutionaries, Eisner's murderer was accommodated in a large, comfortable cell and afforded "fortress imprisonment" status: a privilege customarily granted to white-collar criminals.

The following month, on February 21, a service was held in Munich's eastern cemetery for the one-year anniversary of Kurt Eisner's assassination. As vendors peddled flowers, stickpins, and portraits of the slain minister-president, an estimated eight thousand mourners gathered on the cemetery grounds to pay tribute to the fallen leader.[45] Listening to a chorus sing "Ein Sohn des Volkes" (A Son of the People), they filed past an urn that held Eisner's ashes. Praised for his devotion to the oppressed in a commemorative speech, Eisner was held aloft as a shining hero. Nearly a dozen Bavarian groups showed up to lay claim to his legacy. The presence of so many participants suggested that the Independent Socialists might still have a chance in Bavarian politics.

The following day, in a service at Munich's Tonhalle (concert hall), the USPD held a second memorial for Eisner.[46] Both events were completed without disruption. Unlike the minister-president's grand funeral procession the previous year, neither drew the attendance of Adolf Hitler. The future Nazi dictator was scheming to take advantage of the anniversary in a different way.

"ONLY PEOPLE OF GERMAN BLOOD"

On February 24, 1920, Adolf Hitler and the German Workers' Party staged a mass meeting in the noisy, upstairs Festsaal of Munich's famous Hofbräuhaus. Their timing so close to the one-year anniversary of Eisner's assassination was not accidental: they wanted to emphasize the contrast between their home-grown movement and the failed revolution of an outsider. As Hitler later stated in *Mein Kampf,* "When Kurt Eisner gave the revolutionary uprising in Bavaria a thoroughly conscious impulse against the rest of the Reich, he did not in the slightest degree act on the basis of a Bavarian viewpoint, but only as Jewry's commissar."[47] The meeting at the Festsaal would mark a significant turning point for the fledgling movement. The party changed its name to the National Socialist German Workers' Party (NSDAP), which detractors later shortened to "Nazi."[48] The addition of the words "National" and "Socialist" was meant to emphasize the party's commitment to the common good of the German people, while differentiating the movement from Communism.

In the days before the assembly, party members had slapped up bright red posters all over the city to advertise the meeting. "For our principal color we chose red," Hitler recalled, "as it had an exciting effect on the eye and was therefore calculated to arouse the attention of our opponents and irritate them."[49]

The future Nazi dictator understood that controversy was good for publicity. Drexler intended to chair the event, but, at the last minute, an unexpected health emergency prevented his attendance. Hitler eagerly took his place.[50] By the time he arrived at the Hofbräuhaus fifteen minutes before the meeting was scheduled to begin, the Festsaal was already crammed with two thousand people. The sight of the large crowd must have brought him considerable relief, as the leadership had been obsessing about the attendance.

The Hofbräu Festsaal was a long and narrow chamber in which speakers typically addressed their constituents from the east end. Considering the time and money spent on advertising, it would have been disheartening if the hall had appeared half empty. To preempt this possibility, Hitler had erected a make-shift speaker's podium halfway down one side of the hall, to produce greater intimacy and the illusion of a larger crowd.[51] Now that the auditorium was full, that effort seemed hardly necessary. But not everyone gathered was sympathetic. Dozens of attendees from Bavaria's left wing, including Independent Socialists and Communists, were itching to disrupt the inaugural mass meeting of the new nationalist party. Throughout the postwar period, brawling was common in Munich's beer halls, and speakers were accustomed to dodging flying beer steins thrown by drunken protesters.[52] Hitler was said to be particularly adept at avoiding the ceramic missiles.

When the meeting came to order, Dr. Johannes Dingfelder, a popular writer and ethnic chauvinist delivered the opening remarks. In a tired speech he'd given many times before, Dingfelder, who was twenty-two years older than Hitler, quoted Schiller and Shakespeare before predicting a momentous German awakening.[53] Like many of his generation, Dingfelder thought it uncouth to call out the Jews by name. After he finished, all eyes fell on Hitler as he ascended the podium. Observing the Austrian immigrant with his shock of black hair, thin moustache, and flashing blue eyes, his detractors were ready to pounce. No sooner did he begin speaking than beer steins started flying in his direction and the hall echoed with loud shouts of protest.

Anticipating this possibility, Hitler had peppered the crowd with able-bodied men ready to subdue the agitators at a moment's notice. "A handful of my loyal war comrades and some other followers grappled with the disturbers," he explained in *Mein Kampf*.[54] When the protesters were overpowered and Hitler was able to resume, he unveiled the NSDAP's platform in the form of twenty-five points, articulating the essential program of the Third Reich thirteen years before Hitler became chancellor of Germany. Each was designed to win the support of constituents, including lower and middle class citizens, patriots and nationalists, ethnic chauvinists and anti-Semites, and embittered war veterans.

To begin, Hitler demanded equal status for Germany among all other nations, a repeal of the Treaty of Versailles, and the return of those lands necessary for "the nourishment of our people."[55] These objectives were greeted with hearty applause. Then, Hitler turned to the so-called Jewish question in language that reflected Eckart's philosophy. Stipulating that Jews were mere "guests" in Germany, he stated that only people of "German blood" should be considered citizens and hold public office.[56] According to the Nazi Party platform, all Jews occupying government positions on the local, state, and national levels should be removed. Additionally, the immigration of non-Germans had to be stopped, and any Jews who arrived after August 2, 1914, were to be deported. No objections to these aims were raised. The reaction was in fact quite the opposite. According to *Mein Kampf*, each point was "accepted with increasing enthusiasm."[57]

Next, in language reflecting the theories of Gottfried Feder, Hitler emphasized economic reform, propping up the middle class, and targeting profiteers who allegedly took advantage of German suffering during the war. Since rumors of Jewish war profiteering had been circulating in Germany since 1916, the audience undoubtedly understood that he meant the Jews. Additional points addressed education, law, physical fitness, and the army. Then, Hitler related party objectives for the German press.

All Jews were to be legally removed from newspaper publishing, investment, and influence. The party also demanded legal penalties against subversion in the arts and literature. Though it purportedly identified itself with the Christian faith, the party demanded freedom of religion while opposing "the Jewish materialistic spirit"[58] that had allegedly obstructed Germany's recovery.

In keeping with the party's new name, Hitler stated that the NSDAP was guided by the principle that the "common good" came before the individual. In conclusion, he declared that the Nazi Party demanded a "strong central authority in the Reich," a parliament with unlimited authority, and the formation of state offices to enforce the laws of the nation.[59] To these objectives, he stated, party members would dedicate themselves even if it cost them their lives. "When the last point was reached," Hitler later wrote, "I had before me a hall full of people united by a new conviction, a new faith and a new will. . . . As the masses streamed toward the exits, crammed shoulder to shoulder, shoving and pushing, I knew that a movement was now set afoot among the German people, which would never pass into oblivion."

Despite Hitler's enthusiasm and the success of the meeting, there was no denying that the NSDAP remained a tiny movement with hardly any influence in Bavarian politics. In fact, the local press barely covered the meeting, and, when they did, they focused on Dr. Dingfelder instead of Hitler.[60] The National Socialists still had a long way to go and would require a lot of help if they were going to rise out of obscurity to become a national movement. But they already had a few things going for them: During the meeting, apart from those who were beaten down, no one had objected to Hitler's call for institutionalized anti-Semitism, and no one thought to question how he proposed to define the "common good."

Putting aside for a moment the specter of institutionalized anti-Semitism, when an organization declares the common good as its goal but fails to articulate exactly how the common good will be defined, its membership must, as a matter of faith, trust that its leaders will act in their best interest. But what if they don't? Even with a separation of powers, an informed populace, and a system of checks and balances, the common good can be exploited. After four and a half years of war, this was something that Eisner had been trying to get across to his fellow Bavarians. The Germans had been deceived by a corrupt leadership about the real cause of the First World War—admitting war guilt was a precondition for a restart. The early Nazi platform, which said nothing of public participation in decision-making, was worlds apart from Kurt Eisner's political philosophy, which sought to install the people's voice in government. Whereas Eisner had offered the Bavarians democracy, the NSDAP was proposing fascism. If the reaction in the Festsaal was any indication of the overall temperament of the German people, the dangerous seeds planted by Adolf Hitler were likely to bloom in the coming years.

CHAPTER ELEVEN

THE SHIFT TO THE RIGHT

"TROOPS DO NOT FIRE ON TROOPS"

Though Adolf Hitler's NSDAP attracted two thousand people to its inaugural meeting, it remained obscure when compared to the more popular right-wing political groups in Germany and was in no way ready to challenge the established order. Indeed, in March 1920, one right-wing club was prepared to move against the central government. The Nationale Vereinigung (Nationalist Association), a political group whose membership included government officials and active-duty officers, had been conspiring against the Weimar government since the summer and planned to mobilize seasoned Freikorps units against it. In March, it would stage a putsch in the German capital that would alter the course of national politics and prompt dramatic changes in Bavaria's state government. These changes would prove to be highly advantageous to Hitler. The putsch would also provide him a fantastic opportunity to learn from somebody else's mistakes.

Since the end of the war in 1918, former First Quartermaster General Erich Ludendorff and his wife, Margarethe, had been living like "nomads" in exile.[1] After the general completed his war memoirs in Sweden, the couple returned to Berlin, where they lived incognito as guests at the Hotel Adlon, just a hundred meters from the Brandenburg Gate. Then, in the summer of 1919, the pair moved into a fancy apartment on Viktoriastraße, loaned by the mother-in-law of a loyal subordinate. The flat, with its high ceilings, Persian rugs, and original paintings by Cezanne, Manet, and van Gogh, felt more like a private museum than a residence.[2] Margarethe thought it "magnificently furnished."[3] Her husband described it as "immensely agreeable,"[4] and remarked that its proximity to the Tiergarten encouraged him to exercise. To outsiders, the Luden-dorffs almost appeared like happy retirees. But in private, the former general never stopped scheming, and his Viktoriastraße apartment became one of two central hubs for the Nationale Vereinigung.

Leading the nationalist club with Ludendorff were three key figures: General Walther von Lüttwitz, the commander of the Freikorps that had suppressed the Spartacists in Berlin; Waldemar Pabst, an ultra-nationalist who had ordered the executions of Karl Liebknecht and Rosa Luxemburg; and Wolfgang Kapp, a Prussian bureaucrat who had co-led the Deutsche Vaterlandspartei (German Fatherland Party). The grandson of New York liberals,[5] Kapp wanted to over-turn Germany's parliamentary democracy and bring Ludendorff to power. But the former general was considered too unpopular to lead the uprising.

From the beginning, the Kapp-Lüttwitz Putsch, as it would later come to be known, was fraught with betrayal and intrigue. In July of 1919, Ludendorff had sent a subordinate to inquire if the British might support a putsch against Germany's government.[6] Feigning approval, a British representative said that England would back the coup so long as Ludendorff remained in the shadows.[7] No sooner had Ludendorff's subordinate left the meeting than British intelli-gence warned Reich president Ebert of the impending putsch.

In February 1920, the same month the DAP rebranded itself the NSDAP, the government in Berlin announced that it would begin reductions in the mili-tary in compliance with the Treaty of Versailles. Among the first units targeted for demobilization was the Ehrhardt Brigade, a legendary fighting force led by Captain Hermann Ehrhardt, which had defeated Spartacist revolutionaries in Wilhelmshaven in January 1918.[8] Freikorps Ehrhardt had become the most elite mercenary army in postwar Germany. Well-trained and mobile, the brigade was dispatched to hotspots all over the countryside, including Munich in Bavaria, the Free State of Brunswick in north-central Germany, and Upper Silesia in Poland, where it gained a reputation for savagery.[9] Ehrhardt's mercenaries were said to have a taste for killing and looting. Then, in the winter of 1919–1920, the brigade was brought to Berlin with orders to protect the capital from Com-munist subversion.

Ehrhardt's men were garrisoned in barracks twenty-four kilometers outside the city when the order came through to disband. They felt betrayed: The same government that had asked them to do its dirty work was now abandoning them.[10] Demobilization meant the soldiers would no longer receive pay. Captain Ehrhardt decided to contact his superior officer to see if there was anything he could do. As it turned out, that man was General Lüttwitz, one of the leading conspirators in the Nationale Vereinigung. "Don't do a thing and keep quiet," was the general's slippery reply.[11] Lüttwitz had no intention of allowing the brigade to be dismantled. Instead, he saw an opportunity to take advantage of the discontent caused by reductions in the military. In less than two weeks, Lüttwitz would order the Ehrhardt brigade to march on Berlin with other Freikorps units, for the purpose of overthrowing the government. But a series of unforeseen difficulties would threaten to unravel the putsch before it even started.

On March 8, when Ludendorff's subordinate contacted British authorities to reconfirm their support for the coup, he was snubbed by an official who called it "sheer madness."[12] Two days later, General Lüttwitz was dismissed from his command, and arrest warrants were issued for Kapp and Pabst.[13] Colleagues in the military warned Lüttwitz they would oppose him if he marched against Berlin. Then, the putschists lost the element of surprise when reports of the coup surfaced in the press.[14]

Nevertheless, on the night of March 12, the Ehrhardt Brigade set out for the capital. When the news reached the authorities sometime after midnight, the government called emergency meetings.[15] Defense Minister Noske issued an order to the army to shoot any Freikorps entering the city. But military leaders, including Reichswehr general Hans von Seeckt, were unwilling to authorize it. From behind his trademark monocle, Seeckt admonished, "Troops do not fire on troops. Do you perhaps intend, Herr Minister, that a battle be fought before the Brandenburg Gate between troops who have fought side by side against the common enemy?"[16] Rebuffed, the defense minister joined an exodus of government officials fleeing the capital, including Reich president Friedrich Ebert and German chancellor Gustav Bauer, who escaped to Stuttgart via Dresden.

That same morning, as a light drizzle moistened the predawn air, the Ehrhardt Brigade continued its solemn march into the heart of Berlin. Wearing helmets painted with swastikas—the symbol of German nationalists—the contingent of four thousand men headed confidently toward the government quarter. Along the way, they took a break—set up field kitchens; drank coffee, and smoked in the predawn hours—before resuming their march. Once inside the city limits, however, they were confronted by a local unit of the Einwohnerwehr. But the civilian guards weren't interested in fighting and wished them good luck. As the rays of the morning sun began stretching across the horizon, the brigade arrived in the famous Tiergarten, where they were greeted by Kapp and Ludendorff. After a few words of encouragement, they continued through the Brandenburg

Gate and into the government quarter. Five hours later, Ehrhardt's brigade and other participating Freikorps units controlled the capital. Not a single shot was fired. Now it was up to Kapp—the anointed civilian leader of the putsch—to assume power at the head of a new government. But no sooner had he entered the chancellery than it became apparent Kapp had no idea what he was doing.

Wolfgang Kapp and General Lüttwitz were completely out of synch. The Prussian bureaucrat hadn't even been informed that the Ehrhardt Brigade was marching on Berlin until 6:00 a.m. that morning.[17] The putsch, which had been initiated on a Saturday, when government employees had the day off, left Kapp with no one to type out the announcement for his new government at the chancellery.[18] Not only that, staff workers had removed all the rubber stamps used to authenticate government communications.[19] By the time Kapp's daughter arrived at the chancellery to do the typing, it was already too late to submit an announcement for the Sunday papers.[20] Apparently, it didn't even matter because someone in Kapp's provisional government had already forbidden the local press from printing newspapers.[21] The bureaucrat's problems were only just beginning.

Without access to cash, Kapp lacked the money he needed to pay off the Freikorps. When his subordinates demanded that the Reichsbank release the funds he required, they were told they didn't have the right paperwork. After they filled out the proper forms, the bank refused to recognize their authority. As if this wasn't frustrating enough, labor leaders decided it was a good time to stage a massive strike in the capital, which paralyzed the city. Electricity, water and gas were turned off; municipal services stopped; public transportation ceased; even garbage collectors refused to make their rounds when millions of people took to the streets.[22]

As chaos was enveloping Berlin, a right-wing alliance in Munich decided to take advantage of the situation. Approaching Johannes Hoffmann, they warned the minister-president that a civil war might break out if the military didn't immediately take over and declare martial law in Munich.[23] Hoffmann was flabbergasted: Hadn't he loyally served his fellow Bavarians from exile in Bamberg, defeated the second Soviet Republic, and brought peace and security back to the state?

Unwilling to put up a fight, Hoffmann resigned. Quickly, his Social Democratic colleagues in the cabinet followed suit.[24] Bavaria's Far Right could hardly believe its good fortune: the SPD had been eliminated without a fight. Two days later, Gustav von Kahr, a popular BVP politician and monarchist, was appointed minister-president of Bavaria. Together with his allies, he would transform the state into an oasis for far-right radicals.

Back in Berlin, the situation was not going smoothly for Kapp and Lüttwitz. The cash-strapped putsch remained incapable of paying its forces. Increasingly restless, some of the Freikorps wanted to turn their guns on the labor demonstrators clogging the streets. Eventually, the confluence of setbacks was too much to take and the putschists called it quits on March 17. President Ebert was back in control.

Wolfgang Kapp fled to Sweden and General Lüttwitz escaped to Hungary.[25] Five days after it arrived, the Ehrhardt Brigade received orders to depart the city. For all their efforts, the men had received no pay and no opportunity to vent their frustrations through violence. Retreating grim-faced down Unter den Linden, they marched in silence as crowds of onlookers watched them leave. Suddenly, the quiet was interrupted by the sound of a child laughing. Breaking their ranks, two Ehrhardt soldiers rushed the offending boy and beat him to death with their rifle butts. When a shocked onlooker started to complain, the soldiers fired their machine guns on the crowd before continuing their silent march.[26]

News coming out of the capital was often unreliable during the Kapp-Lüttwitz Putsch. To retrieve a status report and offer fraternal support to Kapp at the height of the coup, Captain Mayr in Bavaria arranged for Hitler and Eckart to travel to Berlin.[27] Eckart's inclusion likely had to do with his familiarity with Kapp who had been an early subscriber to *Auf Gut Deutsch*. In case of trouble, the pair planned to disguise themselves as a traveling businessman and his bookkeeper.[28] Their junket north was Hitler's first trip in an airplane. Enduring a severe thunderstorm that bounced their biplane about, the Austrian immigrant was sickened by turbulence. When they arrived in Berlin, they discovered that the putsch had already failed, and Kapp and Lüttwitz were in exile. Warned that it was dangerous to remain in the capital, Eckart and Hitler decided to return to Munich—this time by train.

"A BLACK MOOD"

Though the Weimar government had survived the coup, its troubles were far from over. Labor strikes had spread across Germany, and workers demanded new national leadership.[29] In late March, Noske resigned as defense minister, Gustav Bauer stepped down as German chancellor, and the strikes dissipated.

But a more threatening crisis was underway in Germany's industrial center. Back on March 14, Communists in the Ruhr Valley—a coal-bearing region in northwestern Germany—had captured four major cities. The revolutionaries hoped to spark a movement in which the red flag of Communism would "wave victoriously over the whole of Germany."[30] Having only just recovered from the Kapp-Lüttwitz Putsch, government representatives weren't exactly thrilled to be dealing with another insurrection. To buy time, local Social Democrats negotiated a ten-day truce with the Communists.

During the ceasefire, Reichswehr general Hans von Seeckt decided to reinstate the Freikorps and send several regiments to support local government forces. Though the Ehrhardt Brigade had participated in the treasonous Kapp-Lüttwitz Putsch just a few days earlier, it too was called up and provided back pay for the wages earlier promised by Kapp.[31] The rehiring of Berlin's aggressors didn't seem to trouble government officials too much, and the mercenaries were happy to learn that their services were still in demand.[32] "[After the Kapp Putsch], we were in a black mood," recalled one of Ehrhardt's men, "and we needed to turn open a valve . . . and let off a lot of steam. Here was an enemy that suited our needs."[33]

On April 3, Freikorps forces loyal to the government launched a military strike against Red Army positions in the Ruhr. The battle was not as one-sided as the attack on Munich. With fifty thousand men, the Ruhr's Red Army was a formidable adversary.[34] Among them were Freikorps units aligned with the Communists. However, in the end, the Red Army was no match for the forces that Seeckt amassed against it. After defeating their enemies, the Freikorps repeated the tactics they'd perfected in Munich: random prisoners and civilians were executed without trial.

With the crisis contained, General Seeckt began reducing the armed forces and demobilizing the Freikorps once more, in accord with the Treaty of Versailles. The Ehrhardt Brigade was officially dissolved. To compensate for the massive reduction, Seeckt created a shadow Reichswehr in which former Freikorps men were given positions in a secret military organization under his control. While some Freikorps officers were willing to join the shadow group, others were not. Hermann Ehrhardt and many of his men decided to immigrate to Bavaria, where they would enjoy the protection of Minister-President Kahr and Munich's police chief, Ernst Pöhner. They wouldn't be the only putschists to seek sanctuary in the Bavarian capital.

On May 17, in the wake of the Kapp-Lüttwitz Putsch, Ludendorff had fled

Berlin for Munich by train. Much as he had at the end of the First World War, the general would blame his failures on somebody else. This time, it was the "unreliability of the officer corps" and "the fickleness of the public" that had doomed the putsch.[35] His wife, Margarethe, blamed her husband for involving himself in such a hopeless undertaking: "I never understood how it was that Ludendorff was the only person to be snared by the alluring eloquence of these men, without demanding guarantees for the success of their great enterprise."[36]

"THE MOST ARTFUL AND CUNNING OF ALL RABBLE-ROUSERS"

The Kapp-Lüttwitz Putsch and its aftermath resulted in significant changes for Bavaria. Not only had members of the Far Right been able to unseat the Social Democratic government of Johannes Hoffmann and elevate Gustav von Kahr to the position of minister-president, the dissolution of the Freikorps had prompted an exodus of mercenaries and nationalists to Germany's southern-most state, infusing it with a defiant and rebellious spirit. Less than a year earlier, the Communists had ruled Munich; now, the Far Right controlled the police, the army, the state government, and the citizen's militia. However, unanimity would elude Bavaria's new masters, as factionalism quickly divided the Right.

Some right-wing leaders, including Kahr and Reichswehr general Arnold Ritter von Möhl, wanted to bring order and stability back to Bavaria. Others, like Mayr and Röhm, yearned to spearhead a counterrevolution against Ebert's Weimar government in Berlin.[37] Bavarian separatists such as Otto Ballerstedt, whom Hitler considered as a rival, argued for secession from the Reich and joining with Austria. And although he counted himself among those who favored counterrevolution, Dietrich Eckart himself—despite his growing regard for Hitler—was still reluctant to commit to a specific person or party.

In his search for Germany's new messiah, Eckart hadn't only considered Hitler. The anti-Semitic publisher had also shown interest in Georg Heim of the BVP, as well as Wolfgang Kapp.[38] In 1920, he devoted an entire issue of *Auf Gut Deutsch* to Kapp. Margarethe Ludendorff had once described the putsch leader as "a man with an insinuating personality" who was "highly gifted as an orator, so that people listened eagerly to his clever speeches."[39] Eckart's eventual rejec-tion of Kapp stemmed not from his political failures, but from his lukewarm commitment to anti-Semitism.[40] The publisher's diligent search for the right spokesman demonstrated that there were other candidates besides the Austrian immigrant. In this light, arguably, the occurrence of Nazi Germany may not have hinged solely on the appearance of Adolf Hitler. Over time, though, it would be hard to dispute the fact that he would grow into the perfect Nazi for the job.

On March 31, 1920, Hitler was discharged from the Reichswehr.[41] While he would continue to work closely with army associates, he decided it was time to devote himself exclusively to the NSDAP and politicking. Renting a flat not far from the Isar Gate in an apartment building on Thierschstraße, Hitler spent much of his time at the Sterneckerbräu, the same tavern where he attended his first DAP meeting, and the site of the party's first headquarters. With apparently enough funds at his disposal to survive, Hitler committed himself day and night to the expansion of the party and soon convinced his colleagues to hold meetings nearly every week. These gatherings, held in beer halls and establishments all over the city, provided him an opportunity to refine his public speaking.

Hitler's talent for oratory was a combination of skill, practice, and observation. He was familiar with stuffy politicians who alienated their audiences by talking down to them in pompous tones and wasn't about to make the same mistake. With a preternatural sensitivity to the moods of his listeners, Hitler articulated feelings and convictions that created emotional resonance and gave his restless audiences a sense of hope. Once he established a rapport, he could direct their hatreds by revealing his own. Hitler's appeal had less to do with the ideas he presented than in the way he presented them. Speaking in the language of ordinary people, he gave the impression that he understood their problems better than they did. Mesmerized by his hypnotic power, even skeptics were transformed into true believers. Though his intuitive facility was extraordinary, Hitler didn't rest on talent alone.

Making a careful study of the acoustics in various beer halls and arenas, Hitler learned how to project his voice for maximum effect at different locations. At the Platzl, a drinking establishment opposite the Hofbräuhaus, Hitler purportedly studied singers and comedians to see how they overcame the din of raucous drunks and clinking steins.[42] With theatrical flair, he made a point of never showing up on time for speaking engagements, and, if possible, he tried to appear from an entrance that no one would expect. Standing above an audience, Hitler endeavored to keep things simple and confined his speeches to three basic points.[43] "Only constant repetition will finally succeed in imprinting an idea on the memory of the crowd," Hitler wrote in *Mein Kampf*.[44] But whether they remembered his ideas or not, Hitler's magic was the impression he left, which compelled his listeners to tell their friends, family, and neighbors about the curious speaker from the Nazi Party. By the spring of 1920, Hitler's name was on everyone's lips in Munich's cafés, beer halls, and restaurants.

Dietrich Eckart was paying close attention to Hitler's development. If the Nazi speaker was going to be successful attracting support from the upper classes, Eckart wagered he would need some refinement. Apart from what he'd learned about decorum in the army, Hitler had little training in social graces since the death of his mother thirteen years earlier. Taking stock of Hitler's rough manners and ill-fitting clothes, Eckart took him out for meals and bought him suits, hats, and a trench coat.[45] More significantly, the publisher continued to tutor Hitler about his anti-Semitic ideology. As the year 1920 progressed, his influence became more pronounced. To differentiate the Nazi Party from other right-wing movements, Hitler started placing greater emphasis on the so-called Jewish question. Arguing that Jewry was a parasitic race, he blamed the Jews for the outcome of the war, the Treaty of Versailles, the postwar revolution, and the Weimar government.

In a speech he gave on April 6, 1920, Hitler suggested that Jews should be "exterminated."[46] The sinister remark was horribly prescient considering the genocide perpetrated two decades later. But at a time when Hitler lacked power or authority, in a culture where anti-Semitic remarks were commonplace, the statement was not yet considered particularly important.

At the same time, Hitler was well aware that many kind-hearted Bavarians were reluctant to join the anti-Semitic chorus. Bavaria was predominately Catholic, and attacking the Jews without provocation betrayed Christian values. In his struggle to awaken Bavarians to the so-called dangers of Judaism, Hitler was familiar with the argument that there were good and bad men among Germans and Jews alike. He knew many Germans had good relations with their Jewish neighbors and sympathized with them. Hitler and Eckart plotted to liberate the Bavarian masses from this purportedly superficial view.

On August 13, 1920, Hitler confronted Jewish sympathies in a speech he delivered entitled, "Why We Are Anti-Semites," at Munich's Hofbräuhaus. In a distorted presentation that lasted two hours, he claimed that the Aryan race had created all of the great civilizations of the ancient world. In contrast, he said, the Jews were nomads and parasites incapable of creating anything resembling a state. Whereas the Aryans performed work out of noble and ethical commitment, Jews saw work as punishment and performed it merely to survive. According to Hitler, the Jews were not greedy, materialistic and egotistical because they were bad people: it was in their blood. "It is not important whether the individual Jew is good or bad," argued the future Nazi leader, "for he has to act according to the laws of his race, just as every member of our people does."[47] Like a modern-day religious ideologue who claims that it's useless to negotiate with an adversary because scripture says he or she is the enemy of God, Hitler claimed the Jew was a destroyer whether he wanted to be or not. Behind Jewish preaching "that all people on earth are equal" and "connected by international solidarity," Hitler saw the self-interest of a race consumed by the desire to dominate all people and become the master race.[48] It was an ironic premise.

If Germans were to rebuild their country, Hitler argued, it was necessary to "take action"[49] against the Jews. He viewed this as the single most important struggle for the German people. The speech received a hearty ovation. But not everyone was pleased with his remarks. In the Social Democratic newspaper, the *Münchener Post*, Hitler was likened to a "comedian," who blamed the Jews "for everything."[50] Despite the bad press, even his critics couldn't deny his uncanny ability: "One thing Hitler has going for him, and it has to be admitted—he's the most artful and cunning of all the rabble-rousers now spreading their poisons around Munich."[51]

THE VÖLKISCHER BEOBACHTER

One of the more important items on Hitler's agenda in 1920 was the acquisition of a party newspaper. In the early twentieth century, Germany was producing more newspapers and magazines than any other country in the world.[52] A significant number of these were published by the country's various political parties, and Hitler understood their influence. In the same way that people in the twenty-first century get their news from websites or cable news stations that reflect their particular political persuasions, Germans in the postwar era tended to read newspapers published by their favorite political party. If you were a Social Democrat in Munich, you read the *Münchener Post*. If you were a Communist, you read *Die Rote Fahne*. Hitler wanted a newspaper that would promote the NSDAP to the German public and announce party meetings. This was also the goal of Eckart, whose commitment to Hitler deepened over the course of the year.

Ever since his early days in Berlin, when he felt sabotaged by a Jewish press that panned his work in the theater, Eckart had been scheming to launch his own anti-Semitic newspaper to reach the masses. Though *Auf Gut Deutsch* was a step in the right direction, the broadsheet wasn't a newspaper. In December 1920,

Hitler became aware that a local newspaper, which catered to the Far Right, was up for sale. First published as the *Münchener Beobachter* (Munich Observer) in 1887, the paper had changed ownership several times before it was sold to the Thule Society's Sebottendorff in 1918 and renamed the *Völkischer Beobachter* (Nationalist Observer), or VB. Sebottendorff and his stockholders had used the paper to advance their racist and nationalist agenda during the postwar period. When Eckart approached Sebottendorff in 1918 to solicit financial support for *Auf Gut Deutsch*, the publisher had denied him because he saw Eckart's venture as a rival publication. According to one source, Hitler had applied for a job at the VB around the same time that he joined the DAP but was turned down.[53]

In late 1920, Sebottendorff and his shareholders decided to put the *Völkischer Beobachter* up for sale for 120,000 marks. It was a hefty price tag: the buyer would also be required to assume the paper's substantial debt, which amounted to an additional 250,000 marks.[54] At first, the Nazi leadership was apprehensive about the purchase. But when news arrived that a rival bidder was making an offer, Hitler persuaded Drexler and Eckart to use their connections to acquire funds. In a meeting with Reichswehr general Franz Ritter von Epp, Eckart convinced the former Life Guards commander to donate 60,000 marks from Reichswehr coffers. This covert use of army funds to support the NSDAP reflected the partisan agenda of the Reichswehr in the period following the Kapp Putsch. Eckart's efforts didn't stop there. He also convinced a notary from Augsburg to guarantee the purchase,[55] and his cousin, an official at Hansa Bank, to facilitate collateral.[56] After Eckart secured another 30,000 marks in donations, Drexler assumed the remaining debt. When the VB's eight shareholders agreed to approve the sale, Drexler became the paper's legal owner. Hitler was overjoyed: Eckart had come through for him. In the *Völkischer Beobachter*, the Austrian immigrant now had a means to influence the public like never before.

CHAPTER TWELVE

A STATE OF EMERGENCY

Violence and terror were powerful tools in postwar German politics. Militias attached to political parties on the left and the right used brute force to intimidate their political rivals. These tactics were not without historical precedent. Back in the seventeenth century, during the Thirty Year's War, when foreign armies of Roman Catholics and Protestants fought a religious struggle on German soil, bands of lawless German mercenaries roamed the countryside selling their services to the highest bidder. In the absence of a centralized military leadership, they served at the behest of their local captains: cunning and charismatic warlords who fought alongside their men.

A German captain was called *der Führer* (the leader), and they functioned under the *Führerprinzip* (leadership principle), which gave them the authority to decide all matters concerning the group. Three centuries later, the Freikorps operated on much the same basis during the counterrevolution. But in 1920, they had outlasted their usefulness, and the Treaty of Versailles demanded their dissolution. Bound by esprit de corps and unwilling to break up, many Freikorps regiments vowed to stay together. Some disguised their activities by forming business fronts such as trucking companies or rental agencies.[1] Others opened youth camps or adopted harmless sounding names like the "Union for Agricultural Instruction."[2]

In Bavaria, some ex-Freikorps members joined the citizen's militia. Despite pressure from Berlin to disband, for example, the Einwohnerwehr had grown to include 400,000 members with 2.5 million weapons.[3] After his Freikorps regiment was disbanded and he moved to Munich, Captain Hermann Ehrhardt formed a new group called the League of Former Ehrhardt Officers. What it intended to do, nobody knew for sure.

Since the end of the war, Munich's beer halls had been arenas for vicious brawls. With demobilized soldiers, disbanded Freikorps fighters, and political extremists in the city, it's not hard to understand why. Trouble usually began with drunken patrons shouting profanities to drown out the speeches of their political rivals. Next, beer steins would start flying, followed by fistfights that often spilled out into the streets. Since its inaugural meeting in the Hofbräu-haus, the Nazi Party had been using the *Saalsschutzabteilung* (hall protection group) to shield Hitler from attackers at his beer hall appearances. Comprised mainly of Hitler's comrades from the war, along with bouncer types, the hall protection group would impose its will with physical violence whenever called upon. Roaming the streets of the Bavarian capital, its members also enjoyed intimidating and sometimes attacking Jews when they could find them.[4] Under the protection of Ernst Pöhner, Munich's sympathetic police chief, they didn't have to worry about arrest or prosecution. Restless for action like their seventeenth century counterparts, members of the hall protection group considered these activities fun and games.

Not everyone in the Nazi leadership approved of Hitler's thugs. Party chairman Anton Drexler groused that Hitler's paramilitaries undermined the legitimacy of the NSDAP as a proper working-class movement.[5] When the hall protection group was renamed the *Turn und Sportabteilung* (Gymnastics and Sports Section), the change didn't satisfy Drexler or conservatives in the party, who were increasingly disturbed by Hitler's leadership style. In 1921, these men would take a stand against Hitler and threaten to divide the Nazi movement before it took off. But before that could happen, a mysterious group of assassins would appear in Bavaria and initiate a murder spree of revenge killings that would raise the stakes of political leadership in Germany.

"THE BLACK HAND HAS JUDGED YOU"

With the piles of orange and yellow leaves that blanketed Munich in the fall of 1920 came a shocking discovery that left many residents frightened. In a popular public woodland just south of the city, the body of woman was found on October 6. Murder was uncommon in Bavaria, and the discovery was highly unusual. The victim had been strangled, and her body had been placed beneath a placard stapled to a tree that read, "You lousy bitch! You have betrayed your Fatherland. The Black Hand has judged you."[6] The woman was identified as nineteen-year-old Marie Sandmeier, a shy and innocent looking young lady who had just recently come to Munich in search of work. Piecing together a narrative of her final days, the police discovered that Fraulein Sandmeier had most recently worked as a servant on an estate in upper Bavaria. While in Munich, she read postings in the streets that ordered Bavarians to turn over all weapons to the Allied Disarmament Commission. Remembering that her former employer was hiding an arms cache on his property, and feeling it her duty to report it, the guileless servant decided to inform the authorities.

Unfortunately, Sandmeier went to the wrong address and gave her report to the shop where the commission's posters had been printed. Instead of reporting to the commission, the print shop told Sandmeier's story to the Einwohnerwehr. After the location of her temporary place of residence was identified, a member of the citizen's militia approached her on October 5 and asked that she accompany him to give a complete report. That was the last time anyone saw her alive. The following day, her dead body was found in the woods. Who was the Black Hand? If the police knew, they weren't saying. The sign placed above Sandmeier's head sent a chilling message: German radicals were now willing to kill anyone—even anonymous servant girls—if they betrayed the nationalist cause by consorting with the Allies.

Not long after, a second terror attack targeted a twenty-one-year-old Reichswehr soldier named Hans Dobner on October 20.[7] Like Sandmeier, Dobner had intended to report a secret weapons cache when an unknown assailant hit him on the head and attempted to strangle him to death.[8] Fighting off his assassin, Dobner escaped with his life and later joined forces with Karl Gareis, the leading USPD politician in Bavaria, to bring his attacker to justice. With the assistance of a lawyer, Dobner and Gareis established that the police had participated in the plot, but they could not uncover the identity of the assassin. In retaliation, the police had Dobner arrested as a nonresident and deported back to his homeland of Czechoslovakia.[9]

Five months later, in March 1921, the body of a thirty-four-year-old waiter named Hans Hartung was discovered at the bottom of Munich's Isar River. Weighted down by paving stones, Hartung had been shot eleven times before being thrown in the water. A member of the Einwohnerwehr, Hartung had recently immigrated to Munich, where he threatened to reveal the location of an arms cache unless the Einwohnerwehr increased his salary.[10] Though two Reichswehr officers were identified in connection with his disappearance, Pöhner, the Munich police chief, delayed their arrests until sufficient time had elapsed for them to flee Bavaria. Unbeknownst to the public, Pöhner shared the same hatreds as the killers and was conspiring with them. He'd been turning over the names of anyone who came forward with information about the murders to the assassins. On one occasion, when an incredulous resident asked Pöhner if he knew that political murder gangs were terrorizing the city, he reportedly retorted, "Yes, but not enough of them."[11]

In June, the assassins were ready to kill a high-profile target. While returning home from a speaking engagement on June 9, Karl Gareis, the prominent USPD leader who had come to the aid of Dobner, and who served in the Bavarian parliament, was gunned down at the front gate of his home in Schwabing. Before his murder, Gareis had made it his mission to investigate secret far-right organizations. As news of the latest assassination spread across Munich, people began to wonder who would be struck down next. Was anyone safe? Before the war, political assassinations had been extremely rare.[12] Everything was different now. In a city that had endured the assassination of its head of state, a massacre in a school gymnasium, and a bloody counterrevolution, the emergence of a political hit squad was just the latest barbarity habituating the people to violence and murder. The disregard for human life was already having a noticeable impact. In the streets of Schwabing, bands of nationalist youth could be heard singing old pogrom songs with fresh lyrics, "O hero brave whose shot made Gareis fall, and brought deliverance again to all."[13]

"UNSER FÜHRER"

In the sixteen months since Hitler unveiled the Nazi party platform in the Hofbräuhaus, the NSDAP had grown from a few hundred followers to three thousand paying members.[14] Hitler had shown himself to be a charismatic speaker, a clever advertiser, and a corporate innovator who drove the purchase of the party's first newspaper. More importantly, he had distinguished the party brand from other far-right organizations through his unique commitment to anti-Semitism.

Despite his successes, Hitler still had to contend with other party leaders when it came decision-making. The NSDAP remained under the primary control of Chairman Anton Drexler, who conferred with an executive committee. While Hitler served on the committee, technically he could not overrule it. The arrangement was paradoxical, considering the fact that the NSDAP stood against democracy and voting. Apart from his past troubles with founding chairman Karl Harrer, Hitler had faced little opposition since joining the DAP.

But in late 1920 that started to change when a clique of conservative opponents started complaining about his aggressive leadership style. Eventually, an argument between the conservatives and the future Nazi dictator would cause such a crisis that it threatened to bring an early end to Hitler's career in the NSDAP.

The conflict had been sparked in August 1920 when Nazi representatives, including Hitler, attended an international, right-wing conference in Salzburg, Austria. When one of the German groups in attendance proposed a merger with the Nazis, Drexler found it hard to resist. Julius Streicher's Deutsche Sozialistische Partei (DSP), which had been created by the Thule Society, was a nationalist, anti-Semitic group with a sizeable following in several prominent German cities. In Drexler's view, a merger with the DSP could extend Nazi Party influence beyond Munich. It would also counterbalance Hitler's influence and satisfy a growing number of critics, including Gottfried Feder, who now complained that the Austrian upstart's vulgar propaganda campaign was jeopardizing party legitimacy.

When Hitler learned of the proposed merger with the DSP, he burst into a fit of anger. According to the Austrian immigrant, the NSDAP didn't need to collaborate with other parties. Anxious that "political kleptomaniacs"[15] were going to steal his ideas and fearing that rivals would try to undermine his authority, or, even worse, turn out to be more qualified, Hitler refused to cooperate with outsiders. First, he wanted to build the NSDAP to his own liking. To achieve this, he insisted on solidifying the movement in Munich before expanding it outward. This time, Drexler backed down. But the party chairman and the anti-Hitler clique weren't ready to give up.

In spring 1921, Drexler met with DSP leaders to consider a new proposal to merge the two parties and relocate NSDAP headquarters to Berlin. When Hitler learned what Drexler had done he became so enraged that he threatened to quit. For a second time, his emotional outburst convinced the party chairman to turn down the DSP proposal. Then, during a subsequent meeting, Hitler erupted in a fiery rant that left negotiators thinking he was a "fanatical would-be big shot."[16] Though he effectively killed the attempt to consolidate the two parties, his tirade hardened the resolve of his adversaries. In June, while he was away with Eckart on a fundraising trip to Berlin, they took steps to orchestrate a merger behind his back.

Hitler's six-week fundraising junket to the German capital was critical to the movement. Though the NSDAP had been collecting membership dues, it was always short of money, and the *Völkischer Beobachter* was barely afloat.[17] Using his connections in the German capital, Eckart took Hitler around to meet prominent figures and wealthy contributors on the far right. Years later, Hitler would recall Eckart introducing him by saying, "This is the man who will one day liberate Germany."[18] By 1921, the anti-Semitic publisher no longer seemed to doubt that he'd found the right protégé.

During their trip to Berlin, Hitler and Eckart received a tip that members of the executive committee were making moves behind their backs. Drexler was proposing to join forces with the DSP and Otto Dickel, the founder of a fascist movement based in Augsburg. Praised for his recent literary work, *The Resurrection of the Western World*, Dickel was a rising star in racist circles. Like Hitler, he was also a convincing orator and a zealous evangelist for the nationalist cause. In late June, Drexler had invited Dickel to speak at the Hofbräuhaus Festsaal while Hitler was away. On the night of the talk before a capacity crowd, Dickel delivered a powerful speech that convinced Drexler's supporters that he was an "outstanding speaker with a popular touch,"[19] second only to Hitler.

Drexler was apparently willing to make special concessions to Dickel if he joined the Nazi Party. Hitler was outraged: the chairman was kowtowing to an outsider and a potential rival. When new talks were opened, Hitler crashed the meeting and told the assembly he would oppose any merger. Though Dickel tried to persuade him of the benefits of a confederation, Hitler stormed off at the suggestion that the Nazi Party platform might require some tweaking. The inference was that the party needed Dickel to amend the twenty-five points because the Austrian immigrant lacked sophistication. Hitler's emotional response, which included sulking, was reportedly so embarrassing that even Eckart cringed. Despite Hitler's histrionics, Drexler refused to drop negotiations, and made plans to bring the merger to a vote in the executive committee. When Hitler learned of Drexler's plan, he submitted a letter announcing his resignation from the Nazi Party.

Hitler's emotional tirades would become legendary. Like a child, he was known to burst into uncontrollable fits of anger when he didn't get his way. According to biographer Ian Kershaw, these tantrums were usually "a sign of frustration, even desperation, not strength."[20] In 1921, Hitler's resignation was a statement telling Drexler and the others that he wouldn't tolerate them scheming behind his back. And it was driven more by emotions than cunning.

Drexler had to consider the consequences of his departure: If Hitler were allowed to resign, a significant number of party members would exit with him, and he would likely start his own movement. Where would the NSDAP be then? Was it really worth the risk? Drexler couldn't deny that Hitler's mesmerizing oratory was the main reason the Nazi Party's mass meetings were so popular. Was a merger with Dickel really worth it if it meant losing Hitler? Certainly Hitler's mercurial outbursts had been childish and exhausting, but was there anyone else on the far right as earnest in his commitment and as able a spokesman? Drexler decided that losing the Austrian immigrant was too great a price to pay and asked Eckart to mediate between them.

In a letter to Drexler on July 14, a much calmer Hitler pledged to rejoin the party if the chairman and executive committee agreed to certain terms: Hitler would replace Drexler as party chairman and be given dictatorial powers, the members of the executive committee would resign, the Nazi Party headquarters would remain in Munich, the Nazi Party platform would be unaltered, and all talk of mergers would be ended. To demonstrate party unity, Hitler demanded that a mass meeting be held within eight days to announce these changes. In conclusion, Hitler wrote, "I do not present these demands because I am power-hungry, but rather because recent events have convinced me more than ever that without an iron-hand at the leadership, this party, even without a change in its name, will within a short time cease to be what it is supposed to be."[21] To underscore his inestimable value as the most popular speaker in the party, Hitler followed his letter with a speech at the Circus Krone auditorium—a six-thousand-seat venue—where he drew a capacity crowd on July 20. Unable to deny his importance to the movement, Drexler and the committee accepted Hitler's demands. But the terms still had to be approved by a party plebiscite.

At a members-only meeting on July 29 at the Hofbräuhaus, Hitler delivered a persuasive speech. Though he'd been offered the position of first party chairman several times before, he explained to the audience that he hadn't been ready to accept responsibility for leading the movement until now. Charmed by his words, the membership granted Hitler dictatorial powers in a vote 554 to 1.[22] All of his demands were met. While Drexler pledged to continue supporting Hitler and the NSDAP, he was forced to step aside and take the title of "honorary chairman."[23]

The outcome was a boost to Hitler's confidence. To reward his teacher for his loyalty, Hitler promoted Eckart to editor-in-chief of the *Völkischer Beobachter*. The selection was the first of many appointments in which Hitler's supporters were rewarded with positions of responsibility. They in turn began to promote him as the ultimate authority in the party. In the pages of the *Völkischer Beobachter*, Eckart got to work elevating Hitler to near mythological status. Shortly after the leadership crisis, he declared that "no man can serve a cause more selflessly, more obediently, and more honestly, than Hitler devotes himself to ours."[24] In time, the newspaper would stop referring to the Nazi leader as "Herr Hitler" and begin calling him "unser Führer" (our leader).[25] The NSDAP was starting to function under the Führerprinzip. Like seventeenth-century freebooters pledging allegiance to their captain, the newspaper's contributing writers fell into lockstep with Hitler.

In July 1921, at roughly the same time that the leadership crisis unfolded in the NSDAP, Bavarian minister-president Gustav von Kahr was forced to dissolve the state's massive citizen's militia, the Einwohnerwehr. After months of pressure, the national government and the Allies had started threatening to send troops to Bavaria if he didn't comply with the dissolution order. Reluctantly, Kahr instructed the militia's leadership to break up the group and turn over its weapons. Since the Allies weren't prepared to go door-to-door to confiscate firearms, most Einwohnerwehr members simply put their guns away for safekeeping. Those that wanted to continue participating in paramilitary activities happily joined one of the many private armies doing the same thing under a false name, such as the Nazi Party's Gymnastics and Sport Section.

Attracting paramilitary support to the NSDAP was one of Adolf Hitler's priorities: the now-undisputed Nazi leader would eventually need an army if he were to launch a coup to unseat the government. The largest paramilitary group in Munich at the time was the pro-monarchist Bund, Bayern, und Reich (League for Bavaria and Empire). Led by prominent far-right leaders, the group attracted recruits with the slogan, "First the homeland, then the world."[26] Despite its smaller size, Hitler's group was about to receive an important infusion. In August, Ernst Röhm convinced Captain Ehrhardt to send some of his most able men into the Gymnastics and Sports Section.[27] As a result, Hitler's paramilitary wing was reinforced with some of the hardiest warriors in Germany.[28] The connection between Ehrhardt, Röhm, and Hitler in the volatile underworld of Bavaria's far-right mercenary movement would have far-reaching, violent consequences.

STRUCK DOWN BY A HAIL OF BULLETS

On August 26, former secretary of state Matthias Erzberger, the hated civilian politician who had crossed enemy lines back in November 1918 to accept Germany's surrender, took a vacation in the Black Forest with his wife, Paula. While on holiday, Erzberger kept up with the latest news from Berlin by receiving visits from political associates. In the years since he affixed his name to the armistice papers in a train car at Compiegne, the Catholic politician had chaired Germany's unpopular armistice commission, supported the humiliating Treaty of Versailles, and pushed unwelcome taxation measures on the German public.[29] Erzberger was willing to play this unpopular role and risk public condemnation because he believed he was saving Germany from anarchy and economic ruin. But his enemies didn't see it that way.

According to the Far Right, Erzberger was one of the "November Criminals": traitorous politicians who negotiated the armistice. He aroused such bitterness that ordinary people said they wanted to "place a couple of handgrenades in his car" or "club him to death."[30] By late summer 1921, the Catholic politician had already survived one assassination attempt, in which an angry naval cadet jumped onto the running board of his automobile and tried to shoot him to death.[31] Lost in conversation one day with a colleague from the Catholic Center Party on the trails of the Black Forest, Erzberger and his companion didn't realize that someone was following them. When they later paused at a summit to take in the view, two hikers approached them and inquired, "Are you Erzberger?"[32] When he replied yes, the young trekkers grabbed guns from their backpacks and started shooting. Uselessly trying to shield themselves with their umbrellas, Erzberger and his colleague were struck down by a hail of bullets. When the assailants stopped to reload, Erzberger tried to hide.[33]

Discovered behind a fir tree, the Catholic politician was finished off with three bullets to the head. Falling to the ground, his lifeless body rolled down a short incline until it settled on the forest floor.[34] Picking up their backpacks, the killers disappeared over a ridge before Erzberger's wounded companion could stagger back down the hill to ask for help. By the time he did, it was too dark to collect Erzberger's body, and it stayed there, exposed to the elements, until the following morning. The much-maligned politician had been shot twelve times. Among those happy to see Erzberger gone was Adolf Hitler. In the weeks before his killing, the Nazi Party leader had suggested that death by firing squad was too good for a traitor like Erzberger, who ought to be hanged.[35]

Since Erzberger's assassination took place in Baden and not Bavaria, Munich's chief of police was unable to orchestrate a cover-up and investigators quickly identified two suspects. The men were former members of the Ehrhardt Brigade and belonged to a secret political hit squad named Organization Consul (OC), which had been formed by Hermann Ehrhardt shortly after his 1920 arrival in Munich.[36] Committed to killing Jews, Social Democrats and leftist radicals, OC took inspiration from the infamous *feme* tribunals of the Middle Ages and was recruiting assassins from all over the country.[37]

Erzberger's killers had fled to Munich.[38] Traveling to Bavaria to seek their extradition, police from Baden were shocked to learn that the pair had been allowed to escape to Hungary. Their passage was made possible by Munich's police chief, Pöhner, who reportedly supplied them with fake passports. Organization Consul and Ehrhardt's role in the killings was kept from the public. In the end, one person was brought to trial in connection with the murder, but he was acquitted by a sympathetic court and served no jail time.

The reaction to Erzberger's assassination in Berlin was quite different from the one in Munich. Government officials could no longer ignore the fact that the Bavarian capital was becoming a terrorist training center for far-right radicals.[39] In response to the murder, a state of emergency was declared and the government invoked Article 48 of the Weimar Constitution, which threatened to prosecute anyone who incited violence against government officials. Bavaria's minister-president, Gustav von Kahr, dismissed the state of emergency but soon found himself at odds with the Bavarian state parliament and officials in his own party. Already weakened by authorizing the dissolution of the Einwohnerwehr, Kahr decided to resign as minister-president in September 1921. His replacement, Count Hugo Lerchenfeld of the BVP, was much more moderate than his predecessor. Accordingly, he would be less inclined to look the other way when the Nazis used violence to intimidate their enemies.

AN ORGANIZATION OF IRON

In his new capacity as first chairman of the Nazi Party, Adolf Hitler wasn't about to curb his rhetoric or restrain the Gymnastics and Sports Section just because the government in Berlin was threatening to prosecute troublemakers. He saw intimidation as a political tool and wasn't afraid to use it. Hoping to silence a political rival in Munich, Hitler made plans to disrupt a meeting of the Bayernbund (Bavarian Association), led by the separatist Otto Ballerstedt, at the Löwenbräukeller on September 14, 1921.

On the night of Ballerstedt's meeting, members of Hitler's Gymnastics and Sports Section seated themselves on benches in the Löwenbräukeller's main hall, closest to the speaker's podium. When Ballerstedt ascended the stage to begin his speech amid cheers from his supporters, the lights were suddenly turned off and Hitler's thugs jumped from their seats to surround him. Chanting their Führer's name over and over again, the men attacked Ballerstedt and threw him from the stage. Whether this had been Hitler's intention is unclear, but when the police arrived and found Ballerstedt bleeding from his head on the floor, they shut the meeting down. Subsequently, Ballerstedt decided to press charges—something Hitler hadn't anticipated. Only a few weeks earlier, the Nazi leader might have escaped prosecution, but the change in government precipitated by the resignation of Kahr had also forced Pöhner to step down. Now, under Lerchenfeld's leadership, Bavaria's state government sought to demonstrate that it administered justice without political bias. Hitler was convicted of breaching the peace and sentenced to three months imprisonment—to be served the following year.

Despite the setback, Hitler and the NSDAP continued efforts to expand the party's paramilitary wing. In October 1921, the Nazi Party's Gymnastics and Sports Section was rebranded the Sturmabteilung (Storm Detachment), or SA. A member of the Ehrhardt Brigade was named as its commander. While neither Ernst Röhm nor Hermann Ehrhardt served the SA in an official capacity, both were providing invaluable leadership from the shadows.[40] Like other paramilitary groups, the SA was secretly being trained as an army unit to participate in a military struggle against the Weimar government. Hitler didn't try to undermine Röhm or Ehrhardt's influence. He recognized Röhm's value as one of the most influential officers in the Bavarian Reichswehr. But he was reticent to allow the paramilitary group to become too independent. Whether or not the SA would remain loyal to Adolf Hitler, or be coopted into a larger nationalist movement, remained to be seen.

CHAPTER THIRTEEN

HITLER'S EXPANDING CIRCLE

n 1922, Hermann Ehrhardt's terrorist group, Organization Consul, was ready to murder its next victim. Philipp Scheidemann, the co-leader of the SPD who had proclaimed Germany a republic back in November of 1918, had been spotted in the city of Kassel, walking with his daughter and nine-year-old niece. Under Reich president Ebert, Scheidemann had opposed the revolution and resigned his post as German chancellor in protest over the terms of the Treaty of Versailles. But this didn't alter his status as a "November Criminal" in the eyes of the Far Right. Vandals had trashed the exterior of his home with graffiti.[1] Right-wing journalists had attacked him in the press. Concerned for his own safety, he carried a concealed firearm.

On June 4, Scheidemann was stalked to a park by OC assassins, who waited until he was a good ten meters ahead of his daughter and niece before launching their attack. The killers planned to use prussic acid to kill their quarry. A precursor to Zyklon B—used in the Nazi gas chambers—prussic acid attacks the nervous, circulatory, and respiratory systems, depleting oxygen and resulting in death. Killing Scheidemann with a deadly toxin was a metaphor for the politician's alleged crime of poisoning the home front against the war. While rich in symbolism, it was highly impractical. His daughter Luise remembered watching a man rush past and approach her father with something hidden in his hand.[2] When he caught up with Scheidemann, the man suddenly produced a bulb syringe and squirted the toxic substance into his face at close range. Perhaps by impulse, Scheidemann managed to cover his mouth and deflect some of the poison. Before falling to the ground, where he lost consciousness, he drew his revolver and fired two shots in the direction of his assassin. It was enough to scare the attacker off, and he ran away, together with another man hiding in the bushes.

Amazingly, the SPD politician survived. Scheidemann's thick moustache presumably helped block most of the poison from entering his nose and mouth. This time, the would-be assassins were caught by the authorities, tried, and sentenced to time in prison. But, as was the case with many convicted criminals on the far right, they received special treatment, were released early, and went on to join the Nazi Party. Press coverage of the terrifying episode was widespread, but it wasn't enough to prompt the government to stop Organization Consul's unobstructed murder spree.

Quite apart from the political violence, in 1922 Germany also was experiencing new financial strains as the government tried to keep the economy afloat while paying heavy reparations in accord with the Treaty of Versailles. French authorities were concerned that if Germany couldn't keep its finances in order a budget crisis might interrupt the expected payments. These circumstances frustrated those already embittered by Germany's capitulation at the end of the war.

"WHAT A POWER I HAVE BEHIND ME"

On June 14, 1922, top leaders of Germany's Far Right assembled in Munich for a secret meeting to conspire against the national government. Though bound by their hatred of the "November Criminals" and the desire to reverse the terms of the Treaty of Versailles,[3] the tense, impatient assembly could hardly see eye to eye on anything else. Some lobbied for a march on Berlin; others wanted to reinstall the monarchy; a handful sought secession.

The June 14 meeting brought together a number of notable figures. Among those present were Gustav von Kahr and Erich Ludendorff. Given the opportunity to return to power, Ludendorff bragged that he intended to hang Berlin's Social Democratic leadership and, "with a clear conscience," watch men like Scheidemann and Ebert dangle.[4] Also present was Franz Ritter von Epp, the steely wartime commander who had recently donated Reichswehr funds to Eckart for the purchase of the *Völkischer Beobachter*. A recipient of Germany's highest military honor, the *Pour le Mérite*, Epp was highly critical of Bavarian separatists. Opposing him were Austrians who dreamed of creating a Danubian State. Among them was a participant who made the absurd suggestion that the Habsburgs be ensconced at the head of a new kingdom that merged Bavaria with Austria.[5] And, of course, the assembly included an initiate from the beer halls of Munich: Adolf Hitler. In this crowd, Hitler's background as a lowly private without a university education must have invited skepticism. The assembled officers, politicians, and representatives were men of distinguished rank and pedigree. Yet there was one quality of Hitler's that no one could deny: The man could speak.

Most of those assembled shared Hitler's anti-Semitism. But none in this group saw him as *their* leader. This creature of the lower classes with his silly trench coat and comic moustache was a relative newcomer among the more established figures. Because they underestimated the extent to which the failed war had undermined Germany's confidence in traditional authority, they couldn't yet appreciate Hitler's public appeal. From the outset, it appeared the organizers feared the secret meeting might be hijacked by political grandstanding. To forestall the danger, a chairman, identified as Herr Keller, was appointed to maintain order. It wasn't the first time the group had met. When Keller took the floor, he urged the participants to stay focused, adding that "this time" he hoped positive results would be achieved.[6] While the precise order of speakers and topics cannot be verified, the main discussion focused on two questions: bringing back Bavaria's monarchy, and seceding from the Reich. Hitler favored neither.

As the meeting unfolded with various leaders pressing their partisan objectives, organizers attempted to create consensus. When one of the participants suggested that "each group would have to make concessions," Hitler interjected by sniping that he sounded like "the Jew government" in Berlin.[7] For his impudence, Hitler was censured, and the assembly was urged to give the "cold shoulder" to "braggarts."[8] The Nazi leader must have been angered. Sitting in his seat, he likely began to boil. Finally, when he was no longer able to restrain himself, he took the floor. Stating that he wished to defend himself against personal attacks, Hitler warned that the group was following in the footsteps of "the capitalist Jew-Government."[9] Given their shared hatred of the Jews, Hitler's affront was quite shocking. Invoking the name of "His Excellency [Erich] Ludendorff," he proposed that the best course of action was to "unite for a time with the extremists of the Left, for the purpose of delivering the latter from the hands of the Jews and of making use of them later to get power into our own hands."[10] Hitler's audience must have had a hard time believing what they had just heard. This was heresy. No one in this crowd was willing to work with the hated Left, not even as a strategy. Ludendorff asserted he'd never said such a thing.[11]

Hitler's remarks provoked pandemonium, and someone howled, "Throw him out!"[12] But the Nazi leader pressed on: "Compromises are half measures, of which the nation has had enough. We must act once and for all. If we do not, others will, and we shall be too late."[13] The beer-hall agitator and his audacity were too much to take. The shouting against him became so disruptive that Chairman Keller finally asked him to leave. Bavaria's most conspicuous right-wing leaders were censoring the future German dictator with the confidence that they could move forward without him. On his way out the door, Hitler turned menacingly on the assembly and shouted, "You will live to regret the treachery which you are committing against the German race today. You will recognize too late what a power I have behind me."[14]

"TO THE GALLOWS WITH THE JEW GOVERNMENT"

Ten days later, Hitler began a three-month jail sentence at Stadelheim Prison for his role in the attack on Otto Ballerstedt the previous year. Incarcerated in a facility full of sympathetic nationalists, his stay was hardly uncomfortable. Meanwhile, at a prison where the conditions were far worse, Ernst Toller was just learning about the Nazi leader.

In his autobiography, Toller claimed a fellow inmate shared some illuminating details about Adolf Hitler. According to the unidentified man, Hitler had referred to himself as a Social Democrat during the revolution of 1918–1919.[15] Though the story was never verified, it offers one explanation of Hitler's apparent neutrality during the time of the Soviet Republic. Since all records of his activities in this period were expunged by the Nazis, we will likely never know. The historian Thomas Weber observed, "Hitler, who in painstaking detail described all other periods of his life in *Mein Kampf*, skated at great speed over the first five months after his arrival back in Bavaria."[16]

Toller's fellow inmate went on to describe Hitler as "conceited and puffed-up," like a person who "read many books and digested none."[17] He even knew details about Hitler's postwar hospitalization and purportedly told the playwright that Hitler's blindness was not the result of mustard gas but of shell shock. "That nervous blindness made me thoughtful," Toller wrote in 1933. "A man who can deliberately go blind in the face of things he does not wish to see must possess extraordinary strength of mind."[18]

At Stadelheim Prison, Hitler was not subjected to the deplorable conditions reserved for leftist prisoners like Toller. His cell even had a private toilet.[19] Hitler's only real torment was not being at liberty to exploit current events for propaganda purposes. No sooner had he entered prison, than far away in Berlin

Hermann Ehrhardt's Organization Consul prepared to execute its next victim and set off a firestorm between the national government and the state of Bavaria.

Foreign Minister Walther Rathenau was an implacable patriot and one of the most brilliant minds in the German government. At the head of the war materials division during the First World War, his leadership had been so exceptional that conservatives called him a "savior of the fatherland."[20] But Rathenau was also a Jew. "I am a German of Jewish descent," he once remarked. "My people is the German people, my fatherland is Germany, my religion that German faith which is above all religions."[21] After the war, Rathenau played a critical role in getting the country back on its feet. An opponent of revolution and Bolshevism, he worked tirelessly in negotiations with the Allies to lessen Germany's reparation payments. Believing in interdependence—that no nation could prosper in isolation—he recognized that countries like France would ultimately suffer by trying to impoverish Germany after the war.[22] But his farsighted vision and support for the payment of reparations was largely misunderstood inside the country.[23]

In April of 1922, as German foreign minister, Rathenau successfully negotiated the terms of the Treaty of Rapallo with the Soviet Union. Recognizing the legitimacy of the Soviet government, the agreement restored diplomatic relations between the two countries, and, unlike of the Treaty of Versailles, saved Germany from having to make monetary payments to its former adversary in the east. Despite this achievement, in the newspapers of the Far Right, Rathenau was characterized as an agent of an alleged international conspiracy of Jews. By the summer of 1922, Ehrhardt's OC was ready to take him out. Unlike the attempts on Scheidemann and Erzberger, who were attacked far outside the capital, Rathenau's public execution was staged in Berlin. In the back of his chauffeured car on the morning of June 24, Rathenau was speeding along his route to the foreign ministry when an open-air touring car pulled up alongside him. Witnesses claimed that two of the assailants wore impressive leather coats, and one looked like a clean-shaven officer.[24] Suddenly pulling in front of Rathenau's car and forcing it to stop, one of the assassins leveled a machine gun at the foreign minister and shot him at point-blank range. To make sure he was dead, another heaved a grenade into his car, and when it exploded witnesses claimed the automobile was lifted straight up in the air.[25] In their haste to get away, the assassins hadn't noticed that they'd left Rathenau's chauffeur alive. Unharmed, he succeeded in starting the car and drove his passenger to a doctor, hoping against all odds to save his life. But the foreign minister had already succumbed to his wounds.

Rathenau's 1922 assassination proved once and for all that if you happened to be Jewish and were a prominent politician at the time of Germany's surrender, no amount of patriotism was going to save you from persecution. Whether you were a loyalist or a revolutionary, a hawk or a pacifist, clear-sighted or idealistic, bloodthirsty nationalists wanted to target and kill you. That being said, when compared to the general population of sixty-five million, the number of far-right radicals perpetrating violence in Germany was actually quite small. The problem was that the radicals had powerful backers and sympathetic supporters. In each of the attacks leading up to the foreign minister's murder, the killers had either been protected by the police or coddled by the courts. But the Rathenau assassination would change that.

After the foreign minister's murder, seven hundred thousand Berliners took to the streets in demonstrations. In a scathing reprimand of the poisonous political atmosphere, which condoned Rathenau's murder, the German chancellor, Joseph Wirth, who came to power in October of 1921, attended a session of parliament, and declared, "There stands the enemy that is dripping his poisons into the wounds of our people. The enemy stands on the Right!"[26] Members of the Reichstag agreed that something drastic had to be done. Shortly thereafter, they passed a new law targeting antigovernment groups and imposing harsh penalties on anyone who incited murder or violence. To ensure that justice was served, the government announced the establishment of a special court in Leipzig to prosecute all future offenders; the perpetrators of political crimes could no longer slink away under the protection of sympathetic states. But these developments aroused great hostility in Bavaria. In response, the state parliament issued its own decree, which asserted that in matters pertaining to politics state law superseded national law. Subsequently, in August 1922, fifty thousand nationalists gathered in Munich's Königsplatz to express their support for state's rights.

Released from prison on July 27—two months early for good behavior—Hitler joined the demonstration on the Königsplatz, where he was invited to deliver a speech. Electrifying the crowd with his boast that Bavaria was "the most German land in Germany,"[27] he urged the assembly to stand united against the government in Berlin. Kurt Ludecke, a Bavarian nationalist who would later join the Nazi Party and travel to America to solicit funds from the automobile manufacturer Henry Ford, recalled his feelings listening to Hitler in the Königsplatz: "I do not know how to describe the emotions that swept over me as I heard this man. . . . I felt sure that no one who had heard Hitler that afternoon could doubt that he was the man of destiny, the vitalizing force in the future

of Germany. . . . At once I offered myself to him and to his cause without res-
ervation."[28] Through his persuasive oratory, Hitler was fast becoming the most
influential public speaker in Munich. His propaganda campaign included seditious leaflets, which read, "Rathenau, now he's dead! Ebert and Scheidemann,
however, are still alive. To the gallows with the Jew government!"[29]

In the aftermath of the assassination, the authorities tracked down Rathenau's murderers to a castle outside of Berlin, where the two killers fired on
police. One of the assassins died in the gun battle, and the other turned his
weapon on himself. Organization Consul had lost two assassins, but between
1919 and 1922 the Far Right had perpetrated 354 murders.[30] From the comforts
of his new residence on the outskirts of Munich, Ludendorff cynically remarked
that Erzberger and Rathenau got what they deserved for plunging Germany
into misery.[31] Eleven years later, when the Nazis seized power, Hitler would pay
tribute to Rathenau's assassins by erecting a memorial in their honor, saluting
them as "advance fighters" who died in the struggle for German redemption.[32]

"DISPOSE OF THE RED TERROR FOR GOOD"

The year of 1922 was turning out to be a great one for recruiting in the Nazi
Party. Craftsmen, merchants, businessmen, and white-collar workers were
joining in record numbers and turning the NSDAP into a middle-class movement.[33] On October 8, Julius Streicher, a prominent anti-Semitic leader in the
German Socialist Party, decided to bring his entire Nuremburg chapter over to
the Nazis, and the rest of the DSP soon followed. Unlike the proposed merger
of 1920 that would have forced Hitler to make concessions, Streicher and his
DSP colleagues were now prepared to serve as the Nazi leader's subordinates.
By the end of the year, NSDAP membership would expand to twenty thousand. Though Hitler's movement was growing steadily, the Nazi leader was
always looking for new ways to expand the ranks. One such opportunity came
in October when he received an invitation to join German Day festivities in the
city of Coburg.

Situated on Bavaria's northern border with Thuringia, the region around
Coburg was rumored to be dominated by Marxist trade unions[34] and was allegedly suffering under the "Red Terror."[35] To infuse German Day with a bit of radicalism, a local leader of Bavaria's largest anti-Semitic organization, the Schutz
und Trutzbund (Nationalist Protection and Defiance Federation), invited the

Nazis and other nationalist groups to come to Coburg.[36] Fearing violence, trade union and SPD representatives asked government officials to ban the celebration. Officials chose instead to forbid the Nazis from marching through the city. But the last-minute decision was apparently made when Hitler's group was already on its way.

Hitler brought with him eight hundred stormtroopers from the SA. To build camaraderie among the men, he made special arrangements for the entire group to be transported together on a chartered train. Though they didn't yet possess uniforms, the SA men wore swastika armbands and carried swastika flags. Some were armed with rubber truncheons. In Hitler's logic, Communists and Socialists across Germany had been interfering with nationalist demonstrations since the end of the war, and the SA was going to Coburg to restore freedom of assembly. After a spirited train ride, Hitler and the SA discovered hundreds of protesters waiting for them at Coburg station. On the platform, the Nazi leader was informed that a decree banning the SA from striking up its band, unfurling its flags, and marching through the city had been ordered.

In the context of freedom of assembly and the proud tradition of holding parades and festivals throughout Germany, the local decree seemed to violate basic rights. Sensing an opportunity to win public support for his movement, Hitler decided to defy the order and march. An SA band broke into music, Nazi flags were unfurled, and the stormtroopers began a disciplined procession through the city center. Local police were unprepared to stop them. As the stormtroopers made their way along the parade route, protesters hurled insults, spat at them, threw rocks, and instigated fights. When the men could no longer take it, violent skirmishes erupted, and the protesters were beaten back. According to police records, local workers were responsible for provoking the violence.[37]

"We had dared to oppose a brutal attack with fists and sticks," Hitler wrote in *Mein Kampf*, "instead of with pacifist songs."[38] Later that evening, while Hitler was speaking to twenty-five hundred people in a beer hall, Marxists were organizing a protest for the following day in Coburg's main square, where they hoped to draw ten thousand workers.[39] When Hitler later learned of the planned protest, he ordered his men to march to the city square and "dispose of the Red Terror for good."[40] However, only a few hundred Marxists showed up. Sporadic street fighting continued, but the opposition proved to be no match for the SA. As Hitler and his entourage made their way back to the train station on October 15, residents were cheering them on.

Later, in the Bavarian parliament, Social Democrats blamed the German Day violence at Coburg on the radical Right. Conservatives countered that freedom of assembly had been violated. In the end, no charges were brought against Hitler. "Thus at Coburg," he later recorded, "the citizens' equality in the eyes of the law was restored for the first time since the year 1914."[41]

The SA had demonstrated fearlessness in the face of intimidation, and their success in winning street battles turned out to be a boon for recruiting. Everyone forgot that the German Day celebration had been organized by a rival party, the Schutz und Trutzbund. For the first time, the Nazis were gaining popularity outside of Munich. More importantly, Hitler's conclusion that violence was an important tool in winning favor with the German people was reinforced.

"THE COURAGE TO ACT"

In late October of 1922, news arrived in Germany that the fascist politician Benito Mussolini had led a stunning march on Rome and seized power in Italy. His achievement reflected the aspirations of German nationalists who dreamed of reversing the humiliation of the Treaty of Versailles and taking power in Berlin. "We march on Rome to give Italy her full liberty," read an Italian *Fascisti* press release, "to give the Italian people an Italy as was dreamed of [by] the half million dead in the great war, and by our own dead who continued at war during peace."[42] Mussolini's National Fascist Party and its military wing, the Black Shirts, had used violence and intimidation against their Socialist adversaries and purportedly "saved Italy from Bolshevism."[43] For Hitler, Mussolini's special role in the takeover underscored the power of a charismatic leader to change the destiny of a nation. "At that time—I admit it openly—I conceived a profound admiration for the great man beyond the Alps," Hitler wrote in *Mein Kampf,* "whose ardent love for his people inspired him not to bargain with Italy's internal enemies but to use all possible ways and means in an effort to wipe them out."[44]

Taking stock of Mussolini's example, Hitler imagined himself leading a march on Berlin to achieve a great German revival. "So it will be with us," he was reported as saying. "We only have to have the courage to act."[45] The Nazis wasted no time appropriating Mussolini's success for their own purposes. At Munich's Festsaal on November 3, Hermann Esser—an able spokesman and party member who had supported Hitler since the early days—declared, "Germany's Mussolini is Adolf Hitler." Inspired by the Italian fascist gesture of extending an arm with a closed fist, the Nazis began using the famous *Sieg-Heil* salute. Mussolini's title, *Il Duce* (the leader), used to denote his absolute authority, further encouraged the practice of referring to Hitler as *unser Führer* (our leader). Inflated in the press, Mussolini's march on Rome was actually far less impressive than the Nazis were led to believe. As it turns out, the Black Shirts never marched on Rome, and Mussolini achieved power primarily because the Italian king had asked him to form a new government in order to avoid bloodshed.[46]

"A MASTERLY PERFORMANCE"

In 1922, some of the most influential and sinister people in the history of the Third Reich joined the movement. These individuals would go on to play indispensable roles in military affairs, diplomacy, fundraising, and propaganda under Hitler. Most conspicuous in this fresh crop of converts was the flamboyant Hermann Göring. Around the time that Mussolini was achieving power in Italy, Göring went to a demonstration in Munich in the hopes of hearing Hitler orate.

Charming and intelligent, the veteran fighter ace of the First World War shared many of Hitler's attitudes. Observing the Nazi leader at close range, the twenty-eight-year-old resolved to attend the NSDAP's weekly gathering the following Monday. Listening to Hitler speak, Göring claimed he was mesmerized by convictions that were spoken "word for word as if from my own soul."[47] Paying a courtesy call to Hitler later that week, Göring introduced himself and inquired if he might be of service to the Nazi movement.

Hitler could hardly disguise his excitement. A recip-

Hermann Göring

ient of the Pour le Mérite, Göring was a public relations godsend. A nationally recognized war hero and fighter pilot, he was Manfred von Richthofen's successor in the Red Baron's fabled fighter squadron. With his blond hair and blue eyes, dashing looks and square jaw, young Göring looked like a prototype for the Aryan race. In his conversation with Hitler, he expressed complete agreement with the Nazi program. Eager to harness the war hero's popularity for recruiting, Hitler proposed that he immediately take a position in the NSDAP. But Göring demurred. Instead, he smartly agreed to assume leadership two months into the future, when it didn't look like he was joining simply to get promoted. At least that is what he told Allied interrogators after the Second World War.

While under psychiatric observation before his war crimes trial at Nuremberg, Göring displayed what is now understood to be "classic psychopathic behavior" and "sociopathic thinking"[48] People with Göring's condition have an extraordinary capacity for manipulation and will go to great lengths to appear humble. As medical journalist Jack El-Hai pointed out in his book *The Nazi and the Psychiatrist*, "His loyalty to the party was not about Hitler, not about Germany, and least of all about the preservation of a supposed Aryan race. His aim was to advance Hermann Göring, and he had joined the Nazis to lead a rising party."[49] Göring told Hitler what he thought the Nazi leader wanted to hear as a means to fulfill his own narcissistic goals. Hitler liked what he was hearing and understood how his alliance with Göring could be beneficial. The former flying ace thought the same thing.

At the end of the two-month waiting period, Hitler promoted Göring to lead the SA. Applying the principle of "divide and conquer," Hitler was securing his own authority by setting Göring against Röhm and Ehrhardt, who had become powerful figures in the SA. The antagonism would go on for twelve more years until it ended abruptly in 1934 when Röhm was killed during the infamous "Night of the Long Knives." But that was far in the future.

The photographer Heinrich Hoffmann, who would do more to enhance Hitler's image than any other artist, also met the Nazi leader in 1922, though his introduction was less cordial. On October 30, Hoffmann received an unusual telegram from an American newspaper agency, saying it was willing to pay one hundred dollars for a picture of Hitler. "What a fee!"[50] Hoffmann marveled in his memoirs. Considering the fact that a glass of beer cost about 5 cents at the time, one hundred dollars was a lot of money. Five dollars was the usual asking price for a photo of a high-profile German politician. Why were the Americans willing to pay so much for a picture of Hitler, who was barely known outside of

Munich? Hoffman wondered. Consulting with his friend and fellow drinker Dietrich Eckart, he was surprised to learn that the Nazi leader didn't allow photographs. When Hoffmann protested that public figures didn't have the right to deny picture taking, Eckart tried to help him understand Hitler's reasoning: "Everybody was hearing and reading about him. But nobody had ever seen a picture of him. People were most curious and intrigued, and that was why they flocked to his meetings. They came out of curiosity; but they left as enrolled members of the movement."[51] Eckart was apparently trying to arouse sympathy because he knew the photographer had joined the Nazi Party two years earlier and thought he took it very seriously. If Hoffmann realized that distributing a picture of Hitler could undermine recruiting, he might refrain from taking one. But Eckart overestimated his friend's devotion to the party and didn't realize he was driven by greed. Ignoring the publisher's plea, the photographer set out to capture Hitler on film.

A few days later, Hoffmann discovered that the printer for the Nazi Party newspaper was right across the street from his photo studio on Schellingstraße. Not only that, Hitler's chauffeured car was often parked outside, suggesting that the Nazi leader paid regular visits. Like the paparazzi that he was, Hoffmann started staking out the location and spending long hours waiting to snap a picture of Hitler. It was tedious and boring work. One day, after obtaining proof that his quarry was inside the building, Hoffmann grabbed his camera and waited anxiously on the street for Hitler to exit the front door. Hours passed, but no Hitler. Hoffmann was getting irritated. Finally, the Nazi leader appeared with three bodyguards and the photographer stiffened.

Click: Hoffmann snapped his photo. "The next moment I found my wrists gripped by pretty rough hands," the photographer wrote in his memoirs. "The escorting three had flung themselves upon me! One of them grabbed me by the throat, and a furious struggle ensued for possession of the camera, which I was determined not to surrender at any cost."[52] But he was no match for the bodyguards, who wrestled his camera away and destroyed his picture. Hoffmann accused them of violating his rights, but the bodyguards were indifferent and climbed into Hitler's car for their getaway. "With my tie awry and my camera ruined I stood there," Hoffmann continued, "and Adolf Hitler just smiled at me."[53] Decades later, in 1942, Hitler would brag that he'd evaded photographers for a total of four years. Though he'd been roughed up, the episode was not convincing enough to dissuade Hoffmann from his goal. In the coming months his obsession would lead him to try a much more elaborate scheme.

The year would also bring an influential and enterprising American busi-nessman into Hitler's orbit. Ernst "Putzi" Hanfstaengl was a half-German Harvard graduate living in Munich. Working as an international art dealer specializing in reproductions, Hanfstaengl was well known in German high society. Receiving a telephone call from an old Harvard schoolmate who had been appointed to the American embassy in Berlin, Hanfstaengl was asked to look after an American military attaché named Truman Smith, who was coming to Munich to check out the political scene. In the Bavarian capital, Captain Smith was taken around and introduced to all the city's Far Right heavyweights, including Ludendorff and Kahr.

Over lunch on the final day of his assignment, Smith told Hanfstaengl that "the most remarkable fellow" he'd met was Adolf Hitler. When Hanfstaengl scoffed, Smith urged him to take his press ticket and go see Hitler speak that night at the Kindl-Keller beer hall. "I have the impression he's going to play a big part," Smith told him, "and whether you like him or not he certainly knows what he wants." Later that evening at the Kindl-Keller, Hanfstaengl took a seat in the press section of the rowdy beer hall. When Hitler arrived, he snickered at the Nazi leader's appearance. Wearing a dark suit, a stiff collar, and his peculiar little moustache, Hitler looked "like a waiter in a railway-station."[54] But when the Nazi leader opened his mouth, Hanfstaengl was transfixed.

"In a quiet, reserved voice," the Harvard graduate later wrote, "he drew a picture of what had happened in Germany since November 1918." One after the other, Hitler described the painful postwar events that had brought shame and misery to the German people. He appealed convincingly to ex-servicemen, patriots, and the impoverished. When he sensed he was winning over the audi-ence, Hitler switched gears and attacked the Jews, the Communists, and the Socialists. "All these enemies of the people, he declared would one day be *beseitigt*, literally removed or done away with," Hanfstaengl wrote in his memoirs. "It was a perfectly proper word to use in the circumstances, and I read no sinister con-notation into it."[55] Observing Hitler's audience, Hanfstaengl noted that, "The hubbub and mug clattering had stopped and they were drinking in every word."

When Hitler finished, Hanfstaengl wrote, "The audience responded with a final outburst of frenzied cheering, hand clapping, and a cannonade of table pounding. It sounded like a demonical rattle of thousands of hailstones rebounding on the surface of a gigantic drum. It had been a masterly perfor-mance."[56] Hanfstaengl hadn't expected to be impressed, and his mind began to flood with questions. "What was in the back of this curious man's brain?"

Hanfstaengl asked himself. "I felt the impulse to meet him in a smaller circle and talk to him alone."[57] Sensing that Truman-Smith was correct and that Hitler was going to play an important role in the future of German politics, he waited around after the speech so that he could speak to the Nazi leader. "He seemed to have no conception of the part America had played in winning the war and viewed European problems from a narrow, continental standpoint," the Harvard graduate later recorded. "Here, at least, I felt I could put him right."[58]

Introducing himself to the Nazi orator, Hanfstaengl offered his friendship by saying, "I agree with ninety-five percent of what you said and would very much like to talk to you about the rest sometime." Replying in a friendly and modest way, Hitler accepted the invitation by saying, "I am sure we shall not have to quarrel about the odd five percent."[59] Tossing and turning in his bed later that night, Hanfstaengl couldn't get Hitler out of his mind: "Where all our conservative politicians and speakers were failing abysmally to establish any contact with the ordinary people, this self-made man, Hitler, was clearly succeeding in presenting a non-Communist program to exactly those people whose support we needed."[60]

A few days later, the Harvard grad brought his wife, Helene, to listen to the Nazi leader at the Circus Krone, and she became an instant supporter as well. Their experience was similar to the one recurring week after week as thousands of newcomers came to hear Hitler and underwent a political awakening. Hanfstaengl had serious connections with the wealthy elite and would soon be willing to help Hitler solicit monetary assistance for the Nazi Party. In fact, he would provide from his own pocket the funds that allowed the *Völkischer Beobachter* to become a daily newspaper.

Göring, Hoffmann, and Hanfstaengl would all go on to play infamous roles in the service of the Führer. Göring and his

Ernst Hanfstaengl (center).

crimes would end up dwarfing the latter two. Yet each was compromised by a blinding self-interest that would allow them to participate in a criminal regime. For Hoffmann and Hanfstaengl, this participation was indirect. Hanfstaengl actually fled Germany before the Second World War, switched sides to help the Americans bring down Hitler, and did not participate in the genocide of the Final Solution. Heinrich Hoffmann's ambitions kept him in the business realm, and he never took a leadership position in the Nazi Party. Nevertheless, each man had helped to create the conditions for Hitler's rise in Germany, contributing their robust energy, dedication, and creativity. None of them would kill the victims of the Third Reich with their own hands. Like many other Hitler confidants, they didn't have to.

CHAPTER FOURTEEN

DELUSIONS OF GRANDEUR

"AN AIR OF RESPECTABILITY"

When Adolf Hitler started spending time with Ernst Hanfstaengl in late 1922, the German-American was afforded a rare opportunity to observe the inner workings of the Nazi Party. In friendly contact with some of Hitler's subordinates, he started attending regular meetings and showing up at various party functions. Determined to become Hitler's close adviser and help him become worldly, he had concluded that it was better to remain outside the party. But not everyone trusted his motives, and presumptuous Nazi officials tried to push him to join and make regular financial contributions.[1] "The affairs of the party seemed surrounded by this air of conspiracy and intrigue," Hanfstaengl wrote in his book *Hitler: The Missing Years*.[2]

One day over lunch, Hitler asked Hanfstaengl about Germany's standing in the world. Responding in detail about the importance of establishing a friend-ship with the United States, the Harvard graduate recalled the Nazi leader "listening with great attention and never attempting to interrupt."[3] Despite Hitler's curiosity, Hanfstaengl believed his new friend suffered from a limited continental mindset encouraged by the "ignorant fanatics who were his closet cronies."[4] While Hanfstaengl approved of Eckart as "a man of education,"[5] he loathed the jealous-minded Rudolf Hess and the Estonian immigrant Alfred Rosenberg, whom he considered a "charlatan" and a "troublemaker."[6]

Masquerading as an expert on Russia and the Balkan States, Rosenberg was telling Hitler what he wanted to hear by falsely claiming that the Jews were behind the Russian Revolution. At one time, he'd even suggested that Vladimir Lenin was Jewish. According to Hanfstaengl, Rosenberg's primary defects were his eastern European filter for analyzing geopolitics and his anticlerical fanaticism, which was alienating Bavarian Catholics. Though Hanfstaengl tried to warn Hitler about Rosenberg's flaws, the Nazi leader didn't seem concerned. He was more interested in Hanfstaengl's company because he was one of the few people who could make him relax.

Unlike party subordinates who were constantly vying for power, Hanfstaengl was easygoing and didn't seem to want anything from him. One day when he was feeling particularly tense, Hitler asked the Harvard graduate to play some music to sooth his nerves. When his six-foot-four friend hunched over an upright piano in the corridor of Hitler's apartment building and began playing *Die Meistersinger*, by Richard Wagner, the Nazi leader was instantly transformed. Since his teenage years in Linz, Hitler had been a devoted fan of Wagner. Strutting about the room, waving his arms like a conductor and whistling to the music in perfect pitch, his spirits were completely restored.[7] From that time forward, whenever Hitler felt like he needed a boost, he would ask Hanfstaengl to play Wagner.[8]

Hitler also developed an infatuation with Hanfstaengl's alluring wife, Helene, and made frequent visits to their flat on the edge of Schwabing. Watching the Nazi leader bring his wife flowers, kiss her hand, and flash her adoring looks, Hanfstaengl tried to brush it off as an innocent crush. "I tell you he is a neuter," Helene insisted when the pair discussed Hitler's sexuality.[9] The Austrian immigrant was also a hit with their one-year-old son, Egon. One time when the boy was inconsolable after scraping his knee on a table leg carved in the shape of a lion, Hitler slapped the offending figurine and admonished it to never bite him again. "And of course, Egon beamed," Hanfstaengl wrote. "It became a regular play between them. Every time Hitler came he would slap the lion and say to the boy, 'Now, has he been behaving himself?'"[10] The Nazi leader's rapport with Egon was no fluke. Hitler was able to be charming when he wished, and his ability to be personable was one of his innate gifts. Curious about his upbringing, Hanfstaengl tried several times to get Hitler to open up about his early life in Vienna, but he always kept his mouth shut. No one could get Hitler to talk about his youth.

In the winter of 1922–1923, Hanfstaengl started taking Hitler to meetings and on visits to the homes of Munich's wealthy elite. A few years earlier, the Nazi leader had disavowed marriage. Agreeing with Eckart that he was more likely to win the female vote if he remained a bachelor, Hitler swore off dating, at least in public.[11] This made him all the more attractive to the wives of affluent nationalists such as Helene Bechstein of the Bechstein piano company and Elsa Bruckmann, whose husband was a wealthy publisher. Hoping to give Munich's most eligible bachelor a proper makeover, the two matrons competed with one another to transform the Nazi leader into a proper gentleman. They offered lessons in etiquette, gave him fashion tips, and bought him expensive clothing to make him presentable in Munich's salons.

The homeless drifter that had once slept on park benches in Vienna was outfitted with dinner jackets, broad-brimmed hats, and patent leather shoes.[12] Hanfstaengl watched in horror as his fashion-clueless friend attempted to integrate some of these items into his everyday attire. The gifts were of little help to the NSDAP. On one occasion, Hanfstaengl joked that the Nazi Party might last a bit longer if only Helene Bechstein would part with the jewelry around her neck. Catching his drift, she gifted Hitler several objects of art that he could sell. "Hitler seemed to think that I would give an air of respectability to his begging expeditions," Hanfstaengl later wrote, "and we went on several trips round Munich and its environs visiting prominent citizens."[13] Surrounded by academics, aristocrats, and industrialists, who all came to see the man that everyone was talking about, Hitler acquired valuable insight into Germany's respectable classes. While his initial efforts to acquire funds were largely unsuccessful, he was learning how to win favor among the elite—a skill that would prove invaluable in the future.

Though few have drawn a direct connection between Hitler's failure to procure financial assistance and Germany's troubled economy, there was no denying that the people were facing tough financial times. Ever since Rathenau's assassination, the value of the German mark had been in sharp decline. In June 1922, seven days after the foreign minister's murder, the exchange rate of German marks to US dollars was 401 to 1.[14] A few weeks later, it had slid to 527 to 1. Only six years earlier, the mark had been worth a hundred times more. Frugal Germans who survived the war and its aftermath without spending their hard-earned cash now wished they had. The cruelty of inflation was embodied by a thousand-mark bank note that could barely pay for a tram ticket.

Seeing an opportunity to win converts to his movement, Hitler blamed the government in Berlin and its weak policies for devaluing the currency and causing the people misery. It was just the sort of situation that the Nazi orator could spin to his advantage. Desperate for encouragement and relief, new audiences flocked to hear him speak. "In describing the difficulties of the housewife without enough money to buy the food her family needed," Hanfstaengl later wrote, "he would produce just the phrases she would have used herself to describe her difficulties, if she had been able to formulate them. Where other national orators gave the painful impression of talking down to their audience, he had this priceless gift of expressing exactly their own thoughts."[15] Hitler was planting the idea that Germany's impoverished classes would be better off when a dictator ruled the fatherland. "Mussolini has shown what a disciplined minority can do," he explained to listeners. "In our country we shall have to do the same if we want to avoid ruin."[16] Then, in January 1923, a new crisis provided Hitler yet another opportunity to win public support.

"NO JEW SHALL EVER TOUCH THIS FLAG"

On January 11, 1923, French and Belgian troops crossed the German border and occupied the Ruhr. The Reich had defaulted on reparations payments by failing to turn over a massive shipment of telegraph poles.[17] In response, the French president sent an army to occupy Germany's industrial heartland and control the nation's rich coal assets. In the streets of Essen, residents watched armed French soldiers dressed in steel helmets and wool overcoats march in a procession of trucks, armored personnel carriers, and tanks. Unwilling to launch a counterstrike against the invaders, the German government in Berlin announced its support for a "passive resistance" campaign. Assured that the government would cover their lost wages, thousands of factory workers in the Ruhr walked off the job, and production ground to a halt.

The crisis had the unintended effect of destabilizing the German economy and caused the currency to plummet like never before: It now took 17,000 marks to buy 1 US dollar.[18] Across the country, nationalists and patriots were outraged and ready to go to war with France. But Hitler had a different idea. He suggested that the real enemy was the government in Berlin. "No matter what form of resistance was decided upon," Hitler later wrote in *Mein Kampf,* "the first prerequisite for taking action was the elimination of the Marxist poison from the body of the nation."[19] According to Hitler, that meant deposing the "November Criminals" still in power.

At a party gathering in mid-January, Hitler suggested that the NSDAP would be ready to take action against the government when the time came and implied that the Nazis were preparing for a march on Berlin.[20] "We are powerful enough to proceed by ourselves," he assured an audience in Munich's Café Neumayer.[21] This was just the sort of thing to fire up young recruits. In Germany, it was the boys who'd been too young to participate in the First World War who were most eager to prove themselves in a battle to defend the fatherland. The response to Hitler's aggressive posturing was so strong that a Nazi Party business office had to shut down for a day because there were too many applications to process.[22] But Hitler's recruiting tactic was also risky. Not only was it untrue that the party was ready to take on the national government by itself, recruits were likely to walk away if Hitler couldn't deliver on his promise.

Later that month, as they made final preparations for Nazi Party Day celebrations scheduled in Munich for the end of January, Hitler and his colleagues received a sudden shock. The planned festivities, which included twelve party rallies in the city's largest beer halls on January 27, leading to a flag consecration ceremony and a parade for the SA on January 28 were being shut down. Twenty-four hours before they were to begin, the Bavarian state government, under a new minister-president, Eugen von Knilling of the BVP, had declared a state of emergency. Having learned that Social Democrats were planning a counter-demonstration, the government authorized the ban to prevent the two groups from colliding in the streets and starting a riot. More importantly, officials feared that Hitler was planning to launch a putsch. The last-minute ban gave the Nazi leader little time to save face. Supporters from all over the country were already arriving in Munich to participate in the festivities. How would it look if the man who'd been campaigning against the government suddenly backed down when it tried to reign him in?

Meeting with police officials, Hitler pledged to defy the ban and stated that if the police opened fire on the SA, he would take the first bullet. "Hitler was in an awkward position," Röhm recalled in his memoirs. "He had stuck his neck out, and to back down now would cause him an intolerable loss of face."[23] Röhm used his connections in the Reichswehr to set up a meeting with General Otto von Lossow, commander of the Bavarian Reichswehr, and Hitler "pledged his word guaranteeing a peaceful rally"[24] if the Nazis were allowed to go forward with their plans. Repeating his promise to former Bavarian minister-president Kahr to forgo a putsch, the Nazi leader succeeded in convincing both men to speak on his behalf to the sitting minister-president. Informed of Hitler's promise, Knilling proposed to lift the ban on the condition that the Nazis refrain from marching through the old city, reduce the number of beer hall meetings to six, and cancel the outdoor rally. Hitler accepted the terms. Over the next three days, he would violate every one of them.

Having acquired a Benz convertible, Hitler crisscrossed the city to attend twelve beer hall rallies in a single day. Decorated with bright new party flags, and filled with animated members wearing swastika armbands and exchanging salutes, the mass meetings gave the impression that the NSDAP had entered a new stage of development. In a homogeneous society beset by inflation and an injured national pride, more and more people yearned for a confident leader with a plan to get the country out of the mire. Few lost sleep wondering if Hitler really intended to remove the Jews from Germany. Participants relished the opportunity to sit down with likeminded friends over beer and sausage and hear a hope-filled message that would take them away from their nagging worries. When the Nazi leader finally made his entrance, supporters leapt to their feet and cheered.

As he made his way to each podium, Hitler cautiously scanned the crowds. In the wake of so many political murders, he'd become more vigilant when making public appearances. "He passed very close to me," recalled a prominent Munich professor, "and I saw that this was a different person from the one I had met here and there in private houses; his narrow, pale features were concentrated in wrath, cold flames leaped from his piercing eyes, which seemed to search right and left for possible enemies, as if to cast them down. Was it the mass audience that gave him this uncanny power? Or did he empower the audience with his own inner strength?"[25]

The following day, on the parade grounds at Marsfeld, six thousand SA troops gathered in the crisp winter air to watch a flag consecration ceremony.[26] The solemn rites of the Nazi Party Day celebrations would later become infamous when they were repeated at Nuremberg and spread throughout the world in black and white newsreels. "No Jew shall ever touch this flag," Hitler assured the assembly, "it shall wave before us throughout all of Germany in the march to victory, and pave the way for the flag of our new German Reich."[27] When the ceremony was over, the SA brazenly marched through the heart of the old city. The police made no attempt to stop it. For better or worse, on this day, the Nazis could do whatever they wanted.

It was no small thing that Röhm had interceded on Hitler's behalf to arrange a meeting with Lossow and overturn the ban on Nazi Party Day celebrations. By taking swift action in support of Hitler, he'd saved the Nazi leader great embarrassment. But Röhm did not subscribe to the idea that the SA was Hitler's private army. He saw the group at the center of a much larger militia movement.[28] In February, Röhm took steps to realize that vision when he promoted an alliance between Bavaria's top paramilitary groups. Participating in joint training maneuvers, the alliance appeared to be getting ready for a fight against the French and the Belgians but was more likely preparing for a confrontation with Berlin.[29] Conspiracies against the Weimar government were afoot, and prominent Reichswehr officers including General von Lossow were involved.

"HE WAS STILL MALLEABLE"

In April 1923, Hitler decided to return to Berlin to solicit financial assistance for the NSDAP from one of Eckart's friends in the capital. Bringing Hanfstaengl and two others with him, his car was suddenly stopped at a roadblock in Saxony where Communists had taken control of the state and placed a bounty on Hitler's head. If the Nazi leader's identity was discovered at the checkpoint, he would likely have been thrown in jail, or even possibly killed. "I don't think any of us said anything, there was no time," Hanfstaengl recorded in his memoirs. "But I saw Hitler tense [up] and his hand take a firm grip on his heavy whip, as we came to a stop." Pretending to be a paper manufacturer on his way to the Leipzig Fair, accompanied by his valet and two other men, Hanfstaengl adopted a broken-German accent and eventually convinced the militia to let them pass. "My papers were written in English," the Harvard graduate wrote, "and they made no attempt to look at the documents of the others, but waved us on in surly fashion."[30]

Though he repeatedly thanked Hanfstaengl for saving his life, Hitler apparently bristled at the suggestion that he was a valet.[31] Later, in Berlin, their efforts to secure funding from Eckart's associate fell flat, and the entourage departed for Munich. Stopping for a picnic on the journey home, Hanfstaengl and Hitler discussed politics. "The most important thing in the next war," the Nazi leader declared, "will be to make sure that we control the grain and food supplies of western Russia."[32] Appalled by this narrow line of thinking, Hanfstaengl suspected that Rosenberg was behind the stupid idea. "Even if you overrun western Russia it will not help in the long run," he countered. "You can have all the wheat in the world but you need more than that to fight wars. The country to reckon with is America, and not only do they have more wheat than you can ever capture, but more iron and more steel and more coal . . . and more people. If you have them on the other side you will lose any future war before you start it."[33]

Though he had made a convincing argument, Hanfstaengl concluded it wasn't sinking in when the Nazi leader grunted and changed the subject. Despite his frustration, the Harvard graduate wasn't prepared to give up trying to shape Hitler's ideas. "I was probably entirely wrong in supposing that they could ever be influenced," he wrote in his book, "but in many respects he was still malleable and I looked on his false conceptions as something that might be successfully combated."[34]

"THE GREATEST HUMILIATION OF HIS LIFE"

In April, Communists and Socialists in Munich received government permission to hold a parade in the city to celebrate International Workers Day on May 1. Outraged that Germany's "mortal enemies"[35] would be allowed to march in the streets, Hitler alerted the government that he would stop the parade in its tracks if it weren't banned. The Red celebration, he warned, was "an insult to the overwhelming majority of the city, who saw in the red flag of May 1 the blood of the [Luitpold] hostages of 1919 and the painful symbol of the collapsed fatherland."[36] To undermine the May Day celebration, the Nazis spread rumors that the Reds intended to use it to launch a putsch of their own. "Throughout April there were persistent rumors that the Communist Party intended to transform their normal May Day demonstration into a coup d'état and to seize power,"[37] Heinrich Hoffmann wrote in his memoirs. But the government would not retract its support for the May Day parade. Consequently, Hitler began a quiet campaign to assemble a strike force comprised of SA men and mercenaries from the recently established paramilitary alliance organized by Röhm.

Early on the morning of May 1, while Communists and Socialists were assembling at the Theresienwiese, seven kilometers away at Oberwiesenfeld (the future site of Munich's Olympic Park) Adolf Hitler and units of the SA were gathering with members of the alliance. A significant portion of these men hailed from the Freikorps. To them, May 1 conjured memories of the defeat of the second Soviet Republic. Awaiting their instructions to march against the parade, two thousand far-right ruffians—armed with rifles and machine guns procured from Reichswehr armories—struck up formations and began mock maneuvers. Still smoldering over Hitler's defiance of Minister-President Knilling back in January, the government was not willing to let the Nazi leader double-cross it again. As the right-wing militias conducted their early morning maneuvers at Oberwiesenfeld, they didn't notice that police and Reichswehr forces were slowly surrounding them.

When Hitler realized that government forces intended to stop them, he started pacing. Colleagues described him as lost in thought, wearing his first class Iron Cross, and carrying a steel helmet.[38] Hours passed but Hitler couldn't decide what to do. When a Reichswehr commando approached him and demanded that his forces turn over their weapons and go home, Hitler decided to back down. Reluctantly, the men began handing in their firearms and departing the field. To cheer them up, the Nazi leader cried out, "Our day will come soon."[39] But he likely knew his words sounded hollow. Decades later, Hitler would describe the May Day defeat as the "greatest humiliation of his life."[40] As they made their way back to Munich through Schwabing, Hitler and his colleagues stumbled onto two Communists coming home from the May Day festivities. Tearing a red flag out of their hands, Hitler's group proceeded to burn it. It was but a small consolation. The May Day parade in Munich had gone off without incident. In Berlin, twenty-five thousand Communists had marched as well; in Dresden, another thousand.[41] The resurgence of the KPD seemed to prove that the Far Right still had a legitimate opposition.

The May Day defeat was a public relations disaster for Hitler and the Nazi Party. Foreign diplomats stationed in Munich suspected that the NSDAP was "on the wane."[42] The former commander of Bavaria's Einwohnerwehr called Hitler "a small time demagogue who can only sling slogans."[43] But the Nazi leader was capable of learning from his mistakes. The episode had taught him a valuable lesson: the key to a successful putsch was the support of the military. Without it, any coup was likely to fail before it got started.

"DELUSIONS OF GRANDEUR"

In May of 1923, Hitler made one of his first trips to the Bavarian Alps to spend a few weeks under the mountains at Obersalzberg. Deposited by train at the popular tourist destination of Lake Königssee, Hitler was reportedly forced to backtrack to Berchtesgaden by foot and make the perilous walk up the hill to Obersalzberg, where he had reservations at the Pension Moritz. There he met up with Eckart, who was ducking an order to appear in the special court at Leipzig to answer charges of sullying the reputation of Reich president Friedrich Ebert in the pages of the *Völkischer Beobachter*. According to Hitler, Eckart was "very much moved"[44] that his protégé came to see him. Arriving after dark, Hitler had no way of knowing how beautiful the Obersalzberg area was. Decades later, he described his astonishment upon waking up the next morning and looking out the window: "What a lovely view over the valley! A countryside of indescribable beauty. I'd fallen in love with the landscape."[45]

Situated just below Hoher Göll Mountain and looking across at the Untersberg, where legend had it that the German king Frederick Barbarossa was buried, Obersalzberg offered spectacular views of Watzmann Mountain to the south and Salzburg Castle in the north. In the 1960s, Robert Wise chose this location to film mountain scenes for *The Sound of Music*. The pristine alpine landscape, dotted with farms, inns, and forested trails, so possessed Hitler that he later rented a chalet just below the Pension Moritz, which was eventually bought and transformed into his state residence, the Berghof. Between 1934 and 1944, he would spend nearly a third of each year at the Obersalzberg. But on this trip, Hitler's respite was interrupted by unsettling news from the occupied Ruhr.

Back in March, Freikorps agitators had entered the Ruhr to carry out acts of sabotage against the French and the Belgians. Among them was a former officer and veteran of the Kapp-Lüttwitz Putsch named Leo Schlageter. With slicked back blonde hair and a tidy appearance, Schlageter looked a bit like Kurt Eisner's killer, Anton Arco-Valley. While visiting Munich the previous November, Schlageter had attended a Nazi rally and heard Hitler speak.[46] Mesmerized by the Nazi orator, he started telling friends and acquaintances in northern Germany about Hitler. Then, on March 15, Schlageter participated in blowing up a bridge vital to the French army. Betrayed by colleagues, he was eventually captured and held prisoner by the occupying army. Later, on May 26, he was brought before a French firing squad and executed in Düsseldorf.

Schlageter had allegedly joined the Nazi Party in Munich after hearing Hitler speak. Whether that was true or not, he became an instant martyr to the Far Right. To claim Schlageter as their own, the Nazis sent thousands of SA men to the Ruhr to participate in his funeral parade.[47] Far away at Obersalzberg, Hitler was unable to attend the funeral. But when news surfaced that various far-right-wing groups were planning to conduct a ceremony in Munich's Königsplatz to commemorate Schlageter's sacrifice, Hanfstaengl felt it was imperative that Hitler attend.[48] Rushing by train to Obersalzberg, he tracked down Hitler and urged him to return to Munich. Finding the Nazi orator in a bad mood, he claimed that Hitler refused on the grounds that he would be only one of many speakers that day.[49]

Unwilling to give up, Hanfstaengl tried to change Hitler's mind by telling the story of US president Abraham Lincoln and the funeral train that carried his body from Washington to his hometown of Springfield, Illinois. The Harvard graduate suggested that Schlageter's coffin might be transported across Germany to whip up sympathy for the Nazi Party. Hitler reportedly warmed to this idea. To drive home his point, Hanfstaengl quoted the Scottish philosopher Thomas Carlyle, who said that "any nation which fails to honor its dead can no longer call itself a nation."[50] Pausing for a moment, Hitler suddenly announced that he'd changed his mind and started putting together his thoughts for the speech.

Since it was already late, Hanfstaengl decided to spend the night at the crowded Pension Moritz but soon discovered that his only option was to take a double room with Eckart. After saying goodnight to Hitler, he found his room-mate "in a most disillusioned mood."[51] As the pair prepared for bed, he remembered Eckart saying, "You know, Hanfstaengl, something has gone completely wrong with Adolf. The man is developing an incurable case of delusions of grandeur. Last week he was striding up and down in the courtyard here with that damned whip of his and shouting, 'I must enter Berlin like Christ in the temple of Jerusalem and scourge out the moneylenders' and more nonsense of that sort. I tell you if he lets this Messiah complex run away with him he will ruin us all."[52]

It wasn't the first time Hanfstaengl had heard the morphine-addicted publisher complain about the Nazi leader. Back in Munich, he recalled walking one day with Eckart across Max-Joseph Platz, with Hitler only a few steps behind, when the publisher blurted out, "I tell you I am fed up with this toy-soldier stuff of Hitler's. Heaven knows the Jews are behaving badly enough in Berlin and the Bolshevists are an even worse lot, but you cannot build a political party on the basis of prejudices alone. I am a writer and a poet and I am too old to go along with him anymore."[53] Hanfstaengl couldn't tell for sure whether or not Hitler had heard what Eckart said. The publisher was also deeply frustrated with Alfred Rosenberg, who had essentially taken over the *Völkischer Beobachter* in his absence. One day, Hanfstaengl had found Eckart in tears, saying, "If only I had known what I was doing when I introduced Rosenberg into the party and then allowed him to take over the editorship here, with his rabid anti-Bolshevism and anti-Semitism. He does not know Germany and I have a very strong suspicion that he does not know Russia either."[54]

While there is no way of knowing whether or not Hanfstaengl's account is entirely accurate, both he and Eckart were sensing changes in Hitler's behavior. Unfortunately, neither man was prepared to do anything about it. Returning to Munich with Hanfstaengl, Hitler participated in the ceremony for Leo Schlageter and gave a rousing speech. The saboteur would later gain infamy as one of the Nazis most celebrated martyrs.

"I LIKE YOU"

Ever since Hitler's bodyguards had foiled his attempt to obtain a picture of the Nazi leader on the Schellingstraße in 1922, Heinrich Hoffmann had been scheming to take another. While the timeline of his early relationship with Hitler remains ambiguous, the photographer claimed that his next best opportunity came at the wedding of Hermann Esser, which took place on July 5, 1923. A former intelligence officer under Captain Karl Mayr, Esser had been instructed to join the DAP back in 1919, and had become a member of Hitler's inner circle. When Hoffmann learned that Esser was getting married and that Hitler had promised to attend the wedding, he offered to host a reception for the newlyweds at his home in Schwabing. With Hitler otherwise distracted at the party, Hoffmann conspired to use his assistant to snap a surreptitious photo of the Nazi leader. "In my own home surely I should succeed in getting the longed-for snap!"[55] Hoffmann recorded in his memoirs.

On the day of the wedding reception, Hoffmann placed himself at the entrance of his home to greet his guests as they arrived. When Hitler came into view, Hoffmann saw that he instantly recognized the photographer. According to Hoffmann's memoirs, the Nazi leader made his introduction by saying, "I am really very sorry that you were so rudely disturbed while taking your picture and I hope today that I shall certainly have the opportunity of giving you a more detailed explanation of the circumstances."[56] Humorously brushing it off as just one of the many inconveniences of the trade, Hoffmann assured his guest that he held no grudge. His willingness to make light of his own misfortune for the sake of Hitler's comfort apparently meant a great deal to the Nazi leader. Later, when the party was winding down, Hoffmann invited Hitler into his office. As the Nazi leader was leafing through his book collection, which contained many titles on painting, Hoffmann explained that he'd once dreamed of being a painter but that his father had put a stop to it. Unbeknownst to the host, his confession struck a deep chord with Hitler. "To me, the career of a painter has also been denied," Hitler replied with a regretful look.[57]

Turning to the subject of photography, Hitler surprised his host by saying, "When I shall permit myself to be photographed I cannot say; but this much I can promise you, Herr Hoffmann—when I do so, you will be allowed to take the first photos."[58] It was an extremely generous offer and the pair shook hands. "But," Hitler continued, "I must ask you to refrain from now on from trying to take any snaps without my permission."[59] As if on cue, a messenger appeared and handed Hoffmann a package, which contained a fresh print of Hitler and its matching photographic plate—taken only moments earlier by his assistant. Presenting the print to Hitler, Hoffmann explained how he obtained it. Then, in an act of bravado, Hoffmann smashed the plate to pieces and said, "A bargain is a bargain, and until you ask me to do so, I will photograph you no more."[60] In this way, Heinrich Hoffmann claimed that he charmed the future Nazi dictator. "Herr Hoffman, I like you!" was Hitler's reported reply. "May I come often and see you?"[61]

Thus began a twenty-two-year-long friendship. Heinrich Hoffmann would go on to establish a publishing monopoly selling Hitler's image, which would make him one of the richest men in Nazi Germany. More significantly, his exceptional talent for capturing larger-than-life photos would be directed exclusively for the purpose of enhancing Hitler's image as Germany's savior. If you can picture a photograph of Hitler in your mind, chances are Heinrich Hoffmann took it.

In the summer of 1923, to escape his many pressures, the Nazi leader liked to spend his afternoons at various cafés with men like Hoffmann and Hanfstaengl in mock-Bohemian reverie. While Hanfstaengl seemed interested in expressing his vast knowledge to win Hitler's favor, Hoffmann was more contented to drink heavily, listen attentively, and crack jokes to make Hitler laugh. "I also realized how lonely he was," Hoffmann later wrote, "how desperately he relied on the outlet that this friendship in an entirely different world afforded him."[62]

On one afternoon, Hanfstaengl and Hitler met up with the photographer at his home in Schwabing. Sitting down at a piano, Hanfstaengl started playing Harvard football marches and described to Hitler what it was like to attend a college football game in America, and how marching bands were used to conjure "hysterical enthusiasm."[63] Painting a picture of cheerleaders dancing with pompoms, and spectators screaming in unison, "Harvard, Harvard, Harvard, rah, rah, rah!" Hanfstaengl demonstrated how German melodies could be infused with the beat of American brass-band music. "I had Hitler fairly shouting with enthusiasm," the Harvard graduate later recalled, "'That is it, Hanfstaengl,' Hitler exclaimed, 'that is what we need for our movement...'"[64] The German-American claimed that he went on to write dozens of marches for the Nazis and the Brown Shirts. It was only years later that the self-indulgent Hanfstaengl, like so many other Hitler sympathizers, would remark, "I must take my share of the blame."[65]

CHAPTER FIFTEEN

HITLER'S COMPETITORS

On the evening of July 14, 1923, Ernst Hanfstaengl found himself sitting with Hitler, Hitler's bodyguard, and Hermann Göring in the Nazi Party offices on Corneliusstraße. The group was frustrated. Earlier in the day a Nazi demonstration in Munich had been broken up by the police, who had brandished "swords and rubber truncheons."[1] Ever since May Day, when Hitler's forces were obliged to back down at Oberwiesenfeld, the police seemed to have had the upper hand in the Bavarian capital. Announcing that he was going outside to see if there were any new reports, Hitler urged his three companions to join him. "You could never keep him off the streets," Hanfstaengl later wrote, as if describing an impulsive teenager.[2]

Around eight that evening, the group arrived at the Hofbräuhaus, where Hitler incited patrons seated in the beer hall's inner courtyard to join in a spontaneous protest march—for what purpose, his companions did not know. According to Hanfstaengl, the Nazi leader was "restless" and wanted to raise some hell. But the plan did not turn out as he expected. "The beer-drinkers would have none of it," Hanfstaengl reported, "and after calling us all the names under the sun and telling us to get out, [they] started bombarding us with their heavy mugs. One whistled past my nose and shattered against the wall, spraying beer all around."[3] A first-time initiate to the perils of beer-hall combat, Hanfstaengl didn't know he should duck and was nearly struck in the head. Unable to rally support in the beer hall, the Nazis departed.

Germany was the scene of desperate impoverishment in the autumn of 1923. The country's economic woes had been accelerating since January, when the German chancellor had encouraged workers in the industrial Ruhr to walk off the job. To compensate their lost wages during the French and Belgian occupation, Berlin had printed reams and reams of paper money. As many as three hundred paper mills and two thousand printing presses had been working around the clock to provide Germany with cash.[4] But the circulation of new bills had a terrible effect on the economy, and hyperinflation was spiraling out of control. In August, the exchange rate dipped to 4 million marks for 1 US dollar. Three months later it would fall to 4 trillion.[5] At that time, it cost 80 billion marks just to purchase an egg.[6]

Everywhere, desperate citizens tried to unload their savings before it was too late.[7] Pensions were suddenly worthless. People used wheelbarrows to transport cash. Watching the depreciation of the mark, farmers became reluctant to part with their food. Hyperinflation intensified German hunger and poverty. "The street is grey in the morning. . . . A lorry full of potatoes passes. People immediately rush from both pavements. Some children clamber onto the back of the heavy vehicle and throw armfuls of the precious vegetables onto the road; these are gathered up at once," read one autumn report. "The street is hungry."[8] Even in Berlin's posh Hotel Adlon, where the price of a formal dinner one night would hardly cover a cup of coffee the next morning, the wealthy had to keep pace with the dizzying changes.[9]

As the situation deteriorated, more and more Germans became hostile toward the national government. Few had examined the cause-and-effect link between the economic crisis and German aggression in the First World War. Having hoped that Weimar's postwar parliamentary democracy would end their economic woes, they began to wonder if they might have been better off under the Kaiser. Before the war, Germany had been a prosperous and feared European power. Now, under a collapsing economy and with foreign troops on German soil, the nation seemed to be falling apart. In these conditions, hundreds of thousands of Germans were vulnerable to extremist ideology.

In 1923, Hitler was the most popular radical ideologue in Bavaria, the only orator admired enough to fill the six-thousand capacity auditorium of Munich's Circus Krone. In August, he told a crowd, "Either Berlin marches and ends up in Munich, or Munich marches and ends up in Berlin! A Bolshevist North Germany and a Nationalist Bavaria cannot exist side by side."[10] Week after week, he had taken advantage of the growing divide between north and south and whipped up support for a march against the government of the Weimar Republic. But his statement belied the truth. The government in Berlin was hardly Bolshevik. Its current chancellor, Wilhelm Cuno, was a former director of the Hamburg-American shipping line and had filled his cabinet with conservatives, democrats and Catholics. In fact, German Communists from the KPD were among his fiercest critics. On August 8, KPD ministers in the Reichstag asked for a no confidence vote to depose him. In Chemnitz, the largest city in Saxony, 150,000 workers demonstrated against his government.[11]

When Social Democratic ministers in the Reichstag joined the KPD's vote of no confidence, the chancellor and his cabinet stepped down. Then, on August 13, Gustav Stresemann was appointed to the chancellery. As chairman of the German People's Party, Stresemann had promoted Christian family values and opposed Marxism. His new cabinet, dubbed the "Grand Coalition," included ministers from his own party, the German Democratic Party, the German Center Party, and the Social Democrats. But neither the Far Right nor the extreme Left were satisfied. The beginning of September saw little change in the direction of Germany's economy. Unemployment continued to rise, and the government was printing larger and larger denominations to keep up with hyperinflation.

In Bavaria, right-wing paramilitary groups, including the SA, gathered in Nuremberg on September 1 to attend a German Day rally, which marked the anniversary of Germany's victory over the French at Sedan in the Franco-Prussian war. This was the first of many mass meetings in Nuremberg that inspired the infamous Nazi Party Day rallies of the 1930s. Among the nationalist leaders in attendance was Hitler. After the May Day debacle, the Nazi leader was looking to create new alliances and expand his influence in military circles. Without the cooperation of other paramilitary groups and the Reichswehr, Hitler understood he had little chance of orchestrating a successful government takeover.

Of all the leaders assembled at Nuremberg, the most conspicuous and celebrated figure was Ludendorff. Placing himself at the general's side, Hitler watched 100,000 nationalists and veterans march through the city for two

Erich Ludendorff and Adolf Hitler, 1923.

hours.[12] Though the date of their first encounter remains a mystery, it appeared that Hitler had been corresponding with Ludendorff since the spring of 1921. "I got to know Hitler before he became famous," wrote Ludendorff in his book *On the Way to the Feldherrnhalle*. "I observed his growth. . . . He knew how to give the nationalist movement its content, which the people instinctively grasped: here we have something of high morality, something that offers salvation."[13]

The following day, leaders of the various nationalist groups held a meeting and formed a new partnership called the Deutsche Kampfbund (German Combat League). Created to coordinate the paramilitary wings of Bavaria's far-right organizations, the Kampfbund was an alliance of professional soldier types who wanted to end the foreign occupation of the Ruhr and unseat the Weimar government in Berlin. Under the command of Hermann Kriebel, it included the forces of Hitler's SA, Friedrich Weber's Bund Oberland, and Ernst Röhm's Reichskriegsflagge (Imperial War Flag Society). Weber, whose father-in-law was Julius Lehmann—an influential Thule member and anti-Semitic publisher—had been instrumental in converting Freikorps Oberland, which had participated in the defeat of the second Soviet Republic, into Bund Oberland, a viable political organization.[14] Since the Treaty of Versailles made paramilitary organizations illegal, the Kampfbund had to watch its step. But if the turnout at the German Day celebration was any measure, it appeared to have a highly motivated rebel army at its disposal.

Three weeks after its conception, Röhm convinced the Kampfbund to nominate Hitler as its political leader. The appointment didn't represent real power, nor did it elevate Hitler over Ludendorff as the organization's choice for a future dictator. Hitler was promoted to provide the Kampfbund with political guidance.[15] "In view of the seriousness of the political situation," read the group's official proclamation, "we have felt the need for a unified political leadership. In full agreement . . . we leaders of the Kampfbund . . . transfer this political leadership to Adolf Hitler."[16] Once again, Röhm had played a critical role helping Hitler to achieve influence, just as he had when he set up a meeting between the Nazi leader and General Lossow to overturn the ban on Nazi Party Day celebrations back in January.

While Bavaria's nationalists were coordinating their efforts for a struggle in the south, German Communists regrouped for their own fight in the north. In September, Germany's KPD leadership consulted in secret with members of the Soviet politburo, including Leon Trotsky.[17] The Soviets were optimistic about developments in Germany and believed the time for a Communist revolution was near. On September 21, *Die Rote Fahne* called for demonstrations and a general strike to depose the Stresemann government.[18] Five days later, the Reich president and chancellor decided to take bold action.

To curb hyperinflation, Chancellor Stresemann ordered a halt to "passive resistance" in the Ruhr on September 26. Workers were told to return to their factories. Later that same day, President Ebert invoked Article 48 of the Weimar constitution and declared martial law across the whole of Germany.[19] Emergency powers were granted to defense minister Otto Gessler and Reichswehr commander General Hans von Seeckt. For the next six months, Germany would be run by the military. Ebert's decision gave the defense minister and the Reichswehr commander the authority to clamp down on both the nationalists and the Communists. It also allowed Stresemann some breathing room to focus exclusively on adjusting the German currency and curbing inflation.[20]

To far-right nationalists, the decision to end "passive resistance" in the Ruhr looked like capitulation. It smacked of weakness and resignation and reminded people of Germany's surrender in 1918. This was the subject that Hitler had been exploiting so effectively in the beer halls of Munich. Fearing that the Nazi leader and the Kampfbund might initiate a putsch, Minister-President Knilling of Bavaria declared a state of emergency and appointed Gustav von Kahr to the position of state commissar.[21] In his new capacity, Kahr received broad, almost dictatorial powers. The former minister-president, who had transformed the state into a protection zone for far-right extremists, was back. This time, the authorities wanted him to stand up to Hitler.

The state commissar didn't waste time getting down to business: he banned a series of Nazi Party mass meetings scheduled for September 27. Then he took decisive action against the Left. Declaring strikes illegal, Kahr demanded that the paramilitary wings of the SPD and the KPD be dismantled. No similar measures were taken against the Right. Next, he accused foreign-born Jews of taking advantage of German hyperinflation to make themselves rich and campaigned for their removal from the state.

During this period, opportunistic individuals had attempted to profit in unsavory ways from the economic crisis. Among them were people lucky enough to have access to foreign currency, who could take advantage of the favorable exchange rate and live like kings. In a climate of resentment toward Munich's nouveau riche, Kahr, a relatively lighter version of Hitler, played upon traditional anti-Semitic biases, accused Jews in Bavaria of inflation profiteering, and began ordering arbitrary expulsions. According to a police report, one of the victims had to go because he had too many bottles of sparkling wine at his house.[22] Another was run out of Bavaria because his maid complained about his "luxurious home décor with heavy carpets."[23] The Association of Bavarian Israelite Communities, which had been seeking legal protections for the Jews since April, tried to defend the victims.[24] But the state turned its back on the accused, and over a hundred Jews were given just fourteen days to leave. As if to promote himself as Bavaria's bona fide anti-Semitic leader, the state commissar personally signed each expulsion order, underscoring the fact that German anti-Semitism did not originate with Hitler.

Tensions in the nationalist camp were evident from the beginning. Kahr, a Bavarian monarchist who wanted to bring back the Wittelsbachs, was no friend of Hitler. In a move that would have far-reaching consequences, Kahr, rather than unite with the Nazis and the Kampfbund, would form an alliance with the leaders of the Bavarian Reichswehr and the state police. Dubbed the "triumvirate," this three-way partnership between Kahr, Reichswehr general Lossow, and state police chief Hans Ritter von Seißer itself plotted against Berlin, without Hitler and Ludendorff. Lossow, who had met with Hitler back in January only to watch him defy the conditions set for the Nazi Party Day celebrations, was, like Kahr, no fan of the Nazi leader.

On September 27, the Nazi Party newspaper, the *Völkischer Beobachter*, ran a front-page article criticizing the German chancellor and Reichswehr commander in chief Seeckt for going along with the state of emergency, implying, in part, that they were under the influence of their Jewish wives. Considering the slight a low blow, Seeckt, from Berlin, ordered Lossow in Munich to shut down the newspaper.[25] However, Lossow knew the ban might spark riots and, in a bold demonstration of loyalty to the Bavarian triumvirate, he refused the order and distanced himself from Seeckt and the Reichswehr leadership in Berlin.

Five days later, Reichswehr commander in chief Seeckt asked for Lossow's resignation. It was a drastic measure, considering that Lossow was the most important military figure in southern Germany and commanded Bavaria's Seventh Division. More shockingly, Lossow refused to step down. Rather, he commanded his forces to declare their allegiance to Bavaria.[26] Technically, this was treason, but Berlin hesitated.

As the divide between north and south grew wider, economic conditions across Germany continued to worsen. Banks started issuing ten billion mark notes. To reduce spending, the government started cutting back on the number of state employees: As many as 135,000 civil servants were set to lose their jobs between October and March.[27]

In central Germany, Marxist revolutionaries toying with the idea of insurrection postponed their uprising. With only rifles to fight against a heavily armed Reichswehr, they decided their energies were better spent supporting their local KPD politicians.[28] When new state governments came to power in Saxony and Thuringia in early October, the Communists succeeded in forming coalition governments with Social Democrats and gained control of two of Germany's fifteen states.

In Bavaria, Hitler found himself in an increasingly difficult position. He desperately wanted to launch a putsch against Berlin, but he hadn't secured the support of the triumvirate, which disdained him, or the Reichswehr. Many of his recruits were expecting action. At Nuremberg, Hitler had promised, "In a few weeks, the dice will roll. What is in the making today will be greater than the World War. It will be fought out on German soil for the whole world."[29] But the Nazis seemed no closer to launching a coup than they had the previous month. This was not good news for the recruits. Struggling to make ends meet, many counted on a successful putsch to lead to employment in the Reichswehr.[30] But when was that going to happen? "The day is coming when I can no longer hold my people," warned the leader of an SA regiment. "If nothing happens now the men will sneak away."[31] Some Nazi lieutenants feared their subordinates might even join the Communists.[32] Hitler wanted to lash out at the triumvirate, but he couldn't risk completely cutting himself off.

As the Nazis were beginning to suspect, the triumvirate was advancing its own agenda for a northern expedition against Berlin. The appearance of leftist governments in Saxony and Thuringia gave it the perfect propaganda cover to initiate military action. Since Berlin seemed frozen, and unwilling to topple the twin leftist regimes, Kahr authorized the combined triumvirate forces to take up positions along Bavaria's northern border. An incursion across the state line into Thuringia to defeat the Communists was the perfect excuse for launching a march on Berlin. Among those sent to the northern border was Hermann Ehrhardt. At the head of the Viking Bund—the latest incarnation of the Ehrhardt Brigade—he commanded 15,000 men.[33] Back on May Day, Ehrhardt had lost faith in, and subsequently parted ways with, Hitler when the Nazi leader capitulated to the authorities and walked away at Oberwiesenfeld.[34] Now, on Thuringia's border, Ehrhardt and his men were ready for battle. But the order from the triumvirate to advance never came.

In late October, German chancellor Stresemann authorized his northern army to join loyal government troops inside Saxony and Thuringia to depose their leftist state governments. When the Communists and Socialists were defeated, the triumvirate no longer had any justification for a northern incursion. Together with the other Reichswehr forces amassed on the border, Ehrhardt and the Viking Bund stood down.

Meanwhile, Hitler, convinced that Kahr was the Nazi's main obstacle to power, began plotting against the state commissar and his associates. When news leaked that the triumvirate, Wittelsbach heir Crown Prince Rupprecht, and other leading dignitaries would participate in Memorial Day festivities in central Munich on November 4, the Nazis saw an opportunity. The dignitaries were scheduled to mount a platform on a narrow street near the Residenz to watch a procession of troops. According to Hitler's subordinate Alfred Rosenberg, the platform could be captured in a pincer move by two groups of stormtroopers if the SA arrived before police forces were in position to protect the dignitaries. Rosenberg suggested that they close off the street and take the triumvirate hostage.[35] Then Hitler could appear, explain their intentions to Crown Prince Rupprecht, and announce a government takeover. According to Rosenberg, the putsch would be "short and painless."[36] But when the fateful day came, the conspirators never made a move. Ernst Hanfstaengl had apparently managed to scuttle the plan before it got started "by arguing that any attack on Rupprecht's person would inevitably bring out the Reichswehr in full force against us."[37] The Nazis went back to the drawing board.

In late October and early November, Hitler waged a two-tiered struggle to wear down the triumvirate and pry it apart. During the day he conducted face-to-face negotiations with its leadership. At night, he applied pressure at Nazi Party rallies. In talks with Lossow and the Seißer, Hitler urged separation from Kahr and unity with the Kampfbund.[38] At a rally at the Circus Krone on the night of October 30, Eckart attacked Kahr in a speech.[39] By November 6, the state commissar had had enough of Hitler and was ready to turn the tables.

Gustav von Kahr thought he could outsmart Hitler. Arranging a secret meeting that excluded Hitler, he sat down with the Kampfbund leadership. The purpose of the conference was to discuss in broad terms the triumvirate's plan for a new government in Berlin. Explaining that regime change would take time since it required careful planning and orchestration, Kahr, in his capacity as state commissar, ordered the Kampfbund to refrain from taking any independent action without his permission. When news of the meeting got back to Hitler, he immediately called the Kampfbund leadership together for his own emergency session.

After receiving a detailed report about the state commissar's secret meeting, Hitler sent Kahr a request for a personal audience. It seemed the Nazi leader was optimistic that he could change the state commissar's mind in a one-on-one dialogue. Kahr said he was willing to meet Hitler, but only after November 8. And why was it so important to wait? On November 8, the state commissar was planning to deliver an important address to a gathering of Munich's political elite in the spacious Bürgerbräukeller.

The guest list for Kahr's special event included the minister-president, prominent business leaders, state officials, academics, newspaper editors, captains of industry, and members of parliament. The contents of his speech was a mystery. Hitler began to suspect that he intended to use the meeting to announce the return of the Wittelsbach monarchy.[40] The Nazi leader had already received an intelligence report to that effect,[41] and this was not something that he could support. Hastily, he decided to launch a putsch, with or without the support of the triumvirate.

Hitler's decision was an early demonstration of the impulsiveness that would later frustrate his generals during the Second World War. Meeting with two trusted subordinates on November 6, he laid out his plans to seize power in Munich, arrest the triumvirate, and compel it to endorse a march on Berlin. The plotters were a bald-headed Balkan strategist named Max Erwin Scheubner-Richter and a supreme court judge and Nazi sympathizer named Theodor von der Pfordten. The judge had penned a new constitution to replace Weimar's should the putsch succeed. The document was an early blueprint for the Third Reich: dictatorship would replace democracy, parliament and the unions would be dissolved, freedom of speech and freedom of the press would be canceled, and Jews would be removed and deported into camps. Those who disobeyed would be executed without due process.[42]

Hitler's plan took greater shape the following day when Kampfbund leaders met in secret to work out the details. Due to security concerns, the group was kept small. The only known participants were Ludendorff, Kriebel, Scheubner-Richter, and Göring. At first, the group considered launching the coup on the weekend of November 10 and 11. Despite the lessons of the ill-fated Kapp-Lüttwitz Putsch in Berlin, which had begun on a Saturday, Hitler believed that the weekend was the best time to strike because government administrators had the day off and the police were typically at half strength.[43] However, the participants soon realized that if their plans were initiated on a weekend, government officials would have to be arrested in their homes and this seemed too cumbersome, so the plan was dropped.

Hitler opted instead to take action on November 8, 1923, at Kahr's Bürger-bräukeller event. The success of the plan hinged on the threat of violence. If the Nazis and the Kampfbund could hijack the meeting at gunpoint and takeover Munich by force, they could compel the triumvirate to give its blessing for a march on Berlin. If the triumvirate demonstrated its support in a public statement, the Bavarian Reichswehr and the state police would likely join with the Kampfbund. If these forces united behind Hitler and Ludendorff and marched on Berlin, tens of thousands of other Germans would join them along the way, transforming the putsch into a "national uprising."[44]

These were a lot of "ifs" that, to the detriment of the world, broke to Hitler's eventual advantage.

CHAPTER SIXTEEN

THE BEER HALL PUTSCH

On November 8, Ernst Hanfstaengl was sitting in the offices of the *Völkischer Beobachter* with Alfred Rosenberg, when he learned of Hitler's intention to launch a putsch. "We could hear Hitler stomping up and down the corridor and heels clicking as he called out 'Where is Captain Göring?'" Hanfstaengl recalled in his memoirs. "It was all very military. Then he burst into our room, pallid with excitement, trench-coat tightly belted and carrying his riding whip. We both stood up. 'Swear you will not mention this to a living soul,' he said in a tone of suppressed urgency. 'The hour has come. Tonight we will act.'"[1]

Located on the outer banks of the Isar River, the Bürgerbräukeller was a well-to-do beer hall about one and a half kilometers from the city center. Its main hall could accommodate as many as three thousand people. Kahr's guest list included Ludendorff, Hitler, and "all the leading Bavarian personalities."[2] Informants had hinted to the Nazis that the state commissar might be preparing to announce a return of the Wittelsbach monarchy, or even secession from the Reich. These were unacceptable outcomes to Hitler. Recently, Reichswehr general Lossow had been overheard suggesting that action against Berlin would be initiated in less than two weeks.[3] Hitler refused to be left out.

Instructing Hanfstaengl and Rosenberg to meet him at the Bürgerbräukeller at 7:30 p.m., the Nazi leader said that they should bring their pistols. Returning to his Munich flat, Hanfstaengl told his wife, Helene, now pregnant, to leave the city with their son and drive seventy kilometers south to their villa in Uffing.

When Hanfstaengl arrived at the Bürgerbräukeller at around 7:00 p.m., the police had already barricaded the front entrance and prohibited people from entering.[4] Though it was a Thursday night, the state commissar had drawn a large crowd, and the main hall was already full. A half hour later, when Hitler pulled up with an entourage, including Rosenberg, he motioned to Hanfstaengl to join him, and the police allowed the group to pass. Once inside, Hanfstaengl observed Hitler quietly conferring with colleagues. The Nazi leader was wearing his Iron Cross. Hanfstaengl had no idea what would happen next.

At a podium, Kahr was delivering a tedious speech. Hanfstaengl said that he was so bored he bought a round of beers for Hitler and his men and then passed the time looking around at the guests. "Sure enough, everyone was there," he later wrote, "the Bavarian provincial cabinet, leaders of society, newspaper editors, and officers."[5] Seated below Kahr's podium were the state commissar's triumvirate colleagues—Lossow and state police chief Seißer. Suddenly, Göring burst into the back of the hall with two dozen stormtroopers armed with machine pistols. This was Hitler's cue.

An astonished audience watched Göring and his Stoßtrupp mount a heavy machine gun in the foyer and take up positions in the hall. Hitler and his bodyguards advanced for the podium. Kahr stopped speaking and glared as Hitler marched toward him. The hall began to echo with cries of protest. Mounting a chair, Hitler pulled a pistol out of his coat and fired a single shot into the air. In his guttural voice, he shouted, "The building is surrounded by six hundred heavily armed men! No one is allowed to leave. If you don't stay calm, I will have a machine gun placed in the balcony!"[6]

Göring's men had already blocked all the exits. Armed Stoßtrupp in steel helmets seemed to be everywhere. Standing above the crowd, Hitler announced, "The Bavarian government is deposed. The national government is deposed. A provisional government is being formed. The Reichswehr and Bavarian state police barracks are occupied. Reichswehr and police units are marching here under the swastika flag." Hitler was grossly exaggerating. But it was all part of his plan.

From his vantage point, Hanfstaengl could see Lossow staring at Hitler with contempt. He later claimed to have turned to Göring and said, "Hermann, watch your step. Lossow is going to double-cross us."[7] The audience was also studying Hitler. With his pale face dripping with perspiration, and his black hair falling messily over his forehead, he hardly resembled a German hero. Unlike the smartly dressed crowd in their tailored outfits, the Nazi leader's suit was baggy, and his swastika lapel button appeared to be oversized.

At this point, Hitler motioned the triumvirate to join him in a side room. Regretting that he "hadn't even brought a sidearm,"[8] Lossow quietly urged his colleagues to play along as they were led away. According to the general, Hitler seemed to be in "a state of ecstasy."[9] As soon as they had left the hall, the audience became contentious and loud. Mounting the podium, Göring fired another

pistol shot into the ceiling and promised that everything would soon be clarified. "Don't worry, we have the friendliest intentions and anyway," he mocked,
"you can be happy, you have your beer."[10]

In the side room of the Bürgerbräukeller, Hitler was sweating profusely.
This was the moment of truth: if the triumvirate could be convinced to join the
putsch, they would bring the police and the army with them. Announcing that
no one could leave without his permission, Hitler explained his intentions: The
putschists would establish political control in Bavaria, then take over Berlin.
In the new national government, Lossow would take the post of defense minister; Seißer would be put in charge of a national police organization, and Kahr
would resume control of Bavaria. In this way, the Nazi leader tried to ply the
triumvirate with the promise of leadership. Further, the Nazi leader explained
that Ludendorff would assume command of a new national army, while Hitler
planned to take political leadership, though he wouldn't reveal what that exactly
meant. Then, brandishing his firearm, he made a threat. "I have four bullets in
my pistol," he warned, "three for my collaborators, if they desert me, and the
fourth one for me."[11] Hitler held the pistol to his ear. Though only moments
earlier he had urged his colleagues to play along, Lossow couldn't take the the-
atrics and rebuked him: "You can arrest me, you can have me shot, and you can
shoot me yourself. Dying or not dying is unimportant."[12]

Seeing that he was getting nowhere, Hitler left the triumvirate under guard
and returned to the main hall. He had hoped that Ludendorff would have arrived
by now, but the general was late. When the audience saw Hitler, some seethed
with hostility. In a crowd filled with many of Munich's most accomplished citizens, the Nazi leader's armed intrusion was considered completely outrageous.
To quiet them down, Hitler fired another round of his pistol into the air and
then took the stage. After detailing his plan to establish a new government that
included the triumvirate, Hitler paused to remind everyone that today was the
fifth anniversary of Kurt Eisner's declaration of the Bavarian Socialist Republic.

This likely gave the audience pause to think. It had been five years since
the Socialists and Communists made a mess of things in Bavaria. Flashing on
all the troubles they had endured from that time until now, many undoubtedly
began to smolder. "Today," Hitler announced, "that disgrace comes to an end!"[13]
It was a dramatic and transformative statement. The audience began to cheer.
Hitler continued, "I ask you now: Are you in agreement with my proposed
solution to the German question? You can see that we are not driven by selfish
motives or personal gain, but only by the battle for the fatherland in the elev-

enth hour. . . . One thing I can say to you: either the German revolution begins tonight or we will all be dead at dawn!" Now under Hitler's spell, the crowd exploded with deafening applause. One observer later called Hitler's speech "an oratorical masterpiece."[14] Hanfstaengl noted, "There were a good many women in the audience, distinguished local matrons with heavy, provincial furs, and they had applauded the loudest."[15] Before returning to the side room, Hitler again addressed the audience: "Outside are Kahr, Lossow, and Seißer. They are struggling hard to reach a decision. May I say to them that you will stand behind them?"[16] The audience responded with cries of "Yes, yes!"[17]

In the adjoining room, the triumvirate could hear the crowd cheering. Then, Erich Ludendorff entered the hall. As Germany's most distinguished military figure strutted down the aisle, the audience stiffened with reverence. Returning to the side room with Ludendorff, Hitler found the triumvirate still unconvinced. "I can only advise you to join with us in this undertaking," the general remarked. Then turning to the head of the Bavarian Reichswehr, he commanded the general to fall in line. That was apparently all that was needed. Lossow reportedly clicked his heels and placed himself at Ludendorff's disposal. Seißer followed in tow. Though Kahr was reluctant, he eventually caved on the condition that he would only serve in the new government until a Bavarian monarch was returned to the throne.

Escorting the triumvirate and Ludendorff back into the main hall and up onto the stage, Hitler appeared to be beaming "with a kind of childish happiness."[18] Explaining to the audience that he was fulfilling a promise that he made to himself five years earlier when he learned of Germany's surrender, Hitler said that he would never rest until the November Criminals were defeated and the German people were returned to "power, greatness, freedom, and joy."[19] The audience was greatly impressed. As Hitler stood proudly next to Ludendorff, no one could see the irony of the statement. For five years, the general had been hiding his role in calling for the armistice and appointing a civilian government to take the blame for Germany's surrender. The so-called November Criminals were literally being killed off while the man who had conjured the myth of their crimes was now beside Hitler basking in applause.

Signaling their agreement, the triumvirate offered words of support and shook hands with Hitler and Ludendorff on stage. To the nationalists assembled in the hall, it was a deeply moving moment. Slowly rising in the chamber came the singing of "Deutschland über Alles." Some audience members were so choked up that they couldn't get the words out. The editor of the *Münchener*

Neueste Nachrichten, Dr. Fritz Michael Gerlich, wrote, "What a magnificent thing, Germany will be united again!"[20] When the singing had finished, armed guards brought the triumvirate back to the side room.

From the audience, Rudolf Hess suddenly appeared and read out a list of dignitaries to be detained in an upstairs room. Among the hostages to be taken was Minister-President Knilling. Later, the prisoners would be transferred by car for safekeeping to the home of the anti-Semitic publisher Julius Lehmann. Apprehending the only Jew the Nazis knew to be in attendance, the storm-troopers hauled off Ludwig Wassermann, a factory owner, and told him he'd be hanged in the Marienplatz the following morning.[21] The remaining crowd was then allowed to depart the hall. Hanfstaengl later reflected that he was "too civilized for this sort of thing."[22]

With the triumvirate and the Bürgerbräukeller safely under his control, Hitler wanted to know how things were going in the rest of Munich. The most encouraging news was that Röhm and three hundred stormtroopers had taken over Lossow's Reichswehr district headquarters on Ludwigstraße. In addition, cadets at Munich's Infantry School had declared their allegiance to the putsch and renamed their company the "Ludendorff Regiment." In the morning they planned to march across the city to the Bürgerbräukeller. At other locations across the city, putschists were busy acquiring hundreds of weapons from illegal arms caches.

Smaller, symbolic Nazi victories were reported elsewhere. At the headquarters of the SPD newspaper, the *Münchener Post*, Nazi Stoßtrupp were ransacking the offices of Hitler's most vociferous opponent in print. Hoping to take the paper's editor captive, they descended on the home of Erhard Auer. The former minister of interior had become a harsh critic of Hitler since recovering from his gunshot wounds in 1919, on the day Eisner was assassinated. When Auer couldn't be located, the Stoßtrupp took sport in harassing his wife and daughters before taking his son-in-law hostage. Another stormtrooper detail in the Bogenhausen district, where Hitler would one day purchase a home for his girlfriend Eva Braun, rounded up approximately twenty Jews and brought them to the Bürgerbräukeller to be held hostage. But in the early hours of the putsch, not everything was going according to plan.

The most serious setback was unfolding at Reichswehr barracks in the north of the city. Sentries had refused to comply with stormtroopers who demanded entry. When Hitler learned of the problem, he decided to go there himself. Leaving Ludendorff with explicit instructions to keep the triumvirate captive, he departed the beer hall. Arriving at the barracks, Hitler was also unsuccessful at convincing the sentries to let him pass. Getting back in his car, he returned to the Bürgerbräukeller. When he arrived, he discovered that the worst had occurred.

In his absence, Ludendorff had allowed the triumvirate to depart. When the trio claimed that they needed to leave in order to attend to their new responsibilities and had given their word of honor that they would uphold their promises, Ludendorff believed them. "Is it safe to let them go?" Scheubner-Richter had questioned. "I forbid you to doubt the word of a German officer," was Ludendorff's stern rebuke.[23]

Learning that the triumvirate had slipped from his grasp, Hitler was crestfallen. He had good reason to be. No sooner had they left the building than Lossow, Seißer, and Kahr rushed to recant their oath of allegiance. Communicating directives to their subordinates to oppose the putsch was not going to be difficult. The putschists had made the critical mistake of failing to capture the city's telephone and wire services. Lossow immediately sent orders for Reichswehr forces to make haste to Munich. "State Commissar Gustav v. Kahr, Col. v Seißer and Gen. v. Lossow repudiate the Hitler putsch," read a cable sent to German wireless stations at 2:55 a.m. "Expressions of support extracted by gunpoint invalid. Caution is urged against misuse of the above names."[24]

In Berlin, Chancellor Stresemann, Reich president Ebert, and General Seeckt were also informed of the putsch. Putting his forces on alert in the German capital, Seeckt cabled Lossow and threatened that if he didn't suppress the putsch, Berlin would do it for him. The warning resembled the one that Defense Minister Gustav Noske had given to Minister-President Johannes Hoffmann four years earlier, when the Soviets controlled Munich. The only real difference was that the enemy now came from the Right instead of the Left. To control the flow of information in Munich and conceal his personal embarrassment, Kahr tried to compel the press to abstain from running articles about the triumvirate's capitulation at the Bürgerbräukeller. But Munich's largest daily rag, the *Münchener Neueste Nachrichten*, had already gone to print.

"WE'LL MARCH!"

At dawn, the scene in the Bürgerbräukeller was grim. A haze of thick cigarette smoke hung in the air as fatigued soldiers and hostages tried to sleep on makeshift beds of benches and chairs. Hitler had stayed up all night pacing the floors, trying to think of a way out of the situation. Reports confirmed that the triumvirate had turned against them. Like the Kapp-Lüttwitz Putsch before it in Berlin, Hitler's coup had failed to secure the unanimous support of the army and the police and had transformed Munich into a landscape of divided loyalties. Now in a situation where clever speeches weren't enough to turn the situation around, Hitler found himself deadlocked. He later said he knew that the putsch was lost when the triumvirate had been allowed to escape.[25] When it was time for breakfast, a band was directed to play marches to lift everyone's mood. But it didn't help. At least Hitler had cash to pay his forces. The Nazis had stolen trillions of marks from two government printing offices to compensate their Kampfbund supporters. Ludendorff had gone home overnight and returned at 8:00 a.m. in fresh clothes. Now he was soothing his stomach with a morning cup of red wine. Outside, a wet snow began to fall. Suddenly, the freshly dubbed "Ludendorff Regiment" from Munich's Infantry School arrived and pledged their allegiance to the general, briefly lifting everyone's spirits. With instructions to capture the state commissar's headquarters, they were sent back over the Isar River and into the center of Munich.

Inside the beer hall, Hitler, Ludendorff, and their fellow conspirators considered their options. As many as eight hundred uniformed men had assembled at the Bürgerbräukeller and were awaiting instructions.[26] Kampfbund groups from as far away as Ingoldstadt, Garmisch, and Weiheim[27] were arriving to lend their support to the coup. The putschists technically had a numerical advantage over the Reichswehr forces currently assembled in Munich, but Hitler's forces were in disarray, and no one knew what their next move was. Reports confirmed that Reichswehr and police units had already taken up key positions around the city. In fact, a police detail was blocking their closest access to the old city at the Ludwig Bridge. Of all the government buildings in Munich, only the Reichswehr district headquarters was under their control, thanks to Ernst Röhm.

The leadership agreed that retreat wasn't an option.[28] Nor was digging in and defending their position. Instead, Hitler and Ludendorff decided to initiate a march. "The sight of a marching column," it had once been said by a stormtrooper, "makes the deepest possible impression on a German and speaks to his heart a more convincing and compelling language than writing or talk of logic can ever do."[29] If Munich's residents saw the putschists proceeding defiantly through the streets, they might rally to their defense. If the public then joined the march in large numbers, the putschists might occupy the old city. This would signal regime change and force the triumvirate to capitulate. In this way, the leadership tried to encourage itself. The matter was settled when Ludendorff exclaimed, "We march!"[30]

The decision was not lacking in historical precedent. After all, Mussolini had allegedly done the same in Rome. Eisner's march into the center of Munich five years earlier had enabled him to seize power. But Eisner had the support of the garrisons. Paradoxically, Hitler would later criticize the November Revolution because it brought a man to power without providing the electorate a chance to signal its approval. Now the putschists were about to try the same thing. But unlike Eisner's venture, this was a last-ditch gambit. Hitler would later recall that it was "the most desperately daring decision of my life."[31]

In preparation for the march, Hanfstaengl was sent on a reconnaissance mission to see what was happening in the old city. The news wasn't good. Police forces were tearing down posters that announced Hitler as Germany's new Reich chancellor.[32] Rumors circulated that the Reichswehr was closing in on the city. Instead of returning to the Bürgerbräukeller, Hanfstaengl hastened home in order to prepare his escape.

Organizing their forces into neat rows in front of the Bürgerbräukeller, the putschists began their parade at noon. As many as two thousand marchers participated.[33] A small detail was left behind at the beer hall to keep watch over the prisoners who had been taken the previous evening. Directly behind a column of flag bearers, Hitler, Hitler's bodyguard Ulrich Graf, Ludendorff, Scheubner-Richter, Göring, the judge Theodor von der Pfordten, Rosenberg, Kampfbund commander Hermann Kriebel, and Friedrich Weber of Bund Oberland, linked arms and marched at the head of the procession. Behind them were Hitler's crack troops. Few were optimistic. One of the marchers later said he felt like it was a funeral procession.[34] Most men carried rifles. Before they departed, Hitler—wanting to avoid antagonizing the Reichswehr further—had ordered the SA to keep their weapons unloaded.

At the Ludwig Bridge, a small detail of policemen made a brief stand but were quickly overwhelmed and taken prisoner. Moments later, the putschists marched under the Isar Gate and entered the old city. As Hitler had hoped, sympathetic bystanders cheered them on. In the Marienplatz, someone had raised the Nazi flag over city hall. Singing patriotic songs, Hitler's stormtroopers felt emboldened. Apart from the police on the Ludwig Bridge, there had been no real altercations, and no opposition had yet appeared to halt their progress. To liberate Röhm's forces at Reichswehr district headquarters, the putschists took a sharp turn to the right at the Marienplatz and headed north. The procession continued unmolested until it reached the side of the Feldherrnhalle at the entrance of the Odeonsplatz, where it was stopped by the Bavarian state police. This was the same square where Hitler had been photographed in a rapturous crowd celebrating the announcement of hostilities at the beginning of the First World War in 1914. Now, positioned between the putschists and the square, state police forces formed neat rows across their path and drew their weapons. "Here they come," warned an onlooker. "Heil Hitler!"[35]

Believing that the police would yield as they had at the Ludwig Bridge, the putschists continued forward. When a police commander instructed his forces to prepare to fire, Hitler's bodyguard, Ulrich Graf, shouted, "Don't shoot, Ludendorff and Hitler are coming."[36] The two forces, brandishing rifle butts and truncheons, started fighting. Suddenly a shot rang out through the air, and the melee became a gun battle. Though it lasted only half a minute, the results were deadly.

The Balkan strategist Scheubner-Richter, who had linked arms with Hitler, was instantly killed with gun shots to the chest. As his lifeless body crashed to the ground, Hitler was jerked violently with him, and his shoulder was dislocated. Jumping on Hitler's body, Graf was riddled with bullets but would survive. Göring took two shots to the thigh and the groin. With a copy of his constitution concealed in his breast pocket, the judge Theodor von der Pfordten was gunned down nearby. In all, thirteen putschists were killed, along with four policemen and one innocent bystander. In the years to come, the fallen would become the Nazi Party's most honored martyrs. Miraculously, Ludendorff was unharmed, although he was immediately arrested. As the state police took him away, he defiantly remarked, "I'll never respect a German officer's uniform again!"[37]

In the confusion, somehow Hitler managed to escape from police and hop into a waiting car that whisked him out of the city. Like Hitler, Göring also managed to flee the Bavarian capital. When Röhm learned what had happened at the Feldherrnhalle, he decided to give up. Together with his men, which included a young recruit named Heinrich Himmler, who would figure prominently in the future of the Third Reich, Röhm handed over his weapons and surrendered to the police. Back at the Bürgerbräukeller, all of the prisoners taken hostage the previous night were released.

In Schwabing, Hanfstaengl was joined by Eckart and a few other Nazis at the home of Heinrich Hoffmann. Neither the photographer nor Hitler's mentor had been informed about the coup. This is the main reason there are so few photographs of the putsch: Hoffmann only learned of Hitler's intentions on November 9 and had missed all the key events. According to Hermann

Esser, Eckart was particularly hurt that his protégé hadn't informed him of the gambit.[38] Having heard an inflated report from the Odeonsplatz, the group was under the impression that Hitler had been killed at the Feldherrnhalle. Concluding that the best thing to do was flee across the Austrian border, they decided to go their separate ways.

Three hours after the march began, Lossow sent news to Kahr that the putsch "had been broken."[39]

"I WILL SHOOT MYSELF FIRST!"

Escaping from Munich in a car driven by NSDAP member Walter Schultze, Hitler decided to go to Uffing, where Hanfstaengl had a villa. Arriving at the door in agonizing pain, Hitler was greeted by Hanfstaengl's wife, Helene, and taken inside. Escorted to an upstairs bedroom, Hitler hid out for the next two days.

Decades later, after two assassination attempts, in 1939 and 1944, a much older Hitler would say that Providence saved him so that he could complete his mission. Did the future Nazi dictator possess the same confident conviction when he cowered behind the walls of the Hanfstaengl villa? What were his thoughts as he replayed the scene at the Feldherrnhalle over and over again in his mind? Did he wonder why he had escaped the bullets when so many others died? Did he think about his first brush with mortality, when his younger brother, Edmund, died of the measles when he was eleven? Why had Edmund died when Adolf was saved? On the twentieth anniversary of the Beer Hall Putsch in 1943, Hitler would declare, "Those who do not pass the trials imposed by Providence, who are broken by them, are not destined by Providence for greater things."[40] But that was the Führer at age fifty-four. The man upstairs with the dislocated shoulder was thirty-four and still unsteady.

Helene had misgivings about Hitler staying in the villa. Despite the presence of servants and her son, Egon, she apparently felt uncomfortable being alone in the house with him and feared he might try something inappropriate. According to her husband, on a recent visit to their Munich flat the Nazi leader had placed his head in Helene's lap and hinted that he wished he had someone like her to take care of him. Moreover, Hitler was in need of medical attention, and surely the authorities would soon be knocking at the door in search of her husband. Helene urged Hitler to find a different hideout and assisted him in contacting the wealthy Bechsteins, who were allegedly sending a car. But before it could reach them, the police arrived on Sunday, November 11.

When Hitler heard that knock on the downstairs door, Helene said he was prepared to kill himself. It's not entirely clear what made him panic. Perhaps it was the realization that if brought to trial he could be facing life in prison or even the death penalty, on various charges that would include treason. How would he handle the ridicule and scorn that surely awaited him for launching such a foolish and costly coup? Some biographers say there's no evidence that Hitler even contemplated suicide when the police showed up. But, according to Hanfstaengl's memoirs, Hitler pulled out his revolver and exclaimed, "This is the end. I will never let those swine take me. I will shoot myself first."[41] The Harvard graduate explained that, with a few basic jujitsu moves she had learned from her husband, Helene deftly wrestled the firearm out of Hitler's hand and deposited it in a bin of flower. As historian David King pointed out, this version is embellished and contradicted by Helene's notes. In her own handwriting, Helene claimed she approached Hitler, rebuked him for thinking of giving up, and took away his gun by grabbing his arm.[42]

Before being escorted away, Hitler jotted down a few instructions for his fellow Nazis. Alfred Rosenberg was selected to take over the movement in his absence. Then, with his arm in a sling and still wearing his Iron Cross, Hitler departed Uffing with the police. Later that night, he was driven to Landsberg Prison, where he would spend the next several months awaiting his fate.

THE TRIAL

Germany experienced profound financial changes in the weeks and months following Hitler's arrest. To stabilize the economy, the national government took the bold step of introducing a new currency dubbed the Rentenmark. By late fall, the new bank notes were starting to have a positive impact: hyperinflation ground to a halt, growth was stimulated, and jobs were created. But Berlin couldn't take all the credit. Under the newly instituted Dawes Plan, the United States had started paying some of the country's massive debt so that reparation payments could be made on time.

In the aftermath of the Beer Hall Putsch, Bavaria's state government banned the Nazi Party and shut down the *Völkischer Beobachter*. The Kampfbund was dissolved, and its weapons were confiscated.[1] Paramilitary activities ground to a halt. Even the triumvirate lost credibility. In a few months, the trio would be removed from power and Bavaria's leading Catholic politician, Heinrich Held, would became the state's new minister-president.[2] Though some of Hitler's colleagues were sitting in jail awaiting trial, others were on the run. Göring took refuge in Austria; Eckart was hiding in the Bavarian Alps near Schönau am Königssee.

When Hitler arrived at Landsberg Prison on November 11, he was still in a considerable amount of pain. The bumpy ride to Landsberg, sixty-one kilometers west of Munich, likely aggravated his dislocated shoulder, which had been reset only the day before.[3] Inside the prison grounds, Hitler was brought to a special wing called die Festung (the Fortress), which housed political prisoners. At the time, there was only one prisoner living in the whitewashed building. Since his conviction for assassinating Kurt Eisner, Anton Arco-Valley had been living in the dorm's most spacious cell. Forced to relocate to accommodations in the prison hospital, Arco-Valley reluctantly gave up his prized room to the Nazi leader. Granted "honorable prisoner" status, Hitler was housed in the two-story minimum-security dormitory.

Early into his incarceration, Hitler initiated a hunger strike. The Nazi leader was depressed. "I've had enough. I'm finished," Hitler reportedly told Landsberg's resident psychologist, Dr. Alois Ott. "If I had a revolver, I would take it [my life]."[4] Usually hunger strikes begin with a demand, but Hitler didn't seem to have one. He just wanted to die. Several days into his strike, when a lack of nourishment began to take a noticeable effect on his appearance, he was moved to the prison's hospital wing, where he would drink only water.[5] As he withered away, starvation turned Hitler's skin more pale than usual, and his breath became so putrid that his jailer had to plug his nose to prevent himself from vomiting. The authorities considered forcing a feeding tube down his throat.[6] When Helene Hanfstaengl learned of his refusal to eat, she sent a message saying "she had not prevented him from committing suicide in order to let him starve himself to death."[7] Anton Drexler purportedly tried to intervene as well.[8]

Then, on November 19, the prison psychologist tried an unorthodox remedy. Bringing Hitler a newspaper, Dr. Ott encouraged the Nazi leader to read an article in which he was accused of "falling victim to the devil of his own vanity and a prima donna complex."[9] Scanning the article, Hitler became so agitated that he started screaming things like, "those who want the best are always crucified and burned at the stake."[10] Allowing him to rant, Dr. Ott listened patiently until Hitler was calm enough to have a conversation. This led to a lengthy exchange of opinions about important topics. The following day, the Nazi leader gave up his hunger strike. Dr. Ott later concluded that Hitler was a psychopath, obsessed with ideology and incapable of hearing any opinion that differed from his own.

Though he was observed by his family doctor in Austria, the doctors at the hospital in Pasewalk, Dr. Ott at Landsberg Prison, and his private doctors Theodor Morrell and Karl Brandt, Hitler never received a proper mental health evaluation. He escaped postwar psychiatric examination when he committed suicide in the Führerbunker in 1945. However, he was the subject of a secret US intelligence profile written by Dr. Walter C. Langer for the Office of Strategic Services in 1943. Langer predicted that Hitler would take his own life, and wrote, "Not only has he threatened to commit suicide, but from what we know of his psychology, it is the most likely possibility."[11] Describing Hitler as a "psychopath," Langer suggested that his conviction "that he was chosen by Providence" to perform a great mission was "the most outstanding characteristic of Hitler's mature personality."[12] His role as Germany's savior, which Langer called a "superman character," was created in his mind to combat intense feelings of self-hatred.[13] Langer's analysis helps explain why Hitler abandoned his hunger strike at Landsberg. When Dr. Ott encouraged him to start talking about things that mattered, the Nazi leader was likely snapped out of his depression and reconnected to his sense of mission.

At what point did Hitler establish unshakeable confidence in his special identity? Did he already possess the "mature personality" that Langer described while awaiting trial at Landsberg? When did he decide to become the Führer? "That decision cannot be dated," wrote the noted German journalist Sebastian Haffner, "nor was it triggered off by one particular event. We may be certain that it was not present during the initial years of Hitler's political career."[14] But was it by late 1923?

During his pretrial incarceration, Hitler received many visitors at Landsberg. Allowed six hours of visitation a week, the Nazi leader enjoyed a constant stream of guests, including Helene Bechstein, who helped restore his spirits. Letters, gifts, and perishables poured in from well-wishers. As an inmate with "honorable prisoner" status, he was allowed to spend several hours each day strolling in the prison gardens. In December, some of Hitler's now-apprehended close associates arrived at Landsberg, including his mentor Dietrich Eckart. Locked up in separate facilities, however, the pair never got a chance to see each other in prison.[15] When Eckart's fragile health began to deteriorate rapidly, prison authorities released him early, and he returned to Berchtesgaden, where he died of a heart attack on December 26. It's not exactly clear how Hitler reacted to Eckart's death. Though he acknowledged his debt of gratitude by dedicating the second volume of *Mein Kampf* to the anti-Semitic publisher, Hitler was estranged from Eckart in the final months of his life.

For his role in the Beer Hall Putsch, Hitler was charged with high treason. His trial rightfully should have been held in the federal court at Leipzig, which was created to litigate crimes against the state after the assassination of Walther Rathenau. But Bavarian authorities intervened to keep the trial in Munich. They knew Hitler and his associates had direct knowledge of Bavarian complicity in the plot against the Weimar government, and they weren't willing to risk exposure in federal court.[16] The decision, however, didn't shield the Nazis from the threat of serious jail time. Hitler specifically, as an Austrian immigrant, faced deportation after serving his sentence.[17]

To prepare the state's case, prosecuting attorney Ludwig Stenglein sent his deputy Hans Ehard to Landsberg Prison to ask Hitler a series of pretrial questions. The Nazi leader refused to cooperate. To get him to change his mind,

Ehard sent his staff out of the room and told Hitler that they could speak in confidence. This led to a five-hour conversation in which the Nazi leader outlined his entire courtroom strategy.[18] According to historian Peter Ross Range, Hitler's defense was to be based on a single question: Was the November revolution of 1918 legal?

To prepare for court, Hitler had been reading many books. Scanning the works of Nietzsche, Kant, Rousseau, Bismarck, Karl Marx, and Houston Stewart Chamberlain, he tried to find corroborating material to back up his arguments. According to his associate, Hans Frank—an early member of the DAP who later became Hitler's personal legal advisor—the Nazi leader boasted that his reading helped confirm "the correctness of my views."[19] Inside Landsberg, Hitler used a typewriter to draft a sixty-page defense statement. The exercise helped clarify his thinking. Hitler believed he had two essential tasks. The first was to implicate the triumvirate, which had also plotted against Berlin. The second was to convince the court that, as a soldier fighting against Marxism, he had taken the appropriate action to defend the fatherland.

"THE COLLISION OF TWO WORLDVIEWS"

On February 22, 1924, Adolf Hitler was driven from Landsberg Prison to Munich, where his highly anticipated trial was scheduled to begin four days later. Just three hundred meters north of the Circus Krone, Munich's Infantry School on Blutenburgstraße had been transformed into a makeshift court and temporary jail for Hitler and his codefendants. Surrounded by armed guards and barbed wire barricades, the campus became an impenetrable fortress. No one was allowed entry without proper identification. Inside the main building, each of the accused was accommodated in his own room. All of the defendants would stay here for the duration of the trial, except Ludendorff, who was spared the indignity of incarceration and permitted to return home each night.

Hitler's trial was highly anticipated in the German press. Not only were German journalists fighting for a seat in the court, The *New York Times*, the London *Times*, and many other news outlets sent correspondents to Munich.

On February 26, the main conspirators, including Hitler, Ludendorff, and Röhm, were led into the makeshift courtroom in the Infantry School for opening statements. The large room, formerly a dining hall, was packed with attorneys, journalists, members of parliament, government officials, and spectators. Before being seated, Hitler paused to survey the crowd with an eerie look of confidence.[20] Next, six members of the judiciary, led by Chief Judge Georg Neithardt, entered the court. A nationalist with Nazi sympathies, Neithardt had presided over the sentencing of Arco-Valley, as well as over Hitler's 1922 trial for the attack on Otto Ballerstedt at the Löwenbräukeller. Like the men who surrounded Hitler when he joined the DAP in 1919, powerful forces seemed poised to protect Germany's future dictator inside the court.

In a ninety-minute opening presentation, the prosecution gave a blow-by-blow description of the failed putsch and accused Hitler of being "the soul of the entire enterprise."[21] Normally, in a group trial, a defendant would be disheartened to learn he was singled out for blame, but not Hitler. Rather, the accusation confirmed his special identity. Hitler wasn't just a member of the chorus; he was the protagonist. However, when the prosecution requested that the trial be conducted in a closed-door session, the Nazi leader's confidence was shaken.

Hitler believed his ultimate vindication depended on exoneration in the court of public opinion. Regardless of the verdict in the courtroom, he felt secure to the extent that he could communicate his version of events to the general population. But now his access to the people was in jeopardy. In a private session, the chief prosecutor warned the judge that the proceedings were likely to expose sensitive information that ought to be kept from the press. If it came out that the Reichswehr had been involved in the training of paramilitary groups plotting against Berlin, for example, the Allies would learn that Germany had violated the terms of the Treaty of Versailles. It was a compelling argument. After listening to both sides, Judge Neithardt ruled that some subjects would be explored in closed session, while others would not. "This trial arises from the collision of two worldviews," he concluded. "We will be committing a grave injustice if we don't let these two points of view have their say in public."[22] The judge didn't realize or didn't care that he'd demonstrated personal bias.

At half past two in the afternoon, Hitler stood up in front of the court, and, with the demeanor of a seasoned lawyer, commenced with his opening statement. Instead of denying his role in the putsch, he admitted his part, and set out to clarify the righteousness of his actions. Describing his service in the German military, Hitler asked the court why a soldier of such good standing would be accused of high treason. In order to answer the question, he started describing his background to explain his state of mind. In Vienna, Hitler claimed that he was exposed to the misery of poverty and the problem of race. These experiences made him an anti-Semite. Pivoting to a critique of Marxism, and drawing a link between Jews and Marxists, he explained that "brutal fanaticism" was the only way to deal with the threat.[23] Hitler had deliberately skipped over his activities during the postwar revolution. According to historian David King, he likely attempted to convince the court that he became an anti-Semite in Vienna and then rushed into an exposé about Marxism in order to avoid questions about his record during the Soviet Republic.[24] Since neither the judge nor the prosecuting attorney pressed him on the subject, Hitler escaped having to explain his neutrality during this pivotal period.

To solve the so-called Jewish problem, Hitler explained the nation needed to do away with bureaucrats and put their weight behind a far-right radical who could inspire and lead the people. He was, of course, referring to himself. "I refuse to be modest," he remarked, "about something that I know that I can do."[25] Challenging the validity of the Weimar government, which according to Hitler came to power as a result of the November Criminals, he denounced the charge of high treason against him as meaningless because the regime itself was traitorous. According to Hitler, the people had been denied the right to choose their government in 1918, and on that basis its successors were illegitimate.

Next, the Nazi leader leveled charges against Bavaria's triumvirate. "If in fact our undertaking was high treason," Hitler reasoned, "then Kahr, Lossow, and Seißer also must have committed high treason because for months on end they agitated for nothing other than that for which we sit in the dock."[26] This was in no way inaccurate. Hitler had implicated some of the highest officials in the Bavarian government, the military, and the police. The statement unnerved the authorities, who feared the Nazi leader would go too far to expose Kahr, Lossow, and Seißer. Their fears were not unfounded. By the time he was finished, Hitler had not only convincingly demonstrated their complicity, he'd ridiculed their wishy-washy behavior.

It was a stunning speech, which ended up lasting four hours. The judge never once tried to interrupt. Hitler told the court that he did not consider himself a traitor but, instead, "just a German who only wanted the best for his people."[27] With this remark, he concluded his opening statement. As the court adjourned, a journalist overheard one of the judges saying, "What a tremendous chap, this Hitler!"[28]

"GUILTY A THOUSAND TIMES"

Over the next few days, shocking details about the Reichswehr's collusion with the putschists were disclosed in court. The testimonies of former police chief Ernst Pöhner and Kampfbund leader Hermann Kriebel were particularly revealing. They described how the Reichswehr and the state police had trained with the Kampfbund in secret exercises, including live-fire and sharpshooting drills. All of it proved that Hitler had not acted alone. Explaining to the court how the triumvirate had been preparing the Kampfbund for offensive purposes, Hitler revealed that Lossow had demanded the "highest state of readiness."[29]

From defendants Pöhner and Wilhelm Frick—a fellow police official and supporter of the putsch—the court learned how Hitler and the Nazis had been protected by the police department since 1919. "We could have easily suppressed it in 1919 and 1920," testified Frick. "But we realized that this little National Socialist movement should not be crushed. . . . We had a protective hand over the NSDAP and Herr Hitler."[30] Referring to Kurt Eisner's revolution as an act of treason against the German people, Pöhner admitted he'd been plotting against Berlin from the beginning. In the gallery, Nazi sympathizers were amused by his gritty and unrepentant style. "If what you're accusing me of is high treason," Pöhner said defiantly, "then we've been in that business for the last five years."[31]

Unlike his codefendants, when Erich Ludendorff was called to the stand, he seemed unsteady. To protect his reputation, the general decided to deny any prior knowledge of the putsch and said he only learned of it while driving to the Bürgerbräukeller that night. But, as his son-in-law Heinz Pernet would later acknowledge, the former First Quartermaster General had been in the know all along.[32] Ludendorff had become so accustomed to lying, he no longer seemed capable of knowing what the truth really was.

As the trial unfolded, it became clear that Judge Neithardt was going to allow Hitler to do almost anything he wished. The Nazi leader was interrupting and even cross-examining the prosecution's witnesses, yet apart from those times when he raised his voice, the judge made no effort to correct him. As more and more damning evidence implicated the triumvirate for its role in the plot against Berlin, pressure mounted on the state prosecutor to indict the three men. A few days before Kahr, Lossow, and Seißer were scheduled to testify in court, Stenglein announced that his office was opening an investigation. It was high drama.

In the pages of Germany's newspapers, reports on the trial read "like install-ments in a serialized novel."[33]

On March 10, 1924, Lossow took the stand at Hitler's trial. Showing no fear, the fifty-six-year-old general dismissed the march on Berlin as childish and suggested that Hitler had "lost all contact with reality and any sense of propor-tion for what was doable."[34] Nevertheless, he did admit that he had been plotting against the Weimar Government with the intent of installing a new regime.[35] He just didn't think Hitler possessed the right temperament to lead the endeavor. Like the psychologist at Landsberg, Lossow said the Nazi leader was incapable of listening to anyone but himself. Not only was Hitler a liar, Lossow claimed he broke his word of honor. Hitler was steaming by the time he finished. But in an unusual act of self-restraint, he said he would wait to cross-examine him until after Lossow's triumvirate colleague Kahr took the stand.

Unlike Lossow, the former Bavarian minister-president Kahr seemed as if he had lost his way. Speaking in a low voice that was difficult to hear, his dispas-sionate statements, troubled memory, and refusal to answer certain questions sucked the energy out of the courtroom. Under cross-examination, he admitted he'd been involved in a long and persistent effort against Berlin. The court real-ized that if Hitler hadn't initiated his putsch on November 8, Kahr's group would have likely instigated another soon thereafter. Hans Ritter von Seißer echoed the testimony of Lossow. Referring to Hitler as a megalomaniac, Seißer claimed he rejected Hitler's march on the basis of practicality.

When Lossow returned to the stand for questioning, he felt confident that he'd put the Nazi leader on his heels. But Hitler was ready. Raising his voice, he accused Lossow of breaking his word of honor as a German officer. The veracity of Hitler's accusation was secondary to its shock value.[36] By addressing Lossow with contempt in a ploy to sully the honor of a high-ranking officer, Hitler was violating military mores. The courtroom was stunned. The Nazi leader had hit the general right where he wanted. Lossow stood up, collected his things, and exited the trial, never to return. Hitler was reprimanded by Judge Neithardt and rebuked in the press. But he'd succeeded in forcing Lossow from the court. To his loyal supporters, who had already lost confidence in the general, Hitler's courage was praiseworthy.

As the trial drew to a close eighteen days after it started, it was difficult to surmise what the outcome would be. The guilt of Hitler was clear. But no one could deny that the triumvirate had conspired against Berlin as well. A week after Lossow abruptly left the court, the chief prosecutor made his final arguments. Stenglein recommended eight years of "fortress imprisonment" for Hitler. Six years was suggested for Kriebel, Pöhner, and Weber. Only two years were recommended for Ludendorff.

Before he finished, Stenglein offered words of praise to the Nazi leader. "Raised in modest circumstances," he announced, "Hitler proved his German patriotism as a brave soldier in the Great War. Filled with glowing, honest enthusiasm for his great German fatherland, he created, with tireless labor after the war and from the tiniest beginnings, a great party, the NSDAP. Its essential program is fighting international Marxism and Judaism, settling accounts with the November Criminals . . . and spreading German nationalism."[37] Stating that it would be "unjust to call him a demagogue in the negative sense of that word," he commended the Nazi leader by saying, "he deserves respect for the way he has kept his private life pristine, given the temptations that naturally come his way as a celebrated party leader." Though he added that Hitler's tragic flaw was an oversized ego, Stenglein missed the mark when he praised the Nazi leader's propriety in private life. While it was true that Hitler didn't smoke, abuse alcohol, or womanize, how he behaved in his private life was completely irrelevant to the crimes he perpetrated against the state. His putsch had resulted in the deaths of four policemen and one bystander. It was like praising a murderer for keeping his garden tidy. When Stenglein was finished, Hitler was allowed the last word.

In a ninety-minute firestorm that resembled his speeches in Munich's beer halls, Hitler restated his case and begged the court not to extradite him to Austria under the Law for the Protection of the Republic.[38] Reminding the court of his service in the Bavarian infantry, Hitler pled to be acknowledged as a German. Then, returning to the main theme of his defense, he concluded his remarks: "Even if you pronounce us guilty a thousand times over, the eternal goddess of the eternal court will laughingly tear up the prosecutor's indictment and the judgment of this court. She will pronounce us not guilty!"[39]

Judge Neithardt waited four days to deliver his verdict. In the interim, wild speculation in the press and rumors of retaliation circled about Munich. Preparing for the worst, the police doubled their defenses around the Infantry School. Then, news leaked that the triumvirate had abruptly skipped town. According to one source, the trio had fled to Italy, then escaped across the Ionian Sea to the island of Corfu. Their departure had the unintended effect of making them look guilty.

On April 1, the final day of the trial, General Ludendorff arrived in full dress uniform. Hermann Kriebel and Ernst Röhm did the same. Joining them at the

Adolf Hitler, Erich Ludendorff, and their fellow defendants at the Beer Hall Putsch trial.

entrance to the school, Hitler and his codefendants paused for a photograph, taken by Heinrich Hoffmann. Inside the court, the gallery was packed and full of anticipation. When the verdicts were read aloud, Adolf Hitler was pronounced guilty of high treason and sentenced to five years of "fortress imprisonment." His codefendants Kriebel, Weber, and Pöhner shared the same fate. Röhm, Brückner, Frick, and two others were convicted of a lesser crime and received fifteen months of imprisonment but were immediately paroled. Erich Ludendorff was acquitted and set free. Then, the judge announced that Hitler and his coconspirators who had received five-year sentences would be eligible for parole in six months. In conclusion, Neithardt declared that Hitler and his cohorts had acted from "a purely patriotic spirit, led by the most noble, selfless will."[40]

The trial was a miscarriage of justice. Throughout the proceedings, no one brought up the four policemen who'd been shot and killed at the Feldherrnhalle. No mention was made of the Jews that were rounded up in the Bogenhausen district and kept prisoner with other detainees. Little was made of the billions of marks that the Nazis stole to pay their soldiers, or the destruction of the offices of the *Münchener Post* and the harassment of Erhard Auer's family. The prosecution even neglected to introduce in court the treasonous constitution that had been discovered in the pocket of the martyred supreme court justice and Nazi sympathizer Theodor von der Pfordten.[41]

But for Hitler, there was still one hurdle to clear: would he be deported to Austria? To clarify the court's position, Judge Neithardt remarked, "Hitler sees himself as a German. Article Nine cannot be applied to a man who thinks and feels as German as Hitler does, who served four and a half years in the German army during the war, who won high honors for bravery in the face of the enemy, who was wounded and otherwise suffered a damage to his health."[42] Hitler would stay in Germany.

When the trial ended, news of the verdicts spread quickly. Supporters were overjoyed to learn that Hitler would be out in as early as six months. From a window in the Infantry School, the Nazi leader electrified a crowd of followers when he suddenly appeared and waived to them. "Those days of his trial," wrote one German war veteran, "became the first days of my faith in Hitler. From that time on I had no thought for anyone but Hitler."[43] Conversely, opponents were outraged when they heard about the court's decision. In an article titled, "At the Grave of Bavarian Justice," the *Münchener Post* accused the court of undermining ethical values and predicted that the "immorality of the state" would have far-reaching consequences.[44] Hitler was unperturbed. Not only had he received a light sentence and escaped deportation, he'd turned the trial into a showcase for his ideology. Millions of Germans now knew his name and understood his message. The trial had been a blessing, and Hitler had achieved victory.

CHAPTER EIGHTEEN

MAN OF PROVIDENCE

"VIOLENCE WOULD NOT WORK"

An energized Hitler returned to Landsberg Prison to serve out his sentence. For the first time in many years, he didn't have to worry about attending meetings or giving speeches. However, he did have a constant stream of visitors. They brought him food and flowers, and his quarters were soon stacked with sweets and pastries. On April 20—his thirty-fifth birthday—there were so many gifts and letters that it took prison censors several days just to go through it all. As the days became weeks, he started to think about what he would do when he was released.

Hitler was still fixating on revenge: He wanted to punish the triumvirate and the November Criminals. But there was little he could do from behind Landsberg's gates. After contributing an article to an anti-Semitic publication, he started thinking about writing a book. The thought had crossed his mind earlier, in 1922, but he'd had no free time to

ADOLF HITLER
in der Festung Landsberg

Phot. Hch. Hoffmann München
Nachdruck verboten.

Adolf Hitler at Landsberg Prison.

pursue it.[1] Now, Hitler wanted to write a manifesto that combined his life story with his ideology. To support his effort, a Remington portable typewriter was sent to the prison, presumably from Helene Bechstein. Soon die Festung was filled with the sound of typing, as Hitler composed an eighteen-page outline for the book that would eventually be titled *Mein Kampf* (My Struggle). Visiting Hitler at Landsberg, Kurt Ludecke remarked that he "appeared calmer and more certain of himself."[2]

When Hitler had been brought back to Landsberg Prison after his conviction, the authorities assigned him the same living quarters he'd used during his pretrial stay. Upstairs in die Festung, his only floor mates were the former Kampfbund commander Hermann Kriebel and Friedrich Weber of Bund Oberland. Then, one month into their incarceration, the trio were joined by forty members of the Stoßtrupp—Hitler's personal bodyguard unit, which operated independently from the SA. The Stoßtrupp had been responsible for ransacking the offices of the *Münchener Post* and taking hostages on the night of the putsch.[3] Convicted as accessories to high treason, the men had been sentenced to fifteen months of "fortress incarceration." Taking up residence on the ground floor, they were soon sharing meals with the Nazi leader. Among them was an early member of the DAP and Hitler's future chauffeur, Emil Maurice. A short while later, Rudolf Hess arrived and took up quarters on the first floor. For the duration of their stay in prison, Maurice and Hess would dutifully attend to the Nazi leader's needs like personal servants. Hess, in particular, played a role in collecting, organizing, and editing Hitler's manuscript.

Hitler and his coconspirators enjoyed extraordinary privileges at Landsberg. Free to wear whatever clothing they wished, they didn't have to work if they didn't want to. Menial chores were completed by inmates from the main prison. They could purchase up to half a liter of beer every day. In the summer months, workers in the prison garden were allowed a full liter. When the inmates wanted hard alcohol, they tricked their jailers into thinking that they required treatment for various ailments, and liquor flowed in die Festung. All of the doors to their cells were open for most of the day, and the inmates were free to congregate as they wished. Early dinners were served in one of the common rooms. "Fortress imprisonment" at Landsberg was quite different than incarceration at Niederschönenfeld Prison, where leftist inmates like Ernst Toller struggled to survive in harsh conditions. However, as historian David King has pointed out, it was their status as fortress prisoners that afforded the Nazis these indulgences, not favoritism.[4]

In May, Hitler started reevaluating his politics. If he was going to seize power in the future, he realized he would have to disavow armed insurrection. Recalling his thoughts at Landsberg years later, Hitler remarked that "violence would not work since the state is too established and has all the weapons in its possession."[5] Only by transforming itself into a respectable organization could the NSDAP win elections. In private, Hitler confessed to Ludecke, "Instead of working to achieve power by an armed coup, we shall have to hold our noses and enter the Reichstag against the Catholics and Marxist deputies. If out-voting them takes longer than out-shooting them, at least the results will be guaranteed by their own constitution."[6] Hitler knew many of his followers would find this transition difficult. The move alienated Röhm and created a gap between the pair. But Hitler reasoned that changes had to be made.

On June 16, Hitler announced that he would withdraw from politics until he was released from prison. It was too difficult to lead the outlawed NSDAP from behind Landsberg's walls. In the months since Rosenberg assumed control of the party, factions had emerged and the movement had become disunified. Allowing his rivals to exhaust themselves with infighting in his absence, Hitler planned to stage a comeback and return to power after his release. In the meantime, he intended to spend all of his time working on his book. The experience would change him forever.

"SCARCELY MORE THAN ONE GENIUS APPEARS IN A CENTURY"

Mein Kampf begins with Hitler's birth in an obscure Austrian border town where, a hundred years prior, a German patriot had been executed for defying French occupiers. According to the author, "destiny"[7] had chosen this town as his birthplace to signify his mission to redeem the German people. Like a screenwriter penning a drama *based* on a true story, Hitler embellished his autobiography to convince readers that "the Goddess of Destiny"[8] had selected him to restore German honor and glory. And the more he wrote, the more he believed it. "I gained clarity about a lot of things that I had previously understood only instinctively," Hitler later remarked.[9] Concluding that great nations were never built by elections or democracy, Hitler theorized that only a man of Providence could lead his people to triumph, and that "[s]carcely more than one genius appears in a century."[10] Powerful feelings of omnipotence surged through him. "One truth which must always be borne in the mind," he wrote in *Mein Kampf*, "is that the majority can never replace the man."[11] Though not a practicing Christian, he believed in a cosmology that rewarded the righteous and punished the wicked. Increasingly certain of his righteousness, his self-image was beginning to meld with the Führerprinzip.

Hitler's fictionalized narrative in *Mein Kampf* is among the many deceptions that have led historians to label him an opportunist. Considering his many fabrications, it's hard to disagree. But his self-possession in *Mein Kampf* has another interpretation: In the act of writing the book, the future Nazi dictator transformed into a true believer in his own special identity.

Hitler's need for certainty was born of a refusal to endure the pain of self-examination. As the psychiatrist M. Scott Peck wrote in his book, *People of the Lie*, "The evil do not serenely bear the trial of being displeasing to themselves. In fact, they don't bear it at all."[12] Hitler became who he was in part because there was no one in Austria or Germany willing to properly guide him during his formative years. Like many youth who fall through the cracks, he learned how to survive in isolation. Besides his father, no one had ever really challenged his assumptions. Corporal punishment and humiliation apparently taught him to keep his inner thoughts private. Only to his teenage roommate, August Kubizek, had the future Nazi leader exposed his private thinking. His proclivity for self-protection continued throughout his time in Vienna, during the First World War, and even during the postwar Socialist revolution. Hitler had no real confidants and no girlfriends in those years.

It was only later when he discovered his gift for oratory that Hitler began to mature. For the first time in his life, people were acknowledging his unique talent. Intoxicated by their feedback, he responded with a furious output of creativity. But the sophisticated network that surrounded him had neither the interest nor the training to analyze his mental health. In need of a spokesperson for their nationalist movement, they were only interested in achieving their political aims. If Hitler didn't serve them, someone else would.

Dietrich Eckart was the most giving and supportive of Hitler's sponsors. Unfortunately, his most enduring contribution turned out to be his twisted anti-Semitic ideology. By the time Eckart discovered that Hitler's megalomania was growing out of control, it was already too late. The Nazi leader had stopped listening to the publisher. In the end, Hitler's energy and ambition would dwarf all of his backers.

"THE RECOGNITION OF POSTERITY"

Deep into the writing of *Mein Kampf*, Hitler had another important realization about his identity. While evaluating the differences between philosophers who set social goals and politicians who carry them out, he started to believe that he was both. "At long intervals of human history," he wrote, "it may occasionally happen that the most practical politician and the political philosopher are one. . . . Such a man does not labor to satisfy demands that are obvious to every commoner; he reaches forward towards ends that are comprehensible only to the few. . . . The protest of the present generation, which does not understand him, wrestles with the recognition of posterity, for which he also works."[13] Hitler's sense of personal power was growing exponentially. Later, he would say that at Landsberg he "gained the level of confidence, optimism and faith that could no longer be shaken by anything."[14]

When Hitler neared the time of his release, some officials in Bavaria were reluctant to let him go. Munich's new police chief warned that he represented a permanent danger to public security. Some authorities wanted him deported to Austria. State representatives had even traveled to Vienna to inquire if the Austrian state would take him off their hands. But the Austrian chancellor refused. Since Hitler had joined the Bavarian infantry during the war, he reasoned that Hitler was no longer Austrian. Finally, on December 19, 1924, Bavaria's court announced that the Nazi leader should be immediately paroled.

The following day, Hitler emerged from Landsberg Prison a free man. Anton Drexler and Gregor Strasser—brother of Otto Strasser—proposed to drive him directly to General Ludendorff so the pair could renew their alliance. But, according to Rudolf Hess, Hitler had no interest in seeing the old general and told them to leave. "He was very angry!" Hess wrote in a letter to his girlfriend. "He wants first his rest and nothing else."[15] Then, Hess prophetically observed, "The race for Hitler had begun sooner than I had expected."[16] It was true. Hitler's popularity had only grown in his absence.

For his ride back to Munich, Hitler asked Adolf Müller—the printer of the *Völkischer Beobachter*—to pick him up. Müller rang Heinrich Hoffmann and asked him to come along too. Grabbing his camera, the photographer was eager to snap the first photo of the paroled leader. Pulling up in front of the prison in a Benz convertible, the pair watched the heavy gates creak open. Leaping from the car, Hoffmann prepared to take a photo but was waved off by prison authorities. "Instructions from the government," he was told. "Hitler is not to be photo-graphed as he leaves the fortress."[17] Disheartened, Hoffmann returned to the car and waited. When Hitler appeared, he climbed into the vehicle, and the three drove away. A little later, he turned to Hoffmann, and said, "I'm glad that you have come along. Now you can photograph me without . . . hindrance."[18]

Driving to a spot near the old city gates, Hoffmann composed a picture of Hitler standing next to the car, dressed in a trench coat, and looking forcefully into the lens. It was a cold December day, and the Nazi leader was starting to shiver. "Get a move on Hoffmann," he chided the photographer, "or we'll have a crowd collecting: and anyway, it's bloody cold!"[19]

It would take another eight years before Hitler would become chancellor of Germany. In the interim, severe economic depression would contribute to his growing popularity. In 1933, politicians and eighty-six-year-old Reich president Paul von Hindenburg believed they could control the Nazi leader in his new position as German chancellor. But events, including a mysterious fire in the Reichstag and Hindenburg's unexpected death from lung cancer, would allow Hitler to seize absolute power. That story is for another book. But if we look back at the formative period between the end of the First World War in 1918 and the writing of the first volume of *Mein Kampf* at Landsberg Prison in 1924, we can see nearly all the elements that would allow Hitler to become the Führer of infamy. What makes this period all the more startling is how many times the Nazi leader might have been stopped.

EPILOGUE

On August 2, 1934, Adolf Hitler seized power in Germany after Reich president Paul von Hindenburg suddenly died in office. From that time until his suicide on April 30, 1945, he was the undisputed dictator of Germany.

To plan the liquidation of European Jewry, Hitler relied not so much on his early supporters but on men who entered his orbit well after his release from Landsberg Prison. The architects of the Final Solution, men like Heinrich Himmler, Reinhard Heydrich, and Adolf Eichmann, were not among his early confidantes. Though his criminal regime would perpetrate genocide against innocent civilians, Hitler avoided personal contact with suffering and never visited the concentration camps.

On November 5, 1945, six months after Hitler's death at the end of the Second World War, the photographer Heinrich Hoffmann was seated in a Nuremberg courthouse, awaiting interrogation by the US Army's Counter Intelligence Corps (CIC). The sixty-year-old had been captured earlier in the year at his country house in Bavaria. Telling himself that he was innocent of war crimes, he was incredulous when Americans came knocking on his door. "Great was my scornful indignation," he later wrote in his memoirs, "when I found that I had been denounced to the Americans and my arrest demanded!"[1] His alibi was that he hadn't involved himself in politics, never held a position in the Third Reich, and didn't know about the death camps. But, for the previous twenty-two years, Hoffmann had been responsible for developing the Führer myth in pictures.

Hoffmann had built a vast publishing empire devoted to the sale of Hitler portraits, and he had become a multimillionaire. Unlike those high-ranking Nazis who lived in constant fear of displeasing the dictator, he enjoyed Hitler's friendship and the resulting privileged lifestyle. It was Hoffmann who had introduced Hitler to Eva Braun, an employee in his Munich store, who later married the Nazi dictator and died with him in Berlin.

The Americans had relocated Hoffmann to a low-security villa in the suburbs of Nuremberg so that he could reconstruct the lost card catalog to his immense Nazi photo archives. The collection served as a forensic record of the criminal regime. Though tedious, the task allowed him to reminisce about his life at the center of Nazi power and was a pleasing diversion from his depressing circumstances. While he enjoyed good food and conjugal visits, he was still a prisoner, suffered mood swings, and even attempted suicide.

At his November interrogation, Hoffmann was asked when he first met Hitler. "I had come to know Hitler early in 1923 but not with any personal intimacy," was his evasive response. "When did you join the Nazi Party?" Hoffmann replied, "[19]23." He was lying; he had joined the Nazi Party three years earlier. "And why was it that you joined the party at that time?" pressed his interrogator. "Primarily, it seemed to be important in regard to my business, because I would have no opportunity to attend any one of the [Nazi] meetings, unless I was a member of the party."[2] Hoffmann was lying again. Whenever interrogated, the photographer tried to diminish the perception that he had willfully participated in the Nazi movement, downplaying his relationship with Hitler.

Eventually, Hoffmann was handed over to Bavarian authorities. In a denazification court he was prohibited from practicing his profession and lost all his assets. He also spent several years in a prison labor camp. Angry and incredulous, the photographer seemed incapable of understanding what he had done wrong. In the 1950s, he would write, "I had joined the Nazi Party in April 1920 . . . for at the time, its program seemed to offer the only possible solution to the chaotic problems with which my country was overwhelmed."[3] Unrepentant to the end, Hoffmann died in 1957 at the age of seventy-two.

Like Hoffmann, many of the Nazis who survived the war and were brought to trial had trouble reconciling the past. The Estonian immigrant Alfred Rosenberg, who helped spread anti-Semitism as a member of Thule and became a vocal advocate for the extermination of Jews in Nazi Germany, declared his conscience "to be completely free from any such guilt," before his hanging for war crimes at Nuremberg.[4] Hermann Göring, who was second only to Hitler in the Nazi hierarchy, asked to be shot by firing squad rather than be hanged like a common criminal after his conviction at Nuremberg.[5] When his request was denied, Göring bit down on a capsule of potassium cyanide that he'd concealed on his body. Incapable of feeling remorse for his role in the Nazi genocide, Göring was ready to commit suicide when he realized he would never regain the esteem of the German people.[6]

Ernst Röhm didn't live long enough to face the tribunal at Nuremberg.

In the early summer of 1934, seventeen months after he became chancellor of Germany, Hitler launched a bloody purge of his political enemies called Operation Hummingbird, aka the Night of the Long Knives. Hummingbird's main target was Röhm. In the years following the Beer Hall Putsch, Röhm had removed himself from public life and taken a job training paramilitaries in Bolivia. Returning to Germany in 1930, he was appointed chief of staff of the SA (Brown Shirts), which boasted nearly a million members.

At the head of the SA—reviled for street violence and drunkenness—Röhm eventually aroused the jealousy and suspicion of Hitler's subordinates, including Göring and Reinhard Heydrich. Alleging that he was plotting a coup, the Nazi leadership decided to eliminate him. At Bad Wiessee in Bavaria, Röhm and the top leadership of the SA were arrested on June 30, 1934. As the story goes, the openly gay Röhm was found in bed with an eighteen-year-old boy. Brought to Stadelheim Prison and provided a pistol, he was encouraged to shoot himself. When he refused, Röhm was gunned down in his cell. Over eight-five victims fell in the purge. Some estimate the number of fatalities was much higher. They included Hitler's old adversary from the Beer Hall Putsch, Gustav von Kahr. The former minister-president and triumvirate leader was captured in Munich and taken to Dachau concentration camp. Tortured and shot by the SS, Kahr's body was found to have been hacked to pieces by axes. Another target in Operation Hummingbird was Hermann Ehrhardt. The former leader of Organization Consul and the Ehrhardt Brigade, who had refused to support Hitler during the Beer Hall Putsch, was on the list of enemies marked for assassination, but he managed to escape the country.[7] He later died at the age of ninety in Austria in 1971.

Operation Hummingbird was particularly significant in the way that it codified state-sanctioned murder. Two weeks after Röhm's death, in a radio address delivered in the Reichstag, Hitler remarked, "If anyone reproaches me and asks why I did not resort to the regular courts of justice, then all I can say is this. In this hour I was responsible for the fate of the German people, and thereby I became the supreme judge of the German people. I gave the order to shoot the ringleaders in this treason . . . let it be known for all time to come that if anyone raises his hand to strike the State, then certain death is his lot."[8] Reich President Hindenburg and Hitler's cabinet raised no objection to the murders. Subsequently, the Reichstag passed a measure legalizing the purge and its executions, making Hitler the primary legal authority in Germany.

After his acquittal for his role in the Beer Hall Putsch, Erich Ludendorff ran for Reich president in 1925 and was defeated by Paul von Hindenburg.

Later, while serving as a Reichstag minister in 1926, he divorced Margarethe and remarried. With his new wife, he published a handful of written works in which they accused Christians, Jews, and Freemasons of various conspiracies. By the time Hitler achieved power in 1933, Ludendorff had become estranged from the Nazi leader and was regarded as an old crank. Before his death in 1937 at the age of seventy-two, he allegedly turned on Hitler, saying that the Nazi leader would "bring our nation to inconceivable misery."[9] But many historians believe these statements were forged.

Despite their status as "November Criminals," Reich president Friedrich Ebert and former chancellor Philipp Scheidemann, who declared Germany a republic in 1918, escaped death by assassination. Ebert continued in the office of the presidency until 1925, when he suddenly died of septic shock at the age of fifty-four.[10] Scheidemann served as a minister in the Reichstag throughout the Weimar period. However, when the Nazis seized power in 1933, he fled into exile. Scheidemann eventually settled in Denmark, where he died in 1939 at the age of seventy-four.

Erhard Auer, the minister of interior who opposed Kurt Eisner and was shot in the Bavarian parliament in 1919 was not as lucky as Scheidemann. Having criticized Hitler and the NSDAP in the pages of the *Münchener Post*, Auer was apprehended by the Nazis when they came to power in 1933 and was sent to Stadelheim Prison. Eventually released, he was re-arrested eleven years later for his support of the assassination attempt on Hitler known as Operation Valkyrie. Though seriously ill at the time of his arrest, Auer was taken to Dachau concentration camp and died in Nazi custody at the age of sixty-nine in 1945.

Auer never satisfied his critics with an acceptable explanation of why he sent flowers to Count Anton Arco-Valley while the pair coincidentally recuperated in the same Munich hospital in 1919. As for Eisner's killer, Arco-Valley was released from Stadelheim Prison in 1925 and pardoned by a Bavarian judge two years later. When the Nazis came to power, he was left alone despite his Jewish background. Surviving the war, the forty-seven-year-old was killed in a traffic accident in Salzburg, Austria, in 1945.

Ernst Hanfstaengl enjoyed a friendly rapport with Hitler until he was cast out of the Führer's inner circle in 1937. The Harvard graduate was at odds with Joseph Goebbels and had been removed from Hitler's staff four years earlier. On a flight to Spain, Hanfstaengl learned that his pilot had been ordered to eject him over enemy territory, where he was certain to die. Landing instead at an airfield near Leipzig, Hanfstaengl was allowed to escape to Switzerland.

According to Hitler and Göring, the incident on the plane had been part of an elaborate joke to scare the German-American. Göring even sent Hanfstaengl a letter explaining the joke and pleading for his return. But the former inner circle advisor was not persuaded and, after securing his son's release from Germany, moved to England. When the Second World War began, Hanfstaengl was arrested and eventually turned over to the Americans, who used him to help write intelligence profiles on the Nazi leadership. His testimony greatly assisted the work of Walter C. Langer, who made a psychoanalytic study of Hitler for the Offices of Strategic Services (OSS). In the late 1950s, Hanfstaengl returned to Germany, where he died in 1975 at the age of eighty-eight.

When Ernst Toller was released from prison in 1925, he was already a famous playwright. His play *Transformation*, which he completed in prison, premiered in Berlin in 1919. Three more plays that he wrote while incarcerated were also staged. In time, he would be renowned as one of the greatest German expressionist playwrights of the twentieth century. But not all Germans appreciated his work. Toller earned the antipathy of the Far Right by writing essays and articles warning of the dangers of Hitler and Nazism.[11] The historian Robert Ellis wrote, "He knew the Nazis were ruthless, would quickly eliminate any institution opposed to them, and establish a reign of terror, and then it would be too late to remove them from the power they had seized."[12] In 1933, the Nazis forced Toller into exile and revoked his citizenship. After living in England, he traveled to the United States and Canada, where he gave lectures against Nazism. Unfortunately, the playwright had difficulty getting his screenplays produced and fell on lean economic times.

Settling in New York City, he worked as a journalist and joined a group of artists living in exile. After learning that his brother and sister had been arrested in Germany and sent to a concentration camp, Toller became depressed.[13] Then in 1939, at the age of forty-five, his sorrow got the better of him and he hanged himself in New York's Mayflower Hotel.[14] Some speculated that the playwright was murdered.[15] But it was never proven.

Though Toller's life ended in despair, his penetrating insight—born of the suffering in the trenches of Verdun—continues to be relevant today. "The words, 'I am proud to be a German' or 'I am proud to be a Jew,' sounded ineffably stupid to me. [I might] as well say, 'I am proud to have brown eyes,'" Toller wrote in his memoirs. "If I were asked where I belonged [or where I came from] I should answer that a Jewish mother had born me, that Germany had nourished me, Europe had formed me, my home was the earth, and the world my fatherland."[16]

Sigmund Fraenkel, the president of Munich's chamber of commerce and trade, who sent a prophetic warning to Ernst Toller and others about the dangers of allowing Judaism to be linked with Bolshevism, didn't live long enough to see Hitler come to power. Six years after he wrote his letter, Fraenkel died in Munich in 1925.

Finally, there is Hitler. Before his downfall in the Second World War, the Nazi dictator had nearly achieved his vision for a Pan-German empire in Europe. He'd conquered almost the entire continent. But the cost was staggering. An estimated 48 million people were killed as a result of the wars he'd started, including six million Jews and other noncombatants in the Nazi concentration camps. Hitler thought future Europeans would thank him for cleansing the continent of Jews. Instead, he is reviled as the worst criminal of the twentieth century; symbols of his regime are banned in Germany, and Nazi concentration camps are preserved as national parks and permanent reminders of the dangers of genocide, totalitarianism, and dictatorship.

The international community wouldn't be what it is today without Hitler. As the German author Sebastian Haffner wrote in 1979, "Today's world, whether we like it or not, is the work of Hitler. . . . Without Hitler there would be no Israel."[17] Without Hitler there would be no United Nations or improved standards for international justice.

And yet, the radical ideas to which Hitler was exposed and that he magnified for the purpose of conquering Europe and murdering Jews are alive and well in today's world. The names, the context, and the scale may be different, but tyrants—large and small—continue to scapegoat the innocent and trample on human rights.

ACKNOWLEDGMENTS

Researching and writing this book was a challenging and deeply meaningful undertaking, and there are many people to thank. First and foremost, I want to acknowledge and thank the editor Steven L. Mitchell, associate editor Sheila Stewart, and all the good staff at Prometheus for their insight and support of this book. Next, I want to thank my agent, Jeff Ourvan, for providing his invaluable encouragement and professional guidance throughout the process. Researchers Monika Malessa in Munich, Simon Fowler in London, and Amy Cheung von Haam in Los Angeles each made important contributions. Monika's research, translations, and familiarity with important archives were particularly exceptional. Andrew McCormick was very helpful with his mapmaking. Jonathan Hall took an early interest in the project and provided timely translations to help capture nuances in German I might have otherwise missed.

The professor and author Peter Longerich, who is among the most accomplished scholars in Germany on the Third Reich and the Holocaust, took time out of his busy schedule to offer me critical guidance. Dr. Klaus Lankheit of the Institut für Zeitgeschichte (Institute for Contemporary History) in Munich went out of his way to facilitate my research and was truly inspiring and supportive. Kurt Eisner's foremost biographer, Bernhard Grau, kindly answered my questions about the former minister-president at his office in Munich. The author Andreas Eichmüller, of the Documentation Center for the History of National Socialism in Munich, was also helpful when we met in the Bavarian capital. At UCLA, I had the privilege of studying under the psychohistorian Dr. Peter Loewenberg, who has made important contributions to our understanding of the history of early-twentieth-century Germany and the Third Reich. In addition, the writings of the philosopher and educator, Dr. Daisaku Ikeda were indispensable in helping me to gain insight into human nature, and formulate an approach to this subject.

Among the institutions, parks, and museums that helped provide historical perspective on Hitler and Nazism were the Institut für Zeitgeschichte, the Documentation Center for the History of National Socialism in Munich and Obersalzberg, Dachau concentration camp, Auschwitz-Birkenau concentration camp, the Bavarian State Library, and the Simon Wiesenthal Center in Los Angeles.

When I began researching this subject, it was the curiosity of my dear friend and fellow filmmaker Darin Nellis that compelled me to pursue the question of how Hitler was made. Alex Ryan was another supportive filmmaker and friend whose creative instincts helped sharpen the narrative. The book wouldn't be what it is without the friendship and influence of Shinji and Donna Ishibashi, Jack and Janet Pickering, and Tom and Valeria Chu, who have also provided invaluable support to me over the years. So have friends like Peter von Haam. My father, Bill, and my brother, Jess, helped spark my initial interest in the subject of the book. In 1978, the past came alive when Dad took us on a tour through Germany and Austria to destinations including Berlin, Bayreuth, Nuremberg, and Vienna. I can still picture him leading us through the center of Munich to the Odeonsplatz, where he read passages from John Toland's *Adolf Hitler* to describe the Beer Hall Putsch. The trip included a visit to Dachau concentration camp, which made a lasting impression on me.

Among the most important contributors to this book is Dr. James Berenson, who helped bring me back from certain death when I was struggling with myeloma (bone marrow cancer) in 2014. At the time, I couldn't walk or sit up because of the degenerative effects of the illness. Dr. Berenson's treatment arrested my disease and stabilized it. It was during the time before I returned to health and started walking again that I began researching this book. At Dr. Berenson's clinic, fellow patients and nurses offered me great encouragement as I continued to write.

Finally, this work would not have been possible without the loving support of my wife and son, to whom the book is dedicated.

NOTES

INTRODUCTION

1. Like much of Munich, the Hofbräuhaus Festsaal was destroyed in Allied bombing raids during the Second World War. Rebuilt in the style of the original and occupying the same real estate, today's Festsaal imitates its predecessor.

2. Anton Drexler, Dietrich Eckart, Gottfried Feder, and Adolf Hitler, "The Program of the NSDAP," in Barbara Miller Lane and Leila J. Rupp, trans. and eds., *Nazi Ideology before 1933: A Documentation* (Austin: University of Texas Press, 1978), p. 89.

3. Adolf Hitler, *Mein Kampf*, trans. James Murphy (1939; Warwickshire, UK: Coda Books, 2011), p. 291.

4. Friedrich von Bernhardi, *Germany and the Next War*, trans. Allen H. Powles (New York: Chas. A. Eron, 1914), p. 81.

5. Ibid., p. 153.

6. Robert B. Asprey, *The German High Command at War: Hindenburg and Ludendorff Conduct World War I* (New York: William Morrow, 1991), p. 23.

7. Otto Strasser, *Hitler and I*, trans. Gwenda David and Eric Mosbacher (Boston: Houghton, 1940), p. 62.

8. Konrad Heiden, *Der Fuehrer: Hitler's Rise to Power*, trans. Ralph Manheim (Boston: Houghton Mifflin, 1944), p. 92.

CHAPTER ONE: THE HORROR OF WAR

1. Adolf Hitler, *Mein Kampf*, trans. James Murphy (1939; Warwickshire, UK: Coda Books, 2011), p. 131.

2. Thomas Weber, *Hitler's First War: Adolf Hitler, the Men of the List Regiment, and the First World War* (Oxford: Oxford University Press, 2010), p. 221.

3. Ibid.

4. Hitler, *Mein Kampf*, p. 133.

5. Ibid., p. 134.

6. Alistair Horne, *The Price of Glory: Verdun 1916* (London: Penguin Books, 1962), p. 36.

7. Frederik Schouten, "Ernst Toller: An Intellectual Youth Biography, 1893–1918" (PhD thesis; Florence: European University Institute, Department of History and Civilization, July 2007), p. 75.

8. Ernst Toller, *I Was a German: The Autobiography of Ernst Toller*, trans. Edward Crankshaw (New York: William Morrow, 1934), p. 62.

9. Robert Ellis, *Ernst Toller and German Society: Intellectuals as Leaders and Critics, 1914–1939* (Madison, NJ: Fairleigh Dickinson University Press, 2013), p. 41.

10. Toller, *I Was a German*, p. 21.

11. Ibid., p. 284.

12. Schouten, "Ernst Toller: An Intellectual Youth," p. 97.

13. Ellis, *Ernst Toller and German Society*, p. 41.

14. Toller, *I Was a German*, p. 80.

15. Horne, *Price of Glory*, p. 42.

16. Ibid., p. 81.

17. Ibid., p. 102.

18. Ibid., p. 36.

19. History Channel, *1916: Total War: The Battle of Verdun*, hosted by British Major General Julian Thompson (New York: A&E Television, 2006).

20. Toller, *I Was a German*, p. 84.

21. Ibid., p. 87.

22. Schouten, "Ernst Toller: An Intellectual Youth," p. 110.

23. Will Brownell and Denise Drace-Brownell, *The First Nazi: Erich Ludendorff, the Man Who Made Hitler Possible*, with Alexander Rovt (Berkeley: Counterpoint, 2016), pp. 41–42.

24. Frank B. Tipton, *A History of Modern Germany Since 1815* (Berkeley: University of California Press, 2003), p. 313.

25. "The Chief of the General Staff was accordingly unshaken in his conviction that a favorable termination of the war was not to be obtained in any other way than by force of arms." Erich von Falkenhayn, *The German General Staff and Its Decisions, 1914–1916* (New York: Dodd, Mead, 1920), pp. 331–32.

26. Schouten, "Ernst Toller: An Intellectual Youth," p. 125.

27. Ibid., p. 119.

28. John Toland, *Adolf Hitler*, 1st Anchor ed. (New York: Anchor Books, 1992), p. 69.

29. Kaiser Wilhelm II, "[Kaiser] Wilhelm II's 'Easter Message' (April 7, 1917)," German History in Documents and Images: Germany at War, 1914–1918: Privation and Ferment on the Home Front, April 7, 1917, http://germanhistorydocs.ghi-dc.org/sub_document.cfm ?document_id=978 (accessed January 12, 2018).

30. Toller, *I Was a German*, p. 93.

31. Schouten, "Ernst Toller: An Intellectual Youth," p. 30.

32. Richard Grunberger, *Red Rising in Bavaria* (London: Arthur Barker, 1973), p. 15.

33. Schouten, "Ernst Toller: An Intellectual Youth," p. 143.

34. Ibid., p. 163.

35. Ibid., p. 170.

36. Ibid.

37. Toller, *I Was a German*, p. 108.

38. Ibid., p. 116.

39. Ibid., p. 119.

CHAPTER TWO: THE GREAT DECEPTION

1. Will Brownell and Denise Drace-Brownell, *The First Nazi: Erich Ludendorff, the Man Who Made Hitler Possible*, with Alexander Rovt (Berkeley: Counterpoint, 2016), p. 72.

2. Paul W. Doerr, "November 1918 as a Transition in Twentieth Century War Termination" (paper, Acadia University, Department of History and Classics, Nova Scotia, 2002), p. 5.

3. David Stevenson, *Cataclysm: The First World War as Political Tragedy* (New York: Basic Books, 2005), p. 324.

4. *World Heritage Encyclopedia*, s.v. "Kerensky Government: April Crisis," quote attributed to Minister of Foreign Affairs Pavel Milukov, April 18, 1917, http://www.world library.org/articles/kerensky_government (accessed January 12, 2018).

5. Brownell and Brownell, *First Nazi*, p. 98.

6. Ibid., p. 101.

7. Ibid., pp. 134–35.

8. Martin Marix Evans, *1918: The Year of Victories* (London: Arcturus, 2002), p. 68.

9. Brownell and Brownell, *First Nazi*, p. 63.

10. G. J. Meyer, *A World Undone: The Story of the Great War, 1914 to 1918*, reprint ed. (New York: Bantam, 2007), p. 648.

11. Evans, *1918*, p. 86.

12. Ibid., p. 113.

13. Ibid., p. 185.

14. Ibid.

15. Erich Ludendorff, *Ludendorff's Own Story: August 1914–November 1918: The Great War from the Siege of Liège to the Signing of the Armistice as Viewed from the Grand Headquarters of the German Army* (1919; San Francisco: Pickle Partners, 2013), p. 332.

16. Brownell and Brownell, *First Nazi*, p. 74.

17. Hugh Cecil and Peter Liddle, *Facing Armageddon: The First World War Experienced* (Barnsley, UK: Leo Cooper/Pen & Sword, 1996), pp. 51–65.

18. Ibid.

19. Paul von Hintze, "Remarks of von Hintze, Secretary of State for Foreign Affairs at That Time, with Regard to Discussions with General Ludendorff in July and August, 1918," in *History of Events Immediately Preceding the Armistice* (Berlin: Official Documents from the Office of the German Chancellor, Crown, 1919), p. 4.

20. Ibid.

21. Ibid.

22. Ibid.

23. Ibid., p. 5.

24. Arthur James Grant and H. W. V. Temperley, *Europe in the Twentieth Century 1905–1970* (London: Routledge, 1985), p. 87.

25. "Eyewitness," *Rheinische Westfälische Zeitung*, September 28, 1918.

26. Ludendorff, *Ludendorff's Own Story*, p. 377.

27. Hintze, "Remarks of von Hintze," p. 16.

28. Ludendorff, *Ludendorff's Own Story*, p. 378.

29. Cecil and Liddle, *Facing Armageddon*, p. 60.

30. Albrecht von Thaer, "Erich Ludendorff Admits Defeat, Diary Entry, October 1, 1918," German History in Documents and Images, Germany at War, 1914–1918: Battle, p. 1, http://germanhistorydocs.ghi-dc.org/sub_document.cfm?document_id=814 (accessed January 12, 2018).

31. Ibid.

32. Ibid.

33. Cecil and Liddle, *Facing Armageddon*, p. 60.

34. Thaer, "Erich Ludendorff Admits Defeat," p. 1.

35. Cecil and Liddle, *Facing Armageddon*.

36. Hintze, "Remarks of von Hintze," p. 22.

37. Ibid., p. iii.

38. Wilhelm Solf, "Correspondence between the United States and Germany," *American Journal of International Law*, October 30, 1918, p. 91.

39. Ibid., p. 93.

40. Thomas Weber, *Hitler's First War: Adolf Hitler, the Men of the List Regiment, and the First World War* (Oxford: Oxford University Press, 2010), p. 221.

41. Ibid.

CHAPTER THREE: A REVOLUTION LED BY GERMAN JEWS

1. Robert B. Asprey, *The German High Command at War: Hindenburg and Ludendorff Conduct World War* I (New York: William Morrow, 1991), p. 461.

2. Ernst Toller, *I Was a German: The Autobiography of Ernst Toller*, trans. Edward Crankshaw (New York: William Morrow, 1934), p. 137.

3. Asprey, *German High Command at War*, p. 468.

4. Richard J. Evans, *The Coming of the Third Reich* (London: Penguin Books, 2005), p. 14.

5. Allan Mitchell, *Revolution in Bavaria 1918–1919: The Eisner Regime and the Soviet Republic* (Princeton NJ: Princeton University Press, 1965), p. 75.

6. David Clay Large, *Where Ghosts Walked: Munich's Road to the Third Reich* (New York: W. W. Norton, 1997), p. 109.

7. Richard Grunberger, *Red Rising in Bavaria* (London: Arthur Barker, 1973), p. 77.

8. Evans, *Coming of the Third Reich*, p. 157.

9. Large, *Where Ghosts Walked*, p. 67.

10. Grunberger, *Red Rising in Bavaria*, p. 31.

11. Mitchell, *Revolution in Bavaria*, p. 91.

12. Grunberger, *Red Rising in Bavaria*, p. 33.

13. Ibid.

14. Ibid.

15. Ibid.

16. Ibid., p. 34.

17. Large, *Where Ghosts Walked*, p. 78.

18. Konrad Heiden, *Der Fuehrer: Hitler's Rise to Power*, trans. Ralph Manheim (Boston: Houghton Mifflin, 1944), p. 20.

19. Grunberger, *Red Rising in Bavaria*, p. 34.

20. Large, *Where Ghosts Walked*, p. 80.

21. Bernhard Grau, *Kurt Eisner, 1867–1919: Eine Biographie* (Munich: Verlag C. H. Beck, 2001), p. 377.

22. Ibid.

23. Grunberger, *Red Rising in Bavaria*, p. 46.

24. Robert Ellis, *Ernst Toller and German Society: Intellectuals as Leaders and Critics, 1914–1939* (Madison, NJ: Fairleigh Dickinson University Press, 2013), p. 90.

25. Grunberger, *Red Rising in Bavaria*, p. 37.

26. Ibid., p. 38.

27. Ibid.

28. Ibid., p. 39.

29. Large, *Where Ghosts Walked*, p. 81.

30. Toller, *I Was a German*, p. 141.

31. Large, *Where Ghosts Walked*, p. 81.

32. Asprey, *German High Command at War*, p. 485.

33. [Gisbert von] Romberg, "To His Excellency von Hintze, G. H. Q., Berlin, October 31, 1918," no. 95 in *History of Events Immediately Preceding the Armistice* (Berlin: Government Printing Works, 1919), p. 106.

34. Ibid., p. 118.

35. Large, *Where Ghosts Walked*, p. 81.

36. Harry Harmer, *Friedrich Ebert: Germany* (London: Haus, 2008), p. 57.

37. Ibid., p. 12.

38. Ibid., p. 56.

39. Ibid., p. 60.

40. Ruth Henig, *The Weimar Republic: 1919–1933* (London: Routledge, 2006), p. 10.

41. Harmer, *Friedrich Ebert*, p. 58.

42. Roger Parkinson, *Tormented Warrior: Ludendorff and the Supreme Command* (New York: Stein and Day, 1978), p. 183.

43. Ibid., p. 184.

44. Ibid., p. 185.

45. Ibid., p. 186.

46. Richard Hanser, *Putsch! How Hitler Made Revolution* (New York: Peter H. Wyden, 1970), p. 131.

47. Harmer, *Friedrich Ebert*, p. 57.

48. Evans, *Coming of the Third Reich*, p. 60.

49. Toller, *I Was a German*, p. 131.

50. Harmer, *Friedrich Ebert*, p. 62.

51. Ibid., p. 60.

52. BBC, *Armistice: The End Game of World War One*, hosted by David Reynolds, Professor of International History, Cambridge University (London: BBC Four, 2008).

CHAPTER FOUR: THE OPPOSITION STIRS

1. Joseph Howard Tyson, *Hitler's Mentor: Dietrich Eckart, His Life, Times, & Milieu* (New York: iUniverse, 2008), p. 128.

2. Ralph Engelman, "Dietrich Eckart and the Genesis of Nazism" (PhD thesis; St. Louis, MO: Washington University, 1971), p. 7.

3. Tyson, *Hitler's Mentor*, p. 3.

4. Engelman, "Dietrich Eckart," p. 13.

5. Ibid., pp. 10–11.

6. Ibid., p. 31.

7. Ibid., p. 42.

8. Ibid., p. 43.

9. Ibid., p. 54.

10. David Luhrssen, *Hammer of the Gods: The Thule Society and the Birth of Nazism* (Washington, DC: Potomac Books, 2012), p. 30.

11. Ibid., p. 40.

12. Engelman, "Dietrich Eckart," p. 66.

13. Tyson, *Hitler's Mentor*, pp. 51–52.

14. Ibid., p. 51.

15. Engelman, "Dietrich Eckart," p. 100.

16. Tyson, *Hitler's Mentor*, p. 119.

17. Ibid., p. 115.

18. Robert Cecil, *The Myth of the Master Race: Alfred Rosenberg and Nazi Ideology* (New York: Dodd Mead, 1972), p. 22.

19. David Clay Large, *Where Ghosts Walked: Munich's Road to the Third Reich* (New York: W. W. Norton, 1997), p. 70.

20. Tyson, *Hitler's Mentor*, p. 118.

21. Ibid., p. 129.

22. Allan Mitchell, *Revolution in Bavaria 1918–1919: The Eisner Regime and the Soviet Republic* (Princeton, NJ: Princeton University Press, 1965), p. 127.

23. Ibid., p. 129.

24. Richard Grunberger, *Red Rising in Bavaria* (London: Arthur Barker, 1973), p. 49.

25. Mitchell, *Revolution in Bavaria*, p. 131.

26. Ibid., p. 129. The source of this misinformation was Eisner's go-between, Friedrich Wilhelm Foerster—coincidentally the same professor whom Ernst Toller had rallied to defend when the teacher was assaulted at LMU in Munich for criticizing the war in 1917.

27. Ibid., p. 132.

28. "The New Books: Peace and World Relations," *Independent* (with *Harper's Weekly*), February 1, 1919, p. 171; Karl Max Lichnowsky, *The Guilt of Germany for the War of German Aggression* (New York: G. P. Putnam's Sons, 1918).

29. Ibid.

30. Ibid., p. 136.

31. Mitchell, *Revolution in Bavaria*, p. 155.

32. Ibid., p. 161.

33. Grunberger, *Red Rising in Bavaria*, p. 55.

34. Mitchell, *Revolution in Bavaria*, p. 166.

35. Large, *Where Ghosts Walked*, p. 86.

36. Mitchell, *Revolution in Bavaria*, p. 174.

37. Luhrssen, *Hammer of the Gods*, p. 108.

38. Ibid., pp. 109–10.

39. Ibid., pp. 108–109.

40. Rudolf von Sebottendorff, *Bevor Hitler Kam* (Munich: Deukula-Verlag Grassinger, 1933), p. 64.

41. Large, *Where Ghosts Walked*, p. 88.

42. Grunberger, *Red Rising in Bavaria*, p. 62.

43. Rosa Luxemburg, "What Does the Spartacus League Want?" in *All Power to the Councils! A Documentary History of the German Revolution of 1918–1919*, ed. and trans. Gabriel Kuhn (Oakland, CA.: PM Press, 2012), p. 103.

44. Rob Sewell, *Germany from Revolution to Counter-Revolution* (London: Fortress Books, 1988), p. 27.

45. Pierre Broué, *German Revolution: 1917–1923*, trans. John Archer (Chicago: Haymarket Books, 2006), p. 205.

46. Harry Harmer, *Friedrich Ebert, Germany* (London: Haus Histories, 2008), p. 70.

47. Grunberger, *Red Rising in Bavaria*, p. 58.

48. Mitchell, *Revolution in Bavaria*, p. 192.

49. Ibid., p. 183.

50. Grunberger, *Red Rising in Bavaria*, p. 57.

51. Ibid., p. 62.

52. Ibid., p. 63.

53. Luhrssen, *Hammer of the Gods*, p. 110.

54. Mitchell, *Revolution in Bavaria*, p. 200.

55. Luhrssen, *Hammer of the Gods*, p. 110.

56. Ibid.

57. Ibid., p. 111.

58. Ibid.

59. Mitchell, *Revolution in Bavaria*, p. 202.

60. Ibid., p. 204.

61. Luhrssen, *Hammer of the Gods*, p. 111.

CHAPTER FIVE: THE DEATH OF IDEALISM

1. Roger Parkinson, *Tormented Warrior: Ludendorff and the Supreme Command* (New York: Stein and Day, 1978), p. 188.

2. Erich Ludendorff, *Ludendorff's Own Story: August 1914–November 1918: The Great War from the Siege of Liège to the Signing of the Armistice as Viewed from the Grand Headquarters of the German Army* (1919; San Francisco: Pickle Partners, 2013), p. 141.

3. Robert G. Waite, *Vanguard of Nazism: The Free Corps Movement in Postwar Germany 1918–1923* (New York: W. W. Norton, 1952), p. 15.

4. Harry Harmer, *Friedrich Ebert: Germany* (London: Haus, 2008), p. 70.

5. Waite, *Vanguard of Nazism*, p. 23.

6. Ibid., p. 42.

7. Harmer, *Friedrich Ebert*, p. 70.

8. Ibid., p. 15.

9. Pierre Broué, *The German Revolution: 1917–1923*, trans. John Archer (Chicago: Haymarket Books, 2006), p. 241.

10. Ibid., p. 244.

11. Waite, *Vanguard of Nazism*, p. 61.

12. Ibid.

13. Harmer, *Friedrich Ebert*, pp. 70–71.

14. Broué, *German Revolution*, p. 255.

15. David Clay Large, *Where Ghosts Walked: Munich's Road to the Third Reich* (New York: W. W. Norton, 1997), p. 88.

16. Heinz A. Heinz, *Hitler: Personal Recollections, Memoirs of Hitler from Those Who Knew Him* (Barnsley, UK: Pen and Sword, 2015), p. 94.

17. Ibid.

18. Konrad Heiden, *A History of National Socialism* (New York: Routledge, 2010), p. 4.

19. David Luhrssen, *Hammer of the Gods: The Thule Society and the Birth of Nazism* (Washington, DC: Potomac Books, 2012), p. 153.

20. Richard Hanser, *Putsch! How Hitler Made Revolution* (New York: Peter H. Wyden, 1970), p. 156.

21. Ibid.

22. Nicholas Goodrick-Clarke, *The Occult Roots of Nazism: Secret Aryan Cults and Their Influence on Nazi Ideology* (London: Tauris Parke Paperbacks, 2004), p. 150.

23. Hanser, *Putsch!* p. 155.

24. Goodrick-Clarke, *Occult Roots of Nazism*, p. 150.

25. Anton Drexler and Karl Harrer, "Guidelines of the German Workers' Party (1919)," *Nazi Ideology before 1933: A Documentation*, trans. and ed. Barbara Miller Lane and Leia J. Rupp (Austin: University of Texas Press, 1978), p. 47.

26. Thomas Weber, *Hitler's First War: Adolf Hitler, the Men of the List Regiment, and the First World War* (Oxford: Oxford University Press, 2010), p. 229.

27. Richard Grunberger, *Red Rising in Bavaria* (London: Arthur Barker, 1973), p. 64.

28. Large, *Where Ghosts Walked*, p. 88.

29. Ibid., p. 87.

30. Allan Mitchell, *Revolution in Bavaria 1918–1919: The Eisner Regime and the Soviet Republic* (Princeton, NJ: Princeton University Press, 1965), p. 212.

31. Large, *Where Ghosts Walked*, p. 89.

32. Grunberger, *Red Rising in Bavaria*, p. 66.

33. Mitchell, *Revolution in Bavaria*, p. 244.

34. Hanser, *Putsch!* p. 150.

35. Ibid., p. 151.

36. Ibid.

37. Mitchell, *Revolution in Bavaria*, p. 246.

38. Ibid., p. 251.

39. Weber, *Hitler's First War*, p. 229.

40. Bruno Naarden, *Socialist Europe and Revolutionary Russia: Perception and Prejudice, 1848–1923* (Cambridge University Press, 1992), p. 324.

41. Ibid., pp. 324–325.

42. John de Kay, *The Spirit of the International at Berne* (1919), p. 3, https://archive.org/stream/spiritofinternat00dekarich/spiritofinternat00dekarich_djvu.txt (accessed January 12, 2018).

43. Ibid., p. 22.

44. Ibid., p. 23.

45. Mitchell, *Revolution in Bavaria*, p. 255.

46. De Kay, *Spirit of the International at Berne*, p. 72.

47. Mitchell, *Revolution in Bavaria*, p. 255.

48. Ibid.

49. Grunberger, *Red Rising in Bavaria*, p. 71.

50. Ibid., p. 72.

51. Adolf Hitler, *Mein Kampf*, trans. James Murphy (1939; Warwickshire, UK: Coda Books, 2011), p. 98.

52. Bernhard Grau, *Kurt Eisner 1867–1919: Eine Biographie* (Munich: Verlag C. H. Beck, 2001), p. 401.

53. Grunberger, *Red Rising in Bavaria*, p. 72.

54. Erich Mühsam, "From Eisner to Leviné: The Emergence of the Bavarian Council Republic," in *All Power to the Councils! A Documentary History of the German Revolution 1918–1919*, ed. and trans. Gabriel Kuhn (Oakland, CA: PM Press, 2012), p. 220.

55. William Gillespie, *Dietrich Eckart: An Introduction for the English-Speaking Student* (Houston: self-pub., June 1975), p. 12.

In 1919, the German mark had depreciated to less than half of its prewar value. According to the historian Laurence Moyer, in 1914 the regular price of a loaf of German bread was fifty pfennig (one half mark), "roughly equivalent to an hour's wages for a semi-skilled worker." Laurence V. Moyer, *Victory Must be Ours: Germany in the Great War, 1914–1918* (London: Leo Cooper, 1995), p. 123.

56. Ralph Engelman, "Dietrich Eckart and the Genesis of Nazism" (PhD thesis; St. Louis, MO: Washington University, 1971), p. 108.

57. Joseph Howard Tyson, *Hitler's Mentor: Dietrich Eckart, His Life, Times, & Milieu* (New York: iUniverse, 2008), p. 131.

58. Alfred Rosenberg, "The Russian Jewish Revolution," *Nazi Ideology before 1933*, trans. and ed. Lane and Rupp, p. 50.

59. Ibid., p. 55.

60. Mühsam, "From Eisner to Leviné," p. 221.

61. Mitchell, *Revolution in Bavaria*, p. 262.

62. Ibid., p. 266.

63. Mitchell, *Revolution in Bavaria*, p. 262.

64. Grunberger, *Red Rising in Bavaria*, p. 76.

65. Ibid.

66. Ibid., pp. 76–77.

67. Mitchell, *Revolution in Bavaria*, p. 271.

68. Ibid.

69. Hanser, *Putsch!* p. 163.

70. Large, *Where Ghosts Walked*, p. 90.

71. Grunberger, *Red Rising in Bavaria*, p. 78.

72. Hanser, *Putsch!* p. 160.

73. Friedrich Hitzer, *Anton Graf Arco: Das Attentat auf Kurt Eisner und die Schüsse im Landtag* (Munich: Knesebeck & Schuler, 1988), p. 387.

74. Large, *Where Ghosts Walked*, p. 91.

75. Luhrssen, *Hammer of the Gods*, p. 114.

76. Large, *Where Ghosts Walked*, p. 91.

77. Ibid.

78. Ibid.

79. Ibid.

80. Grunberger, *Red Rising in Bavaria*, p. 78.

CHAPTER SIX: THE SOVIET REPUBLIC

1. Ernst Toller, *I Was a German: The Autobiography of Ernst Toller*, trans. Edward Crankshaw (New York: William Morrow, 1934), p. 151.

2. Richard Grunberger, *Red Rising in Bavaria* (London: Arthur Barker, 1973), p. 80.

3. Ibid., p. 81.

4. Ibid., p. 80.

5. Erich Mühsam, "From Eisner to Leviné: The Emergence of the Bavarian Council Republic," in *All Power to the Councils! A Documentary History of the German Revolution of 1918–1919*, ed. and trans. Gabriel Kuhn (Oakland, CA: PM Press, 2012), p. 223.

6. Friedrich Hitzer, *Anton Graf Arco: Das Attentat auf Kurt Eisner und die Schüsse im Landtag* (Munich: Knesebeck & Schuler, 1988), p. 311 [author's translation].

7. Toller, *I Was a German*, p. 152.

8. David Clay Large, *Where Ghosts Walked: Munich's Road to the Third Reich* (New York: W. W. Norton, 1997), p. 103.

According to historian Anthony Read, the hostages came from "prominent bourgeois organizations." Shortly thereafter, they were released on the "condition that they remained in Munich." Anthony Read, *The World on Fire: 1919 and the Battle with Bolshevism* (London: W. W. Norton & Company, 2008), p. 118.

9. Allan Mitchell, *Revolution in Bavaria 1918–1919: The Eisner Regime and the Soviet Republic* (Princeton, NJ, Princeton University Press, 1965), p. 283.

10. Ibid., p. 284.

11. Ibid., p. 285.

12. Ibid., p. 275.

13. Large, *Where Ghosts Walked*, p. 104.

14. Thomas Weber, *Hitler's First War: Adolf Hitler, the Men of the List Regiment, and the First World War* (Oxford: Oxford University Press: 2010), p. 251.

Footage of Eisner's funeral procession and the man who resembled Hitler can be viewed at https://www.youtube.com/watch?v=Dem2pvU4AjY (accessed February 6, 2018).

15. Weber, *Hitler's First War*, p. 251.

16. Adolf Hitler, *Mein Kampf*, trans. James Murphy (1939; Warwickshire, UK: Coda Books, 2011), p. 344.

17. Mitchell, *Revolution in Bavaria*, p. 276.

18. Large, *Where Ghosts Walked*, p. 92.

19. William Smaldone, *Confronting Hitler: The German Social Democrats in Defense of the Weimar Republic, 1929–1933* (Lanham, MD: Lexington Books, 2010), p. 150.

20. Mitchell, *Revolution in Bavaria*, p. 286.

21. Mühsam, "From Eisner to Leviné," p. 228.

22. Mitchell, *Revolution in Bavaria*.

23. Ibid., pp. 287–89.

24. Grunberger, *Red Rising in Bavaria*, p. 89.

25. Mitchell, *Revolution in Bavaria*, pp. 290–91.

26. Mühsam, "From Eisner to Leviné," p. 232.

27. Mitchell, *Revolution in Bavaria*, p. 296.

28. Large, *Where Ghosts Walked*, p. 106.

29. Mühsam, "From Eisner to Leviné," p. 235.

30. Large, *Where Ghosts Walked*, pp. 106–107.

31. Mitchell, *Revolution in Bavaria*, pp. 306–307.

32. Large, *Where Ghosts Walked*, p. 107.

33. Ibid.

34. Ibid., p. 108.

35. David Luhrssen, *Hammer of the Gods: The Thule Society and the Birth of Nazism* (Washington, DC: Potomac Books, 2012), p. 118.

36. Toller, *I Was a German*, p. 158.

37. Large, *Where Ghosts Walked*, pp. 108–10.

38. Robert Ellis, *Ernst Toller and German Society: Intellectuals as Leaders and Critics, 1914–1939* (Madison, NJ: Fairleigh Dickinson University Press, 2013), p. 109.

39. Ibid., p. 110.

40. Toller, *I Was a German*, p. 159.

41. Ibid., pp. 160–61.

42. Richard J. Evans, *The Coming of the Third Reich* (London: Penguin Books, 2005), p. 158.

43. Mühsam, "From Eisner to Leviné," p. 251.

44. Grunberger, *Red Rising in Bavaria*, p. 110.

45. Ibid.

46. Evans, *Coming of the Third Reich*, p. 158.

47. Hans Lamm, *Von Juden in München: Ein Gedenkbuch* (Munich: Ner-Tamid-Verlag, 1959), pp. 304–305; Eliza Ablovatski, "The 1919 Central European Revolutions and the Judeo-Bolshevik Myth," in Michael L. Miller and Scott Ury, eds. *Cosmopolitanism, Nationalism, and the Jews of East Central Europe* (London; New York: Routledge, 2015), p. 145; additional trans. by Monika Malessa.

48. Grunberger, *Red Rising in Bavaria*, p. 107.

49. Toller, *I Was a German*, p. 165.

50. Ibid.

51. Ellis, *Ernst Toller and German Society*, p. 112.

52. Luhrssen, *Hammer of the Gods*, p. 121.

53. Ibid., p. 123.

54. Ibid., p. 127.

55. Mitchell, *Revolution in Bavaria*, p. 318.

56. Luhrssen, *Hammer of the Gods*, p. 127.

57. Ibid.

58. Evans, *Coming of the Third Reich*, pp. 158–59.

59. Toller, *I Was a German*, p. 172.

60. Luhrssen, *Hammer of the Gods*, p. 133.

61. Mitchell, *Revolution in Bavaria*, p. 319.

62. Grunberger, *Red Rising in Bavaria*, p. 122.

CHAPTER SEVEN: THE COUNTERREVOLUTION

1. Richard J. Evans, *The Coming of the Third Reich* (London: Penguin Books, 2005), p. 159.

2. David Luhrssen, *Hammer of the Gods: The Thule Society and the Birth of Nazism* (Washington, DC: Potomac Books, 2012), p. 132.

3. Ernst Toller, *I Was a German: The Autobiography of Ernst Toller*, trans. Edward Crankshaw (New York: William Morrow, 1934), p. 174.

4. Luhrssen, *Hammer of the Gods*, p. 133.

5. Ibid., p. 132.

6. Evans, *The Coming of the Third Reich*, p. 159.

7. Allan Mitchell, *Revolution in Bavaria 1918–1919: The Eisner Regime and the Soviet Republic* (Princeton, NJ: Princeton University Press, 1965), p. 321.

8. Robert G. Waite, *Vanguard of Nazism: The Free Corps Movement in Postwar Germany 1918–1923* (New York: W. W. Norton, 1952), p. 84.

9. Ibid.

10. Luhrssen, *Hammer of the Gods*, p. 134.

11. Robert Ellis, *Ernst Toller and German Society: Intellectuals as Leaders and Critics, 1914–1939* (Madison, NJ: Fairleigh Dickinson University Press, 2013), p. 115.

12. Toller, *I Was a German*, p. 175.

13. Ibid., p. 182.

14. Ibid., p. 183.

15. Ibid., p. 186.

16. Richard Grunberger, *Red Rising in Bavaria* (London: Arthur Barker, 1973), p. 122.

17. Tony Atcherley and Mark Carey, *Hitler's Gay Traitor: The Story of Ernst Röhm, Chief of Staff of the S. A.* (Victoria, BC: Trafford, 2007), p. 62.

18. Grunberger, *Red Rising in Bavaria*, p. 123.

19. Ibid., p. 124.

20. Ibid., pp. 124–25.

21. Ibid., p. 126.

22. Heinrich Hoffmann, *Hitler Was My Friend*, trans. R. H. Stevens (London: Burke, 1955), p. 36.

23. Rudolf Herz, *Hoffmann & Hitler: Fotografie als Medium des Führer-Mythos* (Munich: Klinkhardt & Biermann, 1994), p. 26.

24. Ibid., p. 30.

25. Ibid.

26. Ibid.

27. Hoffmann, *Hitler Was My Friend*, p. 36.

28. Heinrich Hoffmann, *Mein Beruf: Meine Arbeit für die Kunst: Mein Verhältnis zu Adolf Hitler* (unpublished manuscript; Archive of the Institut für Zeitgeschichte München-Berlin, MS 2049), p. 5.

29. Ibid., p. 6.

30. Ibid.

31. Hoffmann, *Hitler Was My Friend*, p. 37.

32. Ibid.

33. Herz, *Hoffmann and Hitler*, p. 31.

34. Hoffmann, *Hitler Was My Friend*, p. 37.

35. Mitchell, *Revolution in Bavaria*, p. 322.

36. Waite, *Vanguard of Nazism*, p. 85.

37. Atcherley and Carey, *Hitler's Gay Traitor*, p. 15.

38. Ibid., p. 42.

39. Ernst Röhm, *The Memoirs of Ernst Röhm*, trans. Geoffrey Brooks (Barnsley, UK: Frontline Books, 2012), p. 7.

40. Robert Gerwarth, *The Vanquished: Why the First World War Failed to End* (New York: Farrar, Straus and Giroux, 2017), p. 130.

41. Grunberger, *Red Rising in Bavaria*, p. 128.

42. Atcherley and Carey, *Hitler's Gay Traitor*, p. 62.

43. Waite, *Vanguard of Nazism*, p. 49.

44. Ibid., p. 85.

45. Luhrssen, *Hammer of the Gods*, pp. 122–23.

46. Ralph Engelman, "Dietrich Eckart and the Genesis of Nazism" (PhD thesis; St. Louis, MO: Washington University, 1971), p. 129.

47. Ibid., p. 131.

48. William Gillespie, *Dietrich Eckart: An Introduction for the English-Speaking Student* (Houston: self-pub., June 1975), p. 14.

49. Luhrssen, *Hammer of the Gods*, p. 129.

50. Ibid., p. 135.

51. Grunberger, *Red Rising in Bavaria*, p. 130.

52. Ibid., p. 131.

53. Waite, *Vanguard of Nazism*, p. 87.

54. David Clay Large, *Where Ghosts Walked: Munich's Road to the Third Reich* (New York: W. W. Norton, 1997), p. 118.

55. Grunberger, *Red Rising in Bavaria*, p. 135.

56. Luhrssen, *Hammer of the Gods*, p. 140.

57. Toller, *I Was a German*, p. 199.

58. Grunberger, *Red Rising in Bavaria*, p. 138.

59. Ellis, *Ernst Toller and German Society*, p. 116.

60. Luhrssen, *Hammer of the Gods*, p. 142.

61. Grunberger, *Red Rising in Bavaria*, p. 144.

62. Luhrssen, *Hammer of the Gods*, p. 142.

63. Ibid., p. 145.

64. Large, *Where Ghosts Walked*, p. 121.

65. Evans, *Coming of the Third Reich*, p. 121.

66. Waite, *Vanguard of Nazism*, p. 93.

67. Large, *Where Ghosts Walked*, p. 126.

68. Herz, *Hoffmann & Hitler*, p. 31.

69. Emil Herold and Heinrich Hoffmann, *Ein Jahr bayerische Revolution im Bilde* (Munich: Institut für Zeitgeschichte, 1919), p. 5.

70. Ibid., p. 6.

71. Ibid.

72. Ibid., p. 25.

73. Ibid.

74. Ibid.

75. Ibid.

76. Hoffmann, *Mein Beruf*, p. 4.

77. Herz, *Hoffmann & Hitler*, p. 350n37.

78. Ibid., p. 31.

79. Hoffmann, *Mein Beruf*, p. 4.

CHAPTER EIGHT: HITLER IN AUSTRIA

1. David Clay Large, *Where Ghosts Walked: Munich's Road to the Third Reich* (New York: W. W. Norton, 1997), p. 124.

2. Roger Parkinson, *Tormented Warrior: Ludendorff and the Supreme Command* (New York: Stein and Day, 1978), p. 196.

3. John W. Wheeler-Bennett, "Ludendorff: The Soldier and the Politician," *Virginia Quarterly Review* 14, no. 2 (Spring 1938), http://www.vqronline.org/essay/ludendorff-soldier-and-politician (accessed January 15, 2018).

4. Parkinson, *Tormented Warrior*, pp. 196–98.

5. Stadt-Anzeiger für München, *München-Augsburger Abendzeitung*, no. 73 (May 6, 1919), p. 2.

6. Adolf Hitler, *Mein Kampf*, trans. James Murphy (1939; Warwickshire, UK: Coda Books, 2011), p. 291.

7. Peter Longerich, "Hitler, Munich, and the Early History of the Nazi Party," in *Munich and National Socialism: Catalogue of the Munich Documentation Centre for the History of National Socialism*, ed. Hans Günter Hockerts, Marita Krauss, Peter Longerich, Winifred Nerdinger (Munich: Verlag C. H. Beck, 2015), p. 398.

8. Spartacist and Marxist Newspaper Ban, *Münchener Post* 33, no. 105 (May 6, 1919): 1.

9. Roy G. Koepp, "Conservative Radicals: The Einwohnerwehr, Bund Bayern und Reich, and the Limits of Paramilitary Politics in Bavaria, 1918–1928" (PhD thesis; Lincoln: University of Nebraska, 2010).

10. Large, *Where Ghosts Walked*, p. 127.

11. Karl Mayr, "I Was Hitler's Boss," *Current History* 1, no. 3 (November 1941): 193–99, http://www.history.ucsb.edu/faculty/marcuse/projects/hitler/sources/40s/41currhist/41v CurrHistHitlersBoss.htm (accessed January 15, 2018).

12. Werner Maser, *Hitler's Letters and Notes* (London: Heinemann, 1973), p. 107.

13. Ian Kershaw, *Hitler: 1889–1936 Hubris* (London: W. W. Norton, 1998), p. 10.

14. John Toland, *Adolf Hitler*, 1st Anchor ed. (New York: Anchor Books, 1992), p. 7.

15. Kershaw, *Hitler*, p. 11.

16. Ibid.

17. Ibid.

18. Toland, *Adolf Hitler*, p. 9.

19. Ibid.

20. Ibid., p. 12.

21. Adolf Hitler, *Mein Kampf*, trans. Helmut Ripperger (Boston: Houghton Mifflin, 1941), p. 43.

22. Toland, *Adolf Hitler*, p. 9.

23. Hitler, *Mein Kampf* (Coda Books), p. 16.

24. Ibid., p. 106.

25. Ibid., p. 15.

26. Ibid., p. 107.

27. Ibid., p. 16.

28. Ibid.

29. August Kubizek, *The Young Hitler I Knew* (New York: Tower Book, 1954), p. 53.

30. Ben Novak, *Hitler and Abductive Logic: The Strategy of a Tyrant* (Lanham, MD: Lexington Books, 2014), p. 182.

31. Hitler, *Mein Kampf* (Coda Books), pp. 16–17.

32. Ron Rosenbaum, *Explaining Hitler: The Search for the Origins of His Evil* (Cambridge, MA: Da Capo, 1998), p. xxxii.

33. Hitler, *Mein Kampf* (Coda Books), p. 19.

34. Kershaw, *Hitler*, p. 19.

35. Ibid., p. 19.

36. Kubizek, *Young Hitler I Knew*, p. 51.

37. Ibid., p. 23.

38. Kershaw, *Hitler*, p. 20.

39. Ibid.

40. Ibid., p. 12.

41. Hitler, *Mein Kampf* (Coda Books), p. 22.

42. Ibid., p. 21.

43. Kubizek, *Young Hitler I Knew*, pp. 129–30.

44. Ibid., pp. 136–37.

45. Ibid., p. 145.

46. Hitler, *Mein Kampf* (Coda Books), p. 33.

47. Ibid., p. 34.

48. Ibid., p. 35.

49. Ibid., p. 23.

50. Ibid., p. 42.

51. Ibid., p. 44.

52. Ibid., p. 45.

53. Ibid., p. 49.

54. Kershaw, *Hitler*, p. 85.

55. Richard J. Evans, *The Coming of the Third Reich* (London: Penguin Books, 2005), p. 166.

CHAPTER NINE: THE RIGHT-WING TALENT SEARCH

1. David Clay Large, *Where Ghosts Walked*: *Munich's Road to the Third Reich* (New York: W. W. Norton, 1997), p. 40.

2. Adolf Hitler, *Mein Kampf*, trans. James Murphy (1939; Warwickshire, UK: Coda Books, 2011), p. 109.

3. Thomas Weber, *Hitler's First War* (Oxford: Oxford University Press, 2010), p. 19.

4. Ibid., p. 24.

5. Ibid., p. 53. According to historian Thomas Weber, English-language publications are mistaken when they refer to Hitler as a corporal in the First World War. While Hitler was promoted from "Private" to "Gefreiter" in November of 1914, his new rank was the equivalent of "Private, second grade," and at no time did he have seniority or command over other men. With this understanding, the author refers to Hitler as a "Private" throughout the text.

6. Ibid., p. 49.

7. Ibid., p. 48.

8. Ibid., p. 96.

9. Richard Hanser, *Putsch! How Hitler Made Revolution* (New York: Peter H. Wyden, 1970), p. 83.

10. Weber, *Hitler's First War*, p. 140.

11. Ian Kershaw, *Hitler: 1889–1936 Hubris* (London: W. W. Norton, 1998), p. 93.

12. Werner Maser, *Hitler's Letters and Notes* (London: Heinemann, 1973), pp. 89–90.

13. Weber, *Hitler's First War*, p. 70.

14. Ibid., p. 149.

15. Ibid., p. 154.

16. Hitler, *Mein Kampf*, p. 126.

17. Ibid.

18. Ibid.

19. Weber, *Hitler's First War*, p. 197.

20. Ibid., p. 198.

21. Ibid., p. 202.

22. Hitler, *Mein Kampf*, p. 124.

23. Weber, *Hitler's First War*, p. 217.

24. Ibid., p. 215.

25. Ibid., p. 216.

26. Ibid.

27. Hitler, *Mein Kampf*, p. 133.

28. Ibid., p. 130.

29. Weber, *Hitler's First War*, p. 250.

30. Kershaw, *Hitler*, p. 118.

31. Weber, *Hitler's First War*, pp. 251–52.

32. Peter Longerich, "Hitler, Munich, and the Early History of the Nazi Party," in *Munich and National Socialism: Catalogue of the Munich Documentation Centre for the History of National Socialism*, ed. Hans Günter Hockerts, Marita Krauss, Peter Longerich, Winifred Nerdinger (Munich: Verlag C. H. Beck, 2015), p. 397.

33. Weber, *Hitler's First War*, p. 256.

34. Longerich, "Hitler, Munich, and the Early History of the Nazi Party," p. 398.

35. Ibid.

36. Large, *Where Ghosts Walked*, p. 128.

37. Ibid.

38. Adolf Hitler, *Mein Kampf*, trans. Helmut Ripperger (Boston: Houghton Mifflin, 1941), p. 290.

39. Kershaw, *Hitler*, p. 124.

40. Ibid.

41. Weber, *Hitler's First War*, p. 255.

42. Barbara Miller Lane and Leila J. Rupp, trans. and eds., *Nazi Ideology before 1933: A Documentation* (Austin: University of Texas Press, 1978), p. 16.

43. Ralph Engelman, "Dietrich Eckart and the Genesis of Nazism" (PhD thesis; St. Louis, MO: Washington University, 1971), p. 151.

44. Ibid., p. 149.

45. Joseph Howard Tyson, *Hitler's Mentor: Dietrich Eckart, His Life, Times & Milieu* (New York: iUniverse, 2008), p. 314.

46. Engelman, "Dietrich Eckart," p. 159.

47. Ibid., p. 146.

48. Ibid., p. 159.

49. Ibid.

50. Longerich, "Hitler, Munich, and the Early History of the Nazi Party," p. 398.

51. Ibid.

52. Kershaw, *Hitler*, p. 126.

53. Hitler, *Mein Kampf* (Coda Books), p. 140.

54. Ibid., p. 126.

55. Hanser, *Putsch!* p. 198.

56. Volker Ullrich, *Hitler: Ascent, 1889–1939*, trans. Jefferson Chase, 1st American ed. (New York: Vintage Books, 2017), p. 86.

57. Hitler, *Mein Kampf* (Coda Books), p. 141.

58. Engelman, "Dietrich Eckart," p. 156.

59. Ibid.

60. Ibid., p. 156.

CHAPTER TEN: LAUNCH OF THE NSDAP

1. Robert Ellis, *Ernst Toller and German Society: Intellectuals as Leaders and Critics, 1914–1939* (Madison, NJ: Fairleigh Dickinson University Press, 2013), p. 118.

2. Ernst Toller, *I Was a German: The Autobiography of Ernst Toller*, trans. Edward Crankshaw (New York: William Morrow, 1934), pp. 222–23.

3. Ibid., pp. 205–206.

4. Ibid., p. 212.

5. Ibid., p. 214.

6. Ibid., p. 215.

7. Ellis, *Ernst Toller and German Society*, p. 119.

8. Hans Lamm, *Von Juden in München, Ein Gedenkbuch* (Munich: Ner-Tamid-Verlag, 1959), pp. 305–306 [trans. Monika Malessa].

9. Toller, *I Was a German*, p. 222.

10. Frederik Schouten, "Ernst Toller: An Intellectual Youth Biography, 1893–1918" (PhD thesis; Florence: European University Institute, Department of History and Civilization, July 2007), p. 11.

11. Ellis, *Ernst Toller and German Society*, p. 119.

12. David Clay Large, *Where Ghosts Walked: Munich's Road to the Third Reich* (New York: W. W. Norton, 1997), p. 122.

13. Ellis, *Ernst Toller and German Society*, p. 119.

14. Schouten, "Ernst Toller: An Intellectual Youth Biography," p. 113.

15. Ellis, *Ernst Toller and German Society*, p. 119.

16. Toller, *I Was a German*, pp. 237–38.

17. Ellis, *Ernst Toller and German Society*, p. 119.

18. Large, *Where Ghosts Walked*, p. 133.

19. Ibid.

20. Ibid., p. 132.

21. Ian Kershaw, *Hitler: 1889–1936 Hubris* (London: W. W. Norton, 1998), p. 137.

22. Adolf Hitler, *Mein Kampf*, trans. James Murphy (Warwickshire, UK: Coda Books, 2011), p. 140.

23. Ibid.

24. Kershaw, *Hitler*, p. 127.

25. Adolf Hitler, *Mein Kampf*, trans. Helmut Ripperger (Boston: Houghton Mifflin, 1941), p. 300.

26. Hitler, *Mein Kampf* (Coda Books, 2011), p. 143.

27. Ibid.

28. Ibid.

29. Ibid., p. 208.

30. Kershaw, *Hitler*, p. 140.

31. Richard Hanser, *Putsch! How Hitler Made Revolution* (New York: Peter H. Wyden, 1970), p. 208.

32. Ibid., p. 209.

33. Ibid.

34. Joseph Howard Tyson, *Hitler's Mentor: Dietrich Eckart, His Life, Times & Milieu* (New York: iUniverse, 2008), p. 316.

35. Ibid., p. 333.

36. Ralph Engelman, "Dietrich Eckart and the Genesis of Nazism" (PhD thesis; St. Louis, MO: Washington University, 1971), p. 106.

37. Ibid., p. 144.

38. Ibid., p. 162.

39. Ibid., p. 163.

40. Ibid., p. 160.

41. Kershaw, *Hitler*, p. 143.

42. Benjamin Ziemann, *War Experiences in Rural Germany: 1914–1923, The Legacy of the Great War* (Oxford: Berg Publishers, Bloomsbury Academic, 2007), p. 235.

43. Friedrich Hitzer, *Anton Graf Arco: Das Attentat auf Kurt Eisner und die Schüsse im Landtag* (Munich: Knesebeck & Schuler, 1988), pp. 391–92.

44. Michael Newton, *Famous Assassinations in World History: An Encyclopedia* (Santa Barbara, CA: ABC-CLIO, 2014), p. 132.

45. "The Anniversary of Kurt Eisner's Death," *Münchner Neueste Nachrichten* 73, no. 79 (February 23, 1920) (Archive of the Institut für Zeitgeschichte München-Berlin, Z 007), p. 4.

46. Ibid.

47. Hitler, *Mein Kampf* (Houghton Mifflin), p. 819.

48. Richard J. Evans, *The Coming of the Third Reich* (London: Penguin, 2005), p. 173.

49. Hitler, *Mein Kampf* (Coda Books), p. 232.

50. Kershaw, *Hitler*, p. 141.

51. Ibid., p. 149.

52. Large, *Where Ghosts Walked*, p. 135.

53. Hanser, *Putsch!* p. 214.

54. Hitler, *Mein Kampf* (Coda Books), p. 234.

55. Barbara Miller Lane and Leila J. Rupp, trans. and eds., *Nazi Ideology before 1933: A Documentation* (Austin: University of Texas Press, 1978), p. 89.

56. Ibid.

57. Hitler, *Mein Kampf* (Coda Books), p. 234.

58. Lane and Rupp, *Nazi Ideology before 1933*, p. 92.

59. Ibid.

60. Kershaw, *Hitler*, p. 146.

CHAPTER ELEVEN: THE SHIFT TO THE RIGHT

1. Margarethe Ludendorff, *My Married Life with Ludendorff*, trans. Raglan Somerset (London: Hutchinson, 1930), p. 226.

2. Ibid., p. 227.

3. Ibid.

4. Ingo Bading, "Ludendorff in Berlin 1919 und [and] 1920: Eine schöne Wohnung in der Viktoriastraße, ganz in der Nähe des Tiergartens [A Nice Apartment in the Viktoriastrasse, Very Close to the Zoo]," *Studiengruppe Naturalismus* (blog), January 23, 2012, http://studiengruppe.blogspot.com/2012/01/ludendorff-in-berlin-in-den-jahren-1919.html (accessed January 17, 2018).

5. Richard Hanser, *Putsch! How Hitler Made Revolution* (New York: Peter H. Wyden, 1970), p. 226.

6. Guido Giacomo Preparata, *Conjuring Hitler: How Britain and America Made the Third Reich* (London: Pluto Press, 2005), p. 98.

7. Ibid.

8. Ibid.

9. Ibid., p. 150.

10. Hanser, *Putsch!* p. 224.

11. Robert Waite, *Vanguard of Nazism: The Free Corps Movement in Postwar Germany, 1918–1923* (New York: W. W. Norton, 1952), p. 151.

12. Preparata, *Conjuring Hitler*, p. 103.

13. Waite, *Vanguard of Nazism*, p. 153.

14. Bernard Wasserstein, *The Secret Lives of Trebitsch Lincoln* (New Haven: Yale University Press, 1988), p. 146.

15. Pierre Broué, *The German Revolution 1917–1923* (Chicago: Haymarket Books, 1971), p. 353.

16. Waite, *Vanguard of Nazism*, p. 155.

17. Ibid., p. 157.

18. Hanser, *Putsch!* p. 225.

19. David Clay Large, *Where Ghosts Walked: Munich's Road to the Third Reich* (New York: W. W. Norton, 1997), p. 136.

20. Hanser, *Putsch!* p. 226.

21. Wasserstein, *Secret Lives of Trebitsch Lincoln*, p. 149.

22. Waite, *Vanguard of Nazism*, p. 160.

23. Large, *Where Ghosts Walked*, p. 138.

24. Ibid.

25. Ibid., p. 137.

26. Waite, *Vanguard of Nazism*, p. 163.

27. Ralph Engelman, "Dietrich Eckart and the Genesis of Nazism" (PhD thesis; St. Louis, MO: Washington University, 1971), p. 166.

28. Ibid.

29. Walter Mühlhausen, *Friedrich Ebert 1871–1925: A Social Democratic Statesman*, trans. Christine Brocks (Bonn: Dietz, 2015), p. 85.

30. Waite, *Vanguard of Nazism*, p. 177.

31. John Toland, *Adolf Hitler*, 1st Anchor ed. (New York: Anchor Books, 1992), p. 100.

32. Waite, *Vanguard of Nazism*, p. 171.

33. Ibid., p. 207.

34. Toland, *Adolf Hitler*, p. 100.

35. Nigel Jones, *The Birth of the Nazis: How the Freikorps Blazed a Trail for Hitler* (London: Robinson, 1987), p. 189.

36. Ludendorff, *My Married Life with Ludendorff*, p. 231.

37. Engelman, "Dietrich Eckart," p. 166.

38. Ibid.

39. Ludendorff, *My Married Life with Ludendorff*, p. 227.

40. Engelman, "Dietrich Eckart," p. 167.

41. Thomas Weber, *Hitler's First War: Adolf Hitler, the Men of the List Regiment, and the First World War* (Oxford: Oxford University Press, 2010), p. 258.

42. Hanser, *Putsch!* pp. 250–51.

43. Ibid.

44. Adolf Hitler, *Mein Kampf*, trans. James Murphy (1939; Warwickshire, UK: Coda Books, 2011), p. 122.

45. Joseph Howard Tyson, *Hitler's Mentor: Dietrich Eckart, His Life, Times & Milieu* (New York: iUniverse, 2008), p. 334.

46. Richard J. Evans, *The Coming of the Third Reich* (London: Penguin Books, 2005), p. 174.

47. Reginald H. Phelps, "Hitler's Fundamental Speech on Anti-Semitism," *Vierteljahreshefte für Zeitgeschichte* 16, no. 4 (1968): 406 [trans. Monika Malessa].

48. Ibid.

49. Ibid.

50. Hanser, *Putsch!* pp. 244–45.

51. Ibid.

52. Oron J. Hale, *The Captive Press in the Third Reich* (Princeton, NJ: Princeton University Press, 1964), p. 3.

53. Engelman, "Dietrich Eckart," p. 187.

54. Hale, *Captive Press*, p. 18.

55. Engelman, "Dietrich Eckart," p. 187.

56. Hale, *Captive Press*, p. 19.

CHAPTER TWELVE: A STATE OF EMERGENCY

1. Robert G. Waite, *Vanguard of Nazism: The Free Corps Movement in Postwar Germany 1918–1923* (New York: W. W. Norton, 1952), p. 194.

2. Ibid., pp. 194–95.

3. Ian Kershaw, *Hitler: 1889–1936 Hubris* (London: W. W. Norton, 1998), pp. 171–72.

4. Richard J. Evans, *The Coming of the Third Reich* (London: Penguin Books, 2005), p. 182.

5. Ernst Hanfstaengl, *Hitler: The Missing Years*, 1st Arcade ed. (New York: Arcade, 1994), p. 45.

6. Richard Hanser, *Putsch! How Hitler Made Revolution* (New York: Peter H. Wyden, 1970), pp. 260–61.

7. Ulrike Claudia Hofmann, "Fememorde," in *Historisches Lexikon Bayerns*, May 15, 2006, https://www.historisches-lexikon-bayerns.de/Lexikon/Fememorde (accessed January 17, 2018).

8. Douglas G. Morris, *Justice Imperiled: The Anti-Nazi Lawyer Max Hirschberg in Weimar Germany* (Ann Arbor: University of Michigan Press, 2005), p. 62.

9. Ibid., p. 63.

10. Hanser, *Putsch!* pp. 260–61.

11. David Clay Large, *Where Ghosts Walked: Munich's Road to the Third Reich* (New York: W. W. Norton, 1997), p. 142.

12. Hanser, *Putsch!* p. 261.

13. Ibid.

14. Joseph Howard Tyson, *Hitler's Mentor: Dietrich Eckart, His Life, Times, & Milieu* (New York: iUniverse, 2008), p. 345.

15. Ibid., p. 320.

16. Ibid.

17. Ralph Engelman, "Dietrich Eckart and the Genesis of Nazism" (PhD thesis; St. Louis, MO: Washington University, 1971), p. 205.

18. Ibid., p. 211.

19. Ibid., p. 205.

20. Kershaw, *Hitler*, p. 163.

21. Adolf Hitler, "Letter to Executive Committee of the NSDAP, July 14, 1921," *Documents on Adolf Hitler and the Weimar Republic*, ed. John Heineman, https://www2.bc.edu/john-heineman/Weimar.html (accessed January 17, 2018).

22. Joseph Howard Tyson identified the man who cast the vote against Hitler as Rudolf Posch. Posch reportedly worked as a librarian and was a member of the party. Little is known about his life, and he does not appear to have played an important role in the history of National Socialism apart from his refusal to vote in favor of Hitler on July 29, 1921. Tyson, *Hitler's Mentor*, p. 347.

23. Ibid.

24. Engelmann, "Dietrich Eckart," p. 201.

25. Ibid.

26. Ibid., pp. 171–72.

27. Evans, *Coming of the Third Reich*, p. 182.

28. Ibid.

29. Nigel Jones, *The Birth of the Nazis: How the Freikorps Blazed a Trail for Hitler* (London: Robinson, 1987), p. 213.

30. Ibid.

31. Ibid., p. 214.

32. Ibid., p. 215.

33. Ibid.

34. Ibid.

35. Large, *Where Ghosts Walked*, p. 142.

36. Ibid.

37. During the Middle Ages, secret courts in northwestern Germany called Vehm, also spelled *Feme*, administered justice and issued death sentences, which were carried out in brutal fashion. Feme courts were known to hang the dead from trees as a warning to others. With its motto "Traitors fall to the Feme," Organization Consul invoked the memory of the medieval system as it spread terror and murder across Germany. Jones, *Birth of the Nazis*, p. 211.

38. Hanser, *Putsch!* p. 264.

39. Otis C. Mitchell, *Hitler's Stormtroopers and the Attack on the German Republic, 1919–1933*, repr. ed. (Jefferson, NC: McFarland, 2013), p. 68.

40. Tony Atcherley and Mark Carey, *Hitler's Gay Traitor: The Story of Ernst Röhm, Chief of Staff of the S. A.* (Victoria, BC: Trafford, 2007), p. 82.

CHAPTER THIRTEEN: HITLER'S EXPANDING CIRCLE

1. Richard Hanser, *Putsch! How Hitler Made Revolution* (New York: Peter H. Wyden, 1970), p. 268.

2. Mark Jones, "From 'Skagerrak' to the 'Organization Consul': War Culture and the Imperial German Navy, 1914–22," in *Other Combatants, Other Fronts: Competing Histories of the First World War*, ed. James E. Kitchen, Alisa Miller, and Laura Rowe (Newcastle upon Tyne, UK: Cambridge Scholars, 2011), p. 249.

3. SIS British Intelligence Report, "The Policy of Bavarian Monarchists: Minutes of a Secret Meeting," *Central European Summary*, no. 799 (July 28, 1922), p. 1.

4. Margarethe Ludendorff, *My Married Life with Ludendorff*, trans. Raglan Somerset (London: Hutchinson, 1930), p. 177.

5. SIS British Intelligence Report, p. 8.

6. Ibid., p. 5.

7. Ibid., p. 5.

8. Ibid., p. 7.

9. Ibid., p. 5.

10. Ibid., p. 6.

11. Ibid.

12. Ibid.

13. Ibid.

14. Ibid.

15. Ernst Toller, *I Was a German: The Autobiography of Ernst Toller*, trans. Edward Crankshaw (New York: William Morrow, 1934), p. 260.

16. Ibid., p. 250.

17. Ibid.

18. Ibid.

19. Hanser, *Putsch!* p. 271.

20. Wolfram Wette, *The Wehrmacht: History, Myth, Reality*, trans. Deborah Lucas Schneider (Cambridge, MA: Harvard University Press, 2008), p. 57.

21. Robert G. Waite, *Vanguard of Nazism: The Free Corps Movement in Postwar Germany 1918–1923* (New York: W. W. Norton, 1952), p. 219.

22. Eugene Davidson, *The Making of Adolf Hitler: The Birth and Rise of Nazism* (Columbia: University of Missouri Press, 1997), p. 164.

23. John E. Finn, *Constitutions in Crisis: Violence and the Rule of Law* (Oxford: Oxford University Press, 1990), p. 155.

24. Hanser, *Putsch!* pp. 268–69.

25. Ibid.

26. Ibid., p. 270.

27. David Clay Large, *Where Ghosts Walked: Munich's Road to the Third Reich* (New York: W. W. Norton, 1997), p. 146.

28. Kurt G. W. Ludecke, *I Knew Hitler: The Lost Testimony by a Survivor from the Night of the Long Knives* (Warwickshire, UK: Coda Books, 2011), p. 22.

29. Large, *Where Ghosts Walked*, p. 146.

30. Ian Kershaw, *Hitler: 1889–1936 Hubris* (London: W. W. Norton, 1998), p. 171.

31. Hanser, *Putsch!* p. 270.

32. Julia Jüttner, "Mystery Memorial Honors Far-Right Assassins," *Der Spiegel Online*, July 26, 2012, http://www.spiegel.de/international/germany/memorial-to-far-right-killers-of-jewish-minister-walter-rathenau-a-846604.html (accessed January 17, 2018).

33. Volker Ullrich, *Hitler: Ascent, 1889–1939*, trans. Jefferson Chase, 1st American ed. (New York: Vintage Books, 2017), p. 117.

34. R. H. S. Stolfi, *Hitler Beyond Evil and Tyranny* (Amherst, NY: Prometheus Books, 2011), p. 67.

35. Adolf Hitler, *Mein Kampf*, trans. James Murphy (Warwickshire, UK: Coda Books, 2011), p. 340.

36. Nils Schwarz and Dr. Ing. Rainer Hambrecht, "14–15 Oktober 1922: Der '3 Deutsche Tag' in Coburg, Teil 1," *Coburg Digitales Stadt Gedächtnis*, February 16, 2015, http://www.stadtgeschichte-coburg.de/Startseite/archiv/s-schwarz-26-1.aspx/2061_view-2494/#pretty Photo (accessed January 17, 2018).

37. Kershaw, *Hitler*, p. 178.

38. Hitler, *Mein Kampf*, p. 341.

39. Stolfi, *Hitler Beyond Evil and Tyranny*, p. 68.

40. Ibid., p. 256.

41. Hitler, *Mein Kampf*, p. 341.

42. "Fascisti Enter Rome," *Washington Post*, November 1, 1922, p. 1.

43. Ibid.

44. Hitler, *Mein Kampf*, p. 419.

45. Kershaw, *Hitler*, p. 182.

46. Ibid.

47. Roger Manvell and Heinrich Fraenkel, *Goering: The Rise and Fall of the Notorious Nazi Leader* (New York: Skyhorse, 2011), p. 44.

48. Jack El-Hai, *The Nazi and the Psychiatrist: Hermann Göring, Dr. Douglas M. Kelley, and a Fatal Meeting of Minds at the End of WWII* (New York: BBS Public Affairs, 2013), pp. 75–76.

49. Ibid., p. 74.

50. Heinrich Hoffmann, *Hitler Was My Friend: The Memoirs of Hitler's Photographer* (Barnsley, UK: Frontline Books, 2011), p. 41.

51. Ibid., p. 42.

52. Ibid., p. 45.

53. Ibid.

54. Ernst Hanfstaengl, *Hitler: The Missing Years*, 1st Arcade ed. (New York: Arcade, 1994), p. 33.

55. Ibid., p. 35.

56. Ibid., p. 36.

57. Ibid., p. 38.

58. Ibid., p. 36.

59. Ibid., p. 37.

60. Ibid.

CHAPTER FOURTEEN: DELUSIONS OF GRANDEUR

1. Ernst Hanfstaengl, *Hitler: The Missing Years*, 1st Arcade ed. (New York: Arcade, 1994), p. 43.

2. Ibid., p. 44.

3. Ibid., p. 40.

4. Ibid., p. 21.

5. Ibid., p. 45.

6. Ibid., p. 41.

7. Ibid., p. 49.

8. Ibid., p. 50.

9. Ibid., p. 52.

10. Ibid., p. 39.

11. Joseph Howard Tyson, *Hitler's Mentor: Dietrich Eckart, His Life, Times, & Milieu* (New York: iUniverse, 2008), p. 314.

12. David Clay Large, *Where Ghosts Walked: Munich's Road to the Third Reich* (New York: W. W. Norton, 1997), p. 152.

13. Hanfstaengl, *Hitler: The Missing Years*, p. 55.

14. Large, *Where Ghosts Walked*, p. 158.

15. Hanfstaengl, *Hitler: The Missing Years*, p. 67.

16. Large, *Where Ghosts Walked*, p. 161.

17. Ian Kershaw, *Hitler: 1889–1936 Hubris* (London: W. W. Norton, 1998), p. 191. (The actual number of missing poles was 135,000.)

18. Richard J. Evans, *The Coming of the Third Reich* (London: Penguin Books, 2005), p. 103.

19. Adolf Hitler, *Mein Kampf*, trans. James Murphy (1939; Warwickshire, UK: Coda Books, 2011), p. 419.

20. Large, *Where Ghosts Walked*, p. 162.

21. Ibid.

22. Ibid., p. 166.

23. Ernst Röhm, *The Memoirs of Ernst Röhm*, trans. Geoffrey Brooks (Barnsley, UK: Frontline Books, 2012), p. 81.

24. Ibid., p. 82.

25. Large, *Where Ghosts Walked*, pp. 162–63.

26. Kershaw, *Hitler*, p. 193.

27. Large, *Where Ghosts Walked*, p. 167.

28. Tony Atcherley and Mark Carey, *Hitler's Gay Traitor: The Story of Ernst Röhm, Chief of Staff of the S. A.* (Victoria, BC: Trafford, 2007), p. 82.

29. Kershaw, *Hitler*, p. 193.

30. Hanfstaengl, *Hitler: The Missing Years*, p. 57.

31. Ibid.

32. Ibid., p. 64.

33. Ibid.

34. Ibid., pp. 64–65.

35. Hitler, *Mein Kampf*, p. 419.

36. Large, *Where Ghosts Walked*, p. 168.

37. Heinrich Hoffmann, *Hitler Was My Friend: The Memoirs of Hitler's Photographer* (Barnsley, UK: Frontline Books, 2011), p. 52.

38. Ibid., p. 53. (Note: Heinrich Hoffmann claimed that "He [Hitler] was carrying a steel helmet by its chin-strap, and though I tried to persuade him to put it on, he refused. What a grand snap that would have made!" Otto Strasser had a different recollection and said that Hitler "paced a jittery path before his lieutenants, occasionally removing his steel helmet to wipe away rivulets of perspiration from his face and forehead.")

39. Large, *Where Ghosts Walked*, p. 169.

40. Volker Ullrich, *Hitler: Ascent, 1889–1939*, trans. Jefferson Chase, 1st American ed. (New York: Vintage Books, 2017), p. 138.

41. Pierre Broué, *German Revolution 1917–1923*, trans. John Archer (Chicago: Haymarket Books, 2006), p. 770.

42. Arthur H. Mitchell, *Hitler's Mountain: The Führer, Obersalzberg, and the American Occupation of Berchtesgaden* (Jefferson, NC: McFarland, 2007), p. 17.

43. Ullrich, *Hitler: Ascent*, p. 138.

44. Ralph Engelman, "Dietrich Eckart and the Genesis of Nazism" (PhD thesis; St. Louis, MO: Washington University, 1971), p. 226.

45. Mitchell, *Hitler's Mountain*, p. 18.

46. Nigel Jones, *The Birth of the Nazis: How the Freikorps Blazed a Trail for Hitler* (London: Robinson, 1987), p. 248.

47. Ibid., p. 249.

48. Hanfstaengl, *Hitler: The Missing Years*, p. 82.

49. Ibid.

50. Ibid., pp. 82–83.

51. Ibid.

52. Ibid.

53. Ibid., p. 81.

54. Ibid., p. 80.

55. Hoffmann, *Hitler Was My Friend*, p. 46.

56. Ibid., p. 45.

57. Ibid., p. 48.

58. Ibid., pp. 48–49.

59. Ibid., p. 49.

60. Ibid.

61. Ibid.

62. Ibid., p. 51.

63. Hanfstaengl, *Hitler: The Missing Years*, p. 51.

64. Ibid.

65. Ibid.

CHAPTER FIFTEEN: HITLER'S COMPETITORS

1. Roy G. Koepp, "Conservative Radicals: The Einwohnerwehr, Bund Bayern und Reich, and the Limits of Paramilitary Politics in Bavaria, 1918–1928" (PhD thesis; Lincoln: University of Nebraska, 2010), p. 231.

2. Ernst Hanfstaengl, *Hitler: The Missing Years*, 1st Arcade ed. (New York: Arcade, 1957), p. 89.

3. Ibid.

4. Richard Hanser, *Putsch! How Hitler Made Revolution* (New York: Peter H. Wyden, 1970), p. 304.

5. John E. Finn, *Constitutions in Crisis: Political Violence and the Rule of Law* (Oxford: Oxford University Press, 1990), p. 157.

6. David Clay Large, *Where Ghosts Walked: Munich's Road to the Third Reich* (New York: W. W. Norton, 1997), p. 158.

7. Hanser, *Putsch!* p. 308.

8. Pierre Broué, *German Revolution: 1917–1923*, trans. John Archer (Chicago: Haymarket Books, 2006), p. 793.

9. Richard Hanser, Putsch! p. 307.

10. Adolf Hitler, "Munich: Adolf Hitler Speech, September 12, 1923," *Speeches of Adolf Hitler: Early Speeches, 1922–1924, and Other Selections*, ed. Norman Hepburn Baynes (New York: Howard Fertig, 2006), pp. 76–79.

11. Broué, *German Revolution*, p. 745.

12. Ian Kershaw, *Hitler: 1889–1936 Hubris* (London: W. W. Norton, 1998), p. 199.

13. Erich Ludendorff, *Auf dem Weg zur Feldherrnhalle: Lebenserinnerungen an die Zeit des 9.11.1923* (Munich: Ludendorffs Verlag, 1937), p. 130 [trans. Monika Malessa].

14. Stephen Fritz, *Endkampf: Soldiers, Civilians, and the Death of the Third Reich* (Lexington: University Press of Kentucky, 2004), p. 163.

15. Kershaw, *Hitler*, p. 200.

16. Ernst Röhm, *The Memoirs of Ernst Röhm*, trans. Geoffrey Brooks (Barnsley, UK: Frontline Books, 2012), p. 129.

17. Edward Hallet Carr, *A History of Soviet Russia*, vol. 4, *The Interregnum: 1923–1924* (London: Macmillan, 1954), pp. 204–205.

18. Broué, *German Revolution*, p. 775.

19. Ibid., p. 776.

20. Walter Mühlhausen, *Friedrich Ebert 1871–1925: A Social Democratic Statesman*, trans. Christine Brocks (Bonn: Dietz, 2015), p. 89.

21. Richard J. Evans, *The Coming of the Third Reich* (London: Penguin Books, 2005), p. 192.

22. Reiner Pommerin, *Die Ausweisung von 'Ostjuden' aus Bayern 1923: Ein Beitrag zum Krisenjahr der Weimarer Republik* (Munich: Institut für Zeitgeschichte, 1986), p. 324.

23. Ibid.

24. Ibid., p. 322.

25. Peter Ross Range, *1924: The Year That Made Hitler* (New York: Little, Brown, 2016), p. 58.

26. Large, *Where Ghosts Walked*, p. 174.

27. Evans, *Coming of the Third Reich*, p. 243.

28. Broué, *German Revolution*, p. 809.

29. Ibid., p. 172.

30. Large, *Where Ghosts Walked*, pp. 172–73.

31. Kershaw, *Hitler*, p. 202.

32. Ibid.

33. Nigel Jones, *The Birth of the Nazis: How the Freikorps Blazed a Trail for Hitler* (London: Robinson, 1987), pp. 250–51.

34. Ibid., p. 251.

35. Hanser, *Putsch!* p. 330.

36. Ibid.

37. Hanfstaengl, *Hitler: The Missing Years*, p. 90.

38. Kershaw, *Hitler*, p. 202.

39. Ralph Engelman, "Dietrich Eckart and the Genesis of Nazism" (PhD thesis; St. Louis, MO: Washington University, 1971), p. 229.

40. Hanfstaengl, *Hitler: The Missing Years*, p. 90.

41. Kurt G. W. Ludecke, *I Knew Hitler: The Lost Testimony by a Survivor from the Night of the Long Knives* (Warwickshire, UK: Coda Books, 2011), p. 124.

42. Range, *1924*, p. 60.

43. Hanfstaengl, *Hitler: The Missing Years*, p. 88–89.

44. Range, *1924*, p. 65.

CHAPTER SIXTEEN: THE BEER HALL PUTSCH

1. Ernst Hanfstaengl, *Hitler: The Missing Years*, 1st Arcade ed. (New York: Arcade, 1994), pp. 91–92.

2. Ibid., p. 92.

3. Ian Kershaw, *Hitler: 1889–1936 Hubris* (London: W. W. Norton, 1998), pp. 205–206.

4. Hanfstaengl, *Hitler: The Missing Years*, p. 95.

5. Ibid., p. 96.

6. Peter Ross Range, *1924: The Year That Made Hitler* (New York: Little, Brown, 2016), p. 73.

7. Hanfstaengl, *Hitler: The Missing Years*, p. 97.

8. Range, *1924*, p. 74.

9. Ibid.

10. Konrad Heiden, *Der Fuehrer: Hitler's Rise to Power*, trans. Ralph Manheim (Boston: Houghton Mifflin, 1944), p. 187.

11. David King, *The Trial of Adolf Hitler: The Beer Hall Putsch and the Rise of Nazi Germany* (New York: W. W. Norton, 2017), p. 19.

12. Range, *1924*, p. 76.

13. Ibid., p. 77.

14. Ibid.

15. Hanfstaengl, *Hitler: The Missing Years*, p. 98.

16. Kershaw, *Hitler*, p. 207.

17. David Clay Large, *Where Ghosts Walked: Munich's Road to the Third Reich* (New York: W. W. Norton, 1997), p. 178.

18. Richard Hanser, *Putsch! How Hitler Made Revolution* (New York: Peter H. Wyden, 1970), p. 346.

19. Range, *1924*, p. 79.

20. Hanser, *Putsch!* p. 346.

21. Range, *1924*, p. 81.

22. Hanfstaengl, *Hitler: The Missing Years*, p. 101.

23. Heiden, *Der Fuehrer*, p. 191.

24. Hanser, *Putsch!* p. 356.

25. Kershaw, *Hitler*, p. 209.

26. Hanfstaengl, *Hitler: The Missing Years*, p. 104.

27. Hanser, *Putsch!* p. 349.

28. Kershaw, *Hitler*, p. 209.

29. Hanser, *Putsch!* p. 370.

30. King, *Trial of Adolf Hitler*, p. 88.

31. Hanser, *Putsch!* p. 375.

32. Kershaw, *Hitler*, p. 208.

33. Hanser, *Putsch!* p. 378.

34. Kershaw, *Hitler*, p. 210.

35. Ibid.

36. King, *Trial of Adolf Hitler*, p. 99.

37. Ibid., p. 93.

38. Ralph Engelman, "Dietrich Eckart and the Genesis of Nazism" (PhD thesis; St. Louis, MO: Washington University, 1971), p. 230.

39. Hanser, *Putsch!* p. 388.

40. Adolf Hitler, Speech Commemorating the Twentieth Anniversary of the Beer Hall Putsch, delivered at the Löwenbräukeller, Munich, November 8, 1943.

41. Hanfstaengl, *Hitler: The Missing Years*, p. 108.

42. King, *Trial of Adolf Hitler*, p. 123.

CHAPTER SEVENTEEN: THE TRIAL

1. Ian Kershaw, *Hitler: 1889–1936 Hubris* (London: W. W. Norton, 1998), p. 212.

2. Ibid., p. 213.

3. Volker Ullrich, *Hitler: Ascent 1889–1939*, trans. Jefferson Chase, 1st American ed. (New York: Vintage Books, 2017), p. 156.

4. Kershaw, *Hitler*, p. 214.

5. Peter Ross Range, *1924: The Year That Made Hitler* (New York: Little, Brown, 2016), pp. 104–105.

6. Ibid., p. 105.

7. Ernst Hanfstaengl, *Hitler: The Missing Years*, 1st Arcade ed. (New York: Arcade, 1957), p. 113.

8. Kershaw, *Hitler*, p. 214.

9. Range, *1924*, p. 104.

10. Ibid., p. 106.

11. Walter C. Langer, *The Mind of Adolf Hitler: The Secret Wartime Report* (New York: Basic Books, 1972), p. 216.

12. Ibid., p. 162.

13. Ibid., p. 216.

14. Sebastian Haffner, *The Meaning of Hitler: Hitler's Use of Power, His Successes and Failures*, trans. Ewald Osers (New York: Macmillan, 1979), p. 15.

15. Range, *1924*, p. 114.

16. Kershaw, *Hitler*, p. 215.

17. David King, *The Trial of Adolf Hitler: The Beer Hall Putsch and the Rise of Nazi Germany* (New York: W. W. Norton, 2017), p. xxi.

18. Ullrich, *Hitler: Ascent*, p. 159.

19. Range, *1924*, p. 122.

20. Kershaw, *Hitler*, p. 216.

21. Ibid.

22. Range, *1924*, p. 133.

23. Ibid., p. 136.

24. King, *Trial of Adolf Hitler*, p. 160.

25. Ibid., p. 163.

26. David Clay Large, *Where Ghosts Walked: Munich's Road to the Third Reich* (New York: W. W. Norton, 1997), p. 192.

27. Range, *1924*, p. 143.

28. Kershaw, *Hitler*, p. 216.

29. Range, *1924*, p. 148.

30. Ibid., p. 158.

31. Ibid., p. 149.

32. King, *Trial of Adolf Hitler*, p. 30.

33. Range, *1924*, p. 159.

34. Ibid., p. 163.

35. King, *Trial of Adolf Hitler*, p. 226.

36. Both Hitler and Lossow had accused each other of betraying an oath: Hitler for launching the Beer Hall Putsch after guaranteeing peace to Lossow in January of 1923; Lossow for refusing to give back weapons that Bavarian paramilitary groups had handed over to the Reichswehr for "safe-keeping," which the Nazi leader had hoped to use in a May Day attack on the Communists in 1923. Kershaw, *Hitler*, pp. 193–96.

37. Range, *1924*, p. 172.

38. King, *Trial of Adolf Hitler*, p. xxi.

39. Range, *1924*, p. 175.

40. Ullrich, *Hitler: Ascent*, p. 162.

41. Kershaw, *Hitler*, p. 217.

42. Range, *1924*, p. 180.

43. King, *Trial of Adolf Hitler*, p. 335.

44. "At the Grave of Bavarian Justice," trans. Monika Malessa, *Münchener Post* 38, no. 80 (April 4, 1924): 1–2.

CHAPTER EIGHTEEN: MAN OF PROVIDENCE

1. David King, *The Trial of Adolf Hitler: The Beer Hall Putsch and the Rise of Nazi Germany* (New York: W. W. Norton, 2017), p. 320.

2. Ibid., p. 311.

3. Peter Ross Range, *1924: The Year That Made Hitler* (New York: Little, Brown 2016), p. 198.

4. King, *Trial of Adolf Hitler*, p. 311.

5. Volker Ullrich, *Hitler: Ascent 1889–1939*, trans. Jefferson Chase, 1st American ed. (New York: Vintage Books, 2016), p. 163.

6. Range, *1924*, p. 236.

7. Adolf Hitler, *Mein Kampf*, trans. James Murphy (1939; Warwickshire, UK: Coda Books, 2011), p. 13.

8. Ibid., p. 110.

9. Range, *1924*, p. 217.

10. Adolf Hitler, *Mein Kampf*, p. 65.

11. Ibid., p. 61.

12. M. Scott Peck, *People of the Lie, The Hope for Healing Human Evil* (New York: Touchstone, 1998), p. 73.

13. Adolf Hitler, quoted in H. R. Trevor-Roper, "The Mind of Adolf Hitler," in *Hitler's Table Talk 1941–1944: His Private Conversations*, trans. Norman Cameron and R. H. Stevens (New York: Enigma Books, 2000), p. xxviii.

14. Ullrich, *Hitler: Ascent*, p. 165.

15. Range, *1924*, p. 249.

16. King, *Trial of Adolf Hitler*, p. 331.

17. Heinrich Hoffmann, *Hitler Was My Friend: The Memoirs of Hitler's Photographer* (Barnsley, UK: Frontline Books, 2011), p. 60.

18. Ibid., p. 61.

19. Ibid.

EPILOGUE

1. Heinrich Hoffmann, *Hitler Was My Friend: The Memoirs of Hitler's Photographer* (Barnsley, UK: Frontline Books, 2011), p. 232.

2. Lieutenant John Martin, CIC Interrogation Transcript of Heinrich Hoffmann, Nuremberg, November 5, 1945, interpreted by Alfred H. Booth, available online at https://www.fold3.com/image/231904079 (accessed February 19, 2018).

3. Hoffmann, *Hitler Was My Friend*, p. 41.

4. "The Final Statement of Alfred Rosenberg," International Military Tribunal, Nuremberg 1947, http://www.go2war2.nl/artikel/4538/Final-statement-Alfred-Rosenberg.htm (accessed February 19, 2018).

5. Jack El-Hai, *The Nazi and the Psychiatrist: Herman Göring, Dr. Douglas M. Kelley, and a Fatal Meeting of Minds at the End of WWII* (New York: BBS Public Affairs, 2013), p. 150.

6. Ibid.

7. Robert G. Waite, *Vanguard of Nazism: The Free Corps Movement in Postwar Germany 1918–1923* (New York: W. W. Norton, 1952), p. 279.

8. Joachim C. Fest, *Hitler*, trans. Richard and Clara Winstton (New York: Harcourt, 1974), p. 469.

9. Ian Kershaw, *Hitler: 1889–1936 Hubris* (London: W. W. Norton, 1998), p. 426.

10. Ibid. p. 267.

11. Robert Ellis, *Ernst Toller and German Society: Intellectuals as Leaders and Critics, 1914–1939* (Madison, NJ: Fairleigh Dickinson University Press, 2013), p. 213.

12. Ibid.

13. Thomas S. Hischak, *1939: Hollywood's Greatest Year* (New York: Rowman & Littlefield, 2017), p. 129.

14. Frederik Schouten, "Ernst Toller: An Intellectual Youth Biography, 1893–1918" (PhD thesis; Florence: European University Institute, Department of History and Civilization, July 2007), p. 11.

15. Toller's friend, the English-born biographer Robert Payne, recorded in his diary that the playwright said, shortly before his death, "If ever you read that I committed suicide, I beg you not to believe it." Payne went on to say, "He hanged himself with the silk cord of his nightgown in a hotel in New York two years ago. This is what the newspapers said at the time, but I continue to believe that he was murdered." Robert Payne, "Diary Entry for May 23, 1942," *Forever China* (New York: Dodd, Mead, 1945), quoted in https://www.revolvy.com/main/index.php?s=Ernst%20Toller (accessed February 19, 2018).

16. Ernst Toller, *I Was a German: The Autobiography of Ernst Toller*, trans. Edward Crankshaw (New York: William Morrow, 1934), pp. 285–86.

17. Sebastian Haffner, *The Meaning of Hitler: Hitler's Use of Power, His Successes and Failures*, trans. Ewald Osers (New York: Macmillan, 1979), p. 100.

INDEX